FINISHING
SCHOOL

DEBORAH NEWTON

FINISHING SCHOOL

a master class for knitters

sixth&springbooks
NEW YORK

sixth&springbooks

161 Avenue of the Americas
New York, New York 10013
sixthandspringbooks.com

Managing Editor
WENDY WILLIAMS

Senior Editor
MICHELLE BREDESON

Art Director
DIANE LAMPHRON

Yarn Editor
RENEE LORION

Instructions Editor
BARBARA KHOURI

Instructions Proofreaders
LUCINDA HELLER
PATRICIA YANKEE

Editorial Assistant
ALEXANDRA JOINNIDES

Copy Editor
KRISTIN JONES

Illustrations
DEBORAH NEWTON

Charts and Schematics
BARBARA KHOURI

Model Photography
PAUL AMATO

Still-Life Photography
MARCUS TULLIS

Bookings Manager
and Stylist
SARAH LIEBOWITZ

Hair and Makeup
ALEJANDRA FOR
ARTISTSBYTIMOTHYPRIANO.COM

Vice President, Publisher
TRISHA MALCOLM

Creative Director
JOE VIOR

Production Manager
DAVID JOINNIDES

President
ART JOINNIDES

NOTE: Yarns are occasionally discontinued.
If you are unable to locate a yarn used
in a project or wish to make a substitution,
be sure to knit a gauge swatch to obtain the
correct finished measurements. Take care
that both the stitch and row gauge match
those listed in the instructions. Also
note that yarn amounts may vary depending
on the weight and yardage of the
substitute yarn.

Library of Congress
Cataloging-in-Publication Data
Newton, Deborah.
 Finishing school : a master class for knitters /
Deborah Newton.
    p. cm.
 ISBN 978-1-936096-19-0 (hardback)
 1. Knitting--Patterns. I. Title.
 TT825.N47 2011
 746.43'2--dc23

2011013424

Manufactured in China

3 5 7 9 10 8 6 4

First Edition

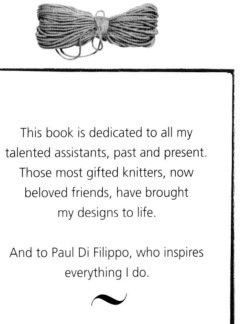

This book is dedicated to all my
talented assistants, past and present.
Those most gifted knitters, now
beloved friends, have brought
my designs to life.

And to Paul Di Filippo, who inspires
everything I do.

~

Contents

page 26   page 31

page 73   page 75

IDEAS & NOTES

"Give us the tools, and we will finish the job."
—WINSTON CHURCHILL

WORKSHOP

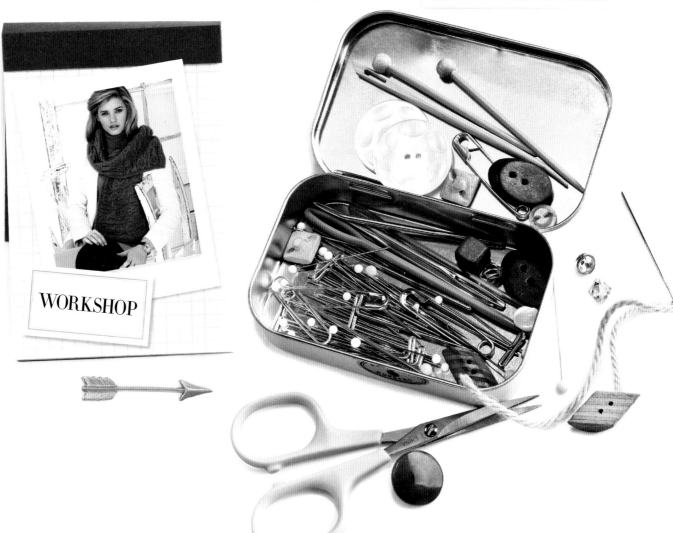

Introduction

As a designer, I create dozens of sweaters each year, and I have done this for two decades. Although I have the help of assistants who knit the pieces of my designs, I do all the finishing myself on almost every design I create.

I am always surprised when I hear someone say, "Oh, I hate finishing," because I have always found this part of making a knitted project so rewarding. I love making the decisions that give a sweater detail and character.

Good finishing is just as important as good fit—without it, my sweaters would look homely rather than stylish. There is nothing worse than a bumpy, uneven seam or sloppy or too-tight edgings— these off-kilter details draw the eye away from the beauty of even the most lovely knitted fabric.

But how do you accomplish good finishing—and enjoy it? I found that it is simply a matter of having a few skills and thinking ahead. Finishing does not have to be hard or tedious or overly time-consuming. Like most knitters—busy with life and work—I don't have endless time for finishing either!

I have a very specific process that I will share here with you. Believe it or not—even though the name of the process implies it—finishing is not something that I wait to think about at the very end of a project. For me, good finishing starts at the beginning of a project, when I consider all aspects of a design: yarn, fabric, seaming, edgings and all the little details that are necessary for a

functional and good-looking knitted project. As I said in my first book, *Designing Knitwear*, swatching is an essential part of my work process. And along with swatching for gauge and fabric, I also rely heavily on my swatch to guide me through the finishing decisions. You'll see throughout this book how testing on swatches helps me envision all aspects of a knitted project.

I will also take you step by step through a number of projects in order to show you how I accomplish flawless finishing in a variety of different situations. Complete instructions for all of the projects are given, and you can use each of these situations as a model for similar projects.

Another component of my love of finishing is respect. I respect the work my knitters do for me, I respect the craft and I value the materials that I use to best express my ideas. Putting a knitted project together carefully, with skill and style, is the only way to do justice to the hours spent knitting the pieces as well as justify the expense of the materials. I do not believe in rushing through finishing. It is a part of the sweater-making process that should be deliberate—and savored.

By building a repertoire of skills—and a vision for what is possible—you can ensure that every sweater you make looks stunning. Instead of avoiding finishing, try to look at each project as a training ground for learning new techniques!

I hope this book helps you to develop some enthusiasm for the all-encompassing process we call finishing, so that you will learn to enjoy it as much as I do. ■

Organza Extravaganza

crystals

slip st texture

fabric ruffles

Fitted Jacket

Plaid Collar + cuffs

Two Scarves — different weights
TRIANGLE TIPS!

BULKY!

Elegant fine gauge

▲ Good finishing starts at the beginning when I consider all aspects of a design: yarn, fabric, seaming, edgings and all the little details necessary for a functional and good-looking project.

11

Preparation is the key to successful finishing. Take time to gather all your tools and materials.

CHAPTER 1

Finishing 101

Before getting into the nitty-gritty of blocking,
seaming, adding edgings and other key steps in
finishing, let's take a moment to plan ahead and get
organized to ensure a successful finish!
We'll learn how to review a pattern, work with a
schematic drawing, make the most of the
all-important swatch and assemble
our essential finishing tools.

Choosing Projects Well

Often the most important step in finishing comes before you even pick up your needles and yarn. Getting into the habit of carefully choosing and reviewing a pattern *before* you begin can save you time and frustration when finishing. I know that most knitters are eager to begin a new project and don't want to take the time to knit a swatch, let alone read the pattern, but you will be glad you did!

The first thing to consider when reviewing a pattern is whether or not you should attempt it at all. Of course you should take your skill and comfort level into consideration when choosing a pattern, but you should also think about the pattern itself and if it is going to give you a satisfactory result. Over the years, many people have shown me projects they have knit from patterns that seem to lack any inherent possibilities for good finishing. "What kind of finishing can I do to make this look better?" they ask. Unfortunately, at that stage in the process it is sometimes too late to remedy the situation. I have seen edges that defy neat seaming; pattern stitches that come right to the edges, leading to bulky seams; no accommodation for the amount of fabric taken up by sewing seams, so that the garment does not fit; stitch counts for edgings that yield less than pretty results; buttonholes that are too loose or too tight; button placement that causes gaping or awkward buttoning. The list goes on!

Just because a pattern exists does not mean it is perfectly planned or well written. Or it might be fine for a particular size but not for additional sizes. *Not every pattern is a good choice.* I am not saying that you shouldn't make a pattern that appeals to you, but consider ahead of time, before you buy yarn, or begin to knit, what a pattern has to offer you. If you study a pattern closely before you begin to knit, with an eye toward the finishing process, you will avoid some of the pitfalls of a less than perfect project.

For example, when I first started designing knitwear, I learned by trial and error which knitting dictionaries, or collections of pattern stitches, to depend on. Those written by Barbara Walker were by far the most comprehensive, had the best editing, clearest presentation and consistently error-free content. Why would I struggle with using another dictionary that was less well organized or well written? Expect the same level of quality with the designs you choose to make. If you do choose to attempt something that looks a little less than perfect in terms of size, shape or finishing, take the time to analyze it first, as I describe below.

These are things that you should look for to help you decide if the project will be successful or if you should make some adjustments.

Pattern Text
Believe it or not, the actual text of a pattern can reveal a lot about finishing, and preparing for it. Make a point of reading through patterns before you choose to make a project. If the directions have been written clearly and with evident care, then that is a good sign. As you are reading the pattern, make sure that you understand the structure of the garment and are familiar with all of the terms and abbreviations used. You won't be able to tell if there are mathematical errors, but if anything seems odd, take a closer look. Look particularly at the finishing instructions. Are they clear? If not, think at the outset how you might want to finish the project.

Schematic
Is there a clear schematic drawing that shows all the major pieces of the garment and their measurements? A good schematic is critical for understanding the shaping and structure of a garment. If a schematic is not provided, you might want to consider drawing your own. (In the next section, we'll discuss in more depth why using a schematic is so important and how to draw your own.)

Pattern Stitches
Are the pattern stitches clearly described? Do the pattern stitches come right to the edge of the piece, or have stitches been added for ease of seaming? (See pages 36–38 for tips on adding seam stitches.) Look at the photo that accompanies the pattern. Does the fabric look strained or bulky in any areas?

Edgings and Extras
Are the instructions for picking up along edges clear? Are the edgings, buttonbands and trims well described in the text? Are there any unusual techniques you are not familiar with, or that you have not had experience incorporating into a project? You might want to do a "test" first to give you confidence with the finishing before you get there. Throughout this book, you will see how your initial swatch can help you test various parts of your finishing, including edgings, buttonholes, embroidery and more. (See Chapters 4 and 5 for more on edgings, buttons, trims and other embellishments.)

Sizing

Is your size well represented? Are you confident that the size you have chosen will give you enough ease for wearing? As anyone who has purchased clothing no doubt knows, sizing terms can be ambiguous. You might, for example, wear a "large" in one design and a "medium" in another. So, before beginning, compare the measurements in the pattern to a sweater that is similar in style and weight to one you already own, and see if the sizing is appropriate for you. If not, you might want to choose a smaller or larger size. Note that if the yarn is fine gauge and makes a lightweight fabric, you will need less ease than for a heavier fabric that is knit from a bulky yarn. Some fibers such as wool and wool blends are more forgiving than less elastic fibers like cotton and silk.

Yarn Alternatives

If you decide not to use the yarn suggested, ask yourself these questions: Does the pattern seem locked into a particular type of yarn—a fiber with unique qualities, such as mohair or a novelty yarn? Consider if a substitution can be easily made. In terms of edgings, or details, if you consider using a contrasting yarn, or one not suggested in the pattern, you must plan for that.

Making Design Decisions

If you generally like a design but want to customize it (other than choosing yarn), now is the time to consider that as well. For instance, if a sweater features close-fitting, very elastic k1, p1 rib cuffs and waistband, and you would like a softer, less close-fitting rib, or vice versa, you should consider that at the outset. Would a different neckline be more flattering on you? Does the length seem right for your proportions? Will you need to alter sleeve length (see page 16)? All of these issues will affect your finishing, so consider them now.

After you have studied the pattern and considered all of the above factors you might decide that the project is not right for you or you will be confident you have all of the information you need to create a successful garment with perfect finishing!

Using a Schematic Drawing

A good pattern always has a schematic drawing for reference. A schematic drawing allows you to compare your pattern to other projects you have already made, size-wise, and it also allows you to check measurements against sweaters that fit you well, in the same weight of fabric. Also, having a schematic for reference enables you to check the width and length of your pieces as you knit.

Have you ever returned to a project and not remembered what you have done? Or what you hoped to do in terms of changing a pattern? Do you know how to calculate the best sleeve length for yourself? Use your schematic to help you.

I refer to my schematic often when finishing and I keep a record of any changes I make, how many rows I knit to reach a particular length and more. Checking measurements helps me calculate gauges for edgings, allows me to envision the neckline, and assists me in plotting buttonhole placement—all very useful things! I save all my schematic drawings because they serve as a record of what I have done. I often refer back to them again for inspiration and ideas for other projects, especially those worked in the same yarn.

You can make a photocopy of a schematic if one is included in your pattern. Enlarging it is a good idea. Or you can draw your own if one is not included.

▼ Make a copy of the schematic drawing for your project and track your changes on it (mine are shown here in red), row counts, pocket placement and any calculations you want to remember. Here I lowered the neckline, added a pocket opening and shortened the sleeve. If I choose to knit the same sweater or base a future design on it, I won't have to rely on my memory.

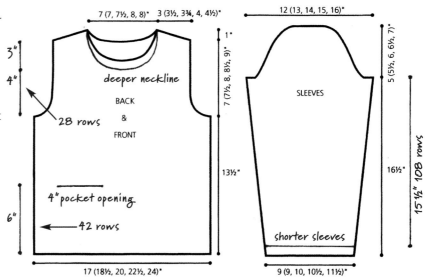

Tutorial
How to Draw Your Own Schematic

If the pattern you are using does not include a schematic, or if you want to draw another one to have as a record of your project and to note any change you want to make, you can draw your own on graph paper. You'll need graph paper to plot the shapes of your project. For schematic drawings I like to use paper that has four squares per inch, large enough to see easily and to aid in planning. Use a pencil and a good eraser!

BODY
Start with the largest body piece: Consider the number of stitches in the body section of your sweater, above any lower edge trim or ribbing.

1. Divide the stitch count for your size by the gauge (stitches per inch) to come up with the width of the body piece.

2. Plot the width on paper. Use one square of graph paper to represent one inch of knitting.

3. Repeat steps 1 and 2 for the shoulder width if it is narrower than the body. Draw in your armhole shaping.

4. Draw in the lengths indicated in the pattern.

5. Calculate, as in step 1, the width of the neckline and shoulders.

6. Draw in the neckline and shoulder shaping. Use the row gauge to calculate neck depth if there are no inch measurements given and only the number of rows is indicated. In other words, divide the number of neckline rows by the given row gauge (rows per inch) to come up with the depth of the neckline.

7. For a longer stretch of bind-offs at the shoulder, calculate in the same way as for the neckline: Divide the number of rows of shoulder shaping by the row gauge.

If the front of the sweater is significantly different from the back, draw a separate schematic. If it is for a cardigan, you should draw both front pieces.

SLEEVES
I like to plot my sleeves so that the armhole shaping is lined up on the graph paper at the same point as the armhole of the body pieces. In this way I can see the relationship of the length of the sleeve to the length of the body. If you are knitting for yourself, this can be a valuable guide to determining sleeve length—you can compare your schematic to a similar sweater that fits you well. Use the calculations above to plot the lengths and widths of the sleeve (keeping in mind that the width probably changes along its length).

Tutorial
Calculating Sleeve Length

Since measurements in patterns are for the "average sleeve," you might need to alter the sleeve length to fit your own personal dimensions. (Who is really "average," after all?). Also, a sleeve is a component of a sweater, and its length is related directly to the shape of the whole sweater, as well as to the ease and fit of the garment. For instance, a wide oversized sweater stands away from the body with a lot of ease, so its sleeve length does not need to be as long as a fitted, more body-conscious sweater. For a more complexly shaped sweater with a fitted sleeve cap, for example, the height of the cap as well as its width must be taken into account.

1. MEASURE YOURSELF
I learned this trick when I worked as a costume designer's assistant and I have altered it a bit to accommodate the nature of knits. When we measured for sewn garments, without the stretch of knits, we took the measurement from center back to the wrist, over a slightly bended elbow. This revealed the total measurement needed for the width of half the upper body, plus any sleeve cap, as well as the length to the wrist. Over the years I have realized that the bended elbow (required for woven fabrics without stretch) is not necessary for knits. Knitted sleeves tend to stretch a little after being worn, so the extra inch or so added by measuring over the bended elbow might result in a sleeve that is droopy and too long. Extend your arm slightly to the side. Have a friend measure the length from center back, starting slightly below the base of the neck, to your wrist. Record this measurement (A).

2. CHECK PATTERN MEASUREMENTS
Fill in these measurements, based on your schematic, in your desired size:
- Half of the upper body width (above any armhole shaping): _____
- Sleeve cap height: _____
- Sleeve length given in pattern for your chosen size: _____
Add these figures together (B).

3. COMPARE
Subtract the smaller of A or B from the other. If your measurement (A) is *larger* than the pattern measurement (B), then that is the number of inches you need to add to the sleeve length, and to the armhole shaping, to *lengthen* your sleeve.

If your measurement is *smaller* than the pattern measurement, then that is the number of inches you need to subtract from the sleeve length, and from the armhole shaping, to *shorten* your sleeve.

Tip YOU CAN CHECK THE LENGTH OF THE BODY of your sweater by measuring from the base of the neck to your waist, taking into consideration the style of the garment (whether it is cropped or tunic-length), any edgings, etc.

Swatching for Success

The next step in a project's success from a finishing point of view is the all-important swatch. Please don't groan. Learn to love your swatches! Mine have gotten bigger and bigger over the years: They are a gold mine of information.

Why I Love Swatches

Throughout this book you'll see many swatches. I have hundreds and hundreds of them that I have made over the years. When I give workshops on finishing, the students are often surprised at the size and detail of the swatches I use to plan my sweater designs. My book *Designing Knitwear* describes my process for designing garments with the swatching process as the key to success. For finishing, the swatch is equally important.

I always say that a good knitted swatch tells the story of a sweater. A large swatch, worked before beginning a sweater, can do so much more than check the gauge! It can be a proving ground for planning edgings, buttonbands, seaming and more. It allows you to see the sweater in miniature form before you begin to knit the actual garment.

I know many knitters cannot wait to jump into a project once a pattern is decided upon and a yarn chosen. But, as is often counseled, making a good-sized swatch, and playing with your yarn, can help you avoid disappointment later. And the swatch aids in finishing as well.

I also see the swatch as an "homage" to my project. It is a token of caring about the success of the project, my respect for my knitting and my knitting helpers. And from a creative and workwoman-like point of view, it embodies my curiosity about my materials. A lot of magic happens for me in the swatch. It is definitely an object of craft for me. I consider it carefully, I design its length and width, and I care about its edges! It reveals the sweater to me.

A well-made swatch is a thing of beauty and pride. And, for me, when the sweater is gone, it is a reminder of the fun and uniqueness of a project, and it captures information in a way that no notebook can. Throughout this book you will see examples of my swatches, and how much detail I put into them.

Swatching has no required skill level—it is an endeavor for all knitters and knitwear garment makers. It should become a labor of love with time and experience. I know this is true—the process of swatching has been the foundation of my career and it never fails. If you take the time to swatch well, you will always produce an outstanding garment.

◀ I work swatches to test aspects of my designs in advance of making them in order to to avoid surprises later. In this example, I tested my fabric (main pattern stitch and ribbing) as well as a cable detail on a shaped collar.

▼ This swatch looks almost like a miniature version of the sweater front it preceded.

Swatching for Gauge

Of course checking gauge is still one of the most important functions of a swatch. If you knit a swatch and find that your gauge is off you will need to change your needle size. You might need to go up or down multiple sizes. Here's the rule: If your gauge is tighter than stated (more stitches or rows per inch), use a larger needle; if your gauge is looser (fewer stitches or rows per inch), use a smaller needle.

Most patterns give the gauge over 4 inches. I think this is much too small. In my experience, from my own knitting and having worked with dozens of excellent knitters, exact gauge is *rarely* determined by an initial swatch that is less than 8 inches tall by 8 inches wide.

Testing Fibers

As knitters we become spoiled by wool. A naturally springy fiber, wool imparts vitality to a knitted fabric. Sweaters knit in most wools reliably keep their shape and often for a long time.

However, some other fibers are not so reliable. Silk, viscose, rayon and other slinky synthetics tend to stretch in a knitted fabric and often the sweater pieces can "grow" even as you are knitting them. One-hundred-percent alpaca can also do this, especially if loosely spun or not plied. How to deal with this issue? First, be aware of it!

Be sure to knit a largish swatch—at least 6 by 6 inches, preferably larger—and carry the swatch around with you for a couple of days in your pocket or purse. Tug at it a little here and there, and give it some wear. When you measure from a swatch that has been handled this way, you will get a more accurate gauge for what your sweater will become!

The Finishing Toolkit

Having the right tools on hand and being prepared will help you enjoy the finishing process. The next chapter will cover the equipment you need to have for blocking, but here are a few other items you should have on hand for other finishing tasks.

Tape Measure

A flexible tape measure, not a ruler, is essential—a true must-have! You'll use it to take your own measurements, check your gauge in your swatch and measure your pieces as you knit.

Tutorial
Get to Know Your Knitting Style!

We all have an individual style in our knitting. Do you know the characteristics of your own knitting? Do you get the same gauge on a straight needle as you do with a circular needle of the same size? I suggest you really get to know your knitting texture as this will shine a light on what kind of finishing is best for you.

I personally tend to have a tighter than average row gauge, and the left side of my knitted pieces tends to be looser than the right. I also have a firm hand, so my texture emerges more prominently than that of knitters with a softer "hand" to their knitting. I can control synthetics and droopier yarns without much effort, and the fabrics I knit from them need little or no blocking. Some of this is my natural knitting "gait" and some I have worked at to firm up my looser tendencies in some patterns. I do not need to block my pieces as firmly as some knitters do.

I have come to learn the various qualities inherent in my knitting possibly because I have had so many knitters assist me over the years. Some knitters create smooth and wonderful colorwork. Some knitters with softer hands work cables in a relaxed way, whereas others who are firmer (even at the same gauge) lend their cables a firmer, more structured look. As a designer, I like to use these subtle differences to enhance a design.

It is possible to even out the texture of your knitting by paying attention. I have found this to be true with my own knitting over the years. Here are some tips:
● Some knitters who work back and forth have a tendency to knit one of their rows more firmly than the other, either right-side rows or wrong-side rows. If this is the case, try using a different needle size for one of your rows.
● If you have a softer hand, or have a hard time getting a handle on softer yarns, try different needles. A wood or bamboo needle may "grab" yarns better and help you even out your tension. If your fabrics are tight and firm, and you would like a softer look, try a slick metal needle.
● Just knitting more mindfully, paying attention at the beginning of rows and taking the time to really study your knitting will make you more aware.

Changing your personal texture is not essential or necessarily even desirable, but it is good to be aware of it. I have a friend who learned to knit by working into the back of his stitches. He didn't know that his twisted-stitch knitting was different. After learning this, he has no desire to change because his fabrics have a look and feel that is distinctive!

Sewing Needles

I have a little tin box that I use to carry a variety of needles and pins and I keep it near at hand at all times. I am always searching for new needles and have an assortment of metal, plastic, bamboo and wooden needles. I am always looking for needles with different "eye" sizes. My personal Holy Grail is to find the perfect needle for sewing on small-holed buttons! Some thin needles with a slightly bigger eye will just not go through the holes or shanks on smaller buttons. Everyone's needle kit will be a little bit different, but here is what is in mine:

TAPESTRY NEEDLES

These blunt needles have large eyes and are thick and easy to hold for seaming. I also use them for "pinning" pieces together to hold them in place while seaming or measuring. Curved needle tips are nice, but I also like straight needles—it's a personal choice! I have a couple of huge bamboo needles for heavy projects with very bulky yarns.

EMBROIDERY NEEDLES

Large-eyed embroidery needles (sometimes called "crewel" needles) are perfect for seaming fine-gauge fabrics.

HAND-SEWING NEEDLES

I use large hand-sewing needles with the largest eyes I can find for sewing woven fabric to a knitted fabric with yarn. Small sewing needles can be used with sewing thread when necessary.

Pins

You'll need a few types in your kit to be ready for any finishing scenario. A sewing-supply or dime store should be able to supply any pins you need.

SAFETY PINS

Safety pins of different sizes are a staple of any finishing toolkit. I used large-size pins for holding pieces together, and small ones for pinning shank buttons (see pages 82–83) in place.

T-PINS

I have a few of these in my kit reserved for general use—pinning pieces together and for final spot "steaming" at the ironing board. I also have a full box in reserve for blocking lace. (See pages 24–25 for more on blocking with T-pins.)

SEWING PINS

I occasionally use sewing pins with large, round, easy-to-grab heads. They are best used for holding zippers in place while sewing by hand.

Knitting Needles

You probably already own all of the knitting needles you need for finishing, including a range of circular needles and straights. And since everyone has a

favorite needle, I believe this is largely a matter of personal choice. However, a few specialty needles are nice to have at hand.

NEEDLES WITH EXTRA-SHARP POINTS

Finishing often requires a good sharp point for picking up stitches, especially for fine-gauge fabrics, so I often save an odd needle for that purpose, even if its twin has been lost.

FINE-GAUGE NEEDLES

These are useful for picking up stitches in edges that are loose or uneven to tighten the join between an edging and the main body of a piece. (See pages 59–61 for more on picking up stitches.)

CIRCULAR NEEDLES

Circular needles are most often used in finishing for knitting edgings in the round at neckline edges. It is useful to have a range of sizes in 16-inch- and 24-inch-long circular needles. I insist, as most experienced knitters will, that the join between the needle ends and the cord that links the needles be smooth and ridge-free, to avoid the yarn getting caught.

Since I often choose to pick up trims at the lower edge of a seamed garment at the very end of a project instead of working the trim at the beginning, I like to have a range of 36-inch needles, too, for either working in the round, or back and forth along a lower edge of a cardigan or open garment. Some garments have edgings that go around a long stretch of fabric (see the striped cardigan vest on page 73), and in those cases a longer-than-average needle is essential.

▼ My little finishing box used to hold Italian licorice candies. It is the perfect size to carry in my purse or knitting bag. I use it to store sewing needles of all sizes, a variety of pins, a few buttons for a current project and any helpful tool of the moment.

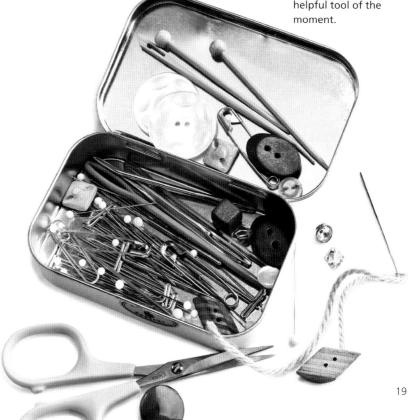

Crochet Hooks

I barely know how to crochet and rarely use a crochet hook in finishing. However, you can use a hook to join pieces in a creative way (see the crochet-edge pullover on pages 54–55) or add a crocheted edging. I most often use a crochet hook when I create a fringed trim (see page 97).

Dress Form

The advantage of a dress form is that you can pin pieces to it, check lengths and steam a finished garment in 3-D. I use my dress form all the time, and I depended on it in my early years of designing to help me envision placement of details and refine measurements. I especially like to use it when pinning attached collars in place.

If you are serious about designing for the yarn industry, or you just want to give yourself the best gift for sweater-making help, invest in a good dress form in your size. You can also make one! I have a friend who went to a sewing workshop where everyone made a cast of their own bodies and then a form that they could use for fitting purposes. There are articles online that explain the process.

A used dress form can be a good buy even if it does not mimic your body exactly. Or if your body differs from a standard size—and whose doesn't?—you can pad out the hips or bust or waist to your own measurements with some fiberfill and then cover it with muslin.

Getting Ready to Finish

Just as the models in a fashion show get a thorough once-over before they hit the runway, so do my sweater pieces before I begin any finishing, including blocking. This is a crucial point in the process!

Nothing is worse than discovering the back armhole depth is an inch shorter than the fronts after the neckline and front bands are complete. I know this sinking feeling from experience. Take the time to check your pieces before you do any assembly work.

Arrange the Pieces

Lay out all your pieces on a table. Place the front(s) next to the back and align the sleeves flat next to the armholes. First look over all the pieces for fabric and pattern errors. Are there any errors that pop out at you? If there is an error in colorwork, perhaps it can be fixed with duplicate stitch. If something is really off, you might have to rip out. Better now than later!

Refer to Your Schematic Drawing

Consulting a schematic drawing is essential with blocking of any type. Lay out your pieces and measure them, then compare the measurements to the schematic. At this point, really scrutinize the pieces. If you find any discrepancy in size, take care of it now, not after you have started to put the pieces together. ■

Tutorial Weaving In Ends

Weaving in ends is another task that most knitters don't relish and put off for as long as possible. It can be done at different stages of finishing. I usually weave the ends into the seams after the sweater is seamed. This way the ends do not add thickness to the body of a piece. I prefer to join new yarn at the beginning of a row, so that this extra weight of yarn at the edge can be easily put into the seam.

However, when doing colorwork, I prefer to weave in ends at the beginning of rows where they are joined. I like to leave a little end hanging. After blocking or steaming, when the ends settle into the fabric, I clip them close. When yarns are joined in the middle of a row, by choice or necessity, weave them in before blocking to help set them in place with the blocking. If you are felting a garment, it is best to settle all the ends into the fabric first. The thinner the needle, the more firmly the end will be imbedded. Weave ends as invisibly as possible when both sides of a piece can be seen.

Tip IT CAN BE TRICKY TO WEAVE IN A SHORT END with a large needle. So, here's a tip that everyone loves: Just weave the large needle along through a path, without the yarn in the eye, then thread the end through the needle's eye and pull it through. No end is too short to weave this way.

CHAPTER 2

Blocking
Basics

Blocking is often the first step in finishing,
and many knitters swear by blocking as an essential
element of the knitting process. In this section,
I explain the various methods of blocking,
describe how blocking affects different yarns
and stitch patterns and make a case for why
I believe less is more when it comes to blocking.

~

To Block or Not to Block?

Blocking is a process in which you use water or steam to even out irregularities or surface unevenness in a knitted fabric. Knitted fabrics can become uneven as a result of knitting tension, yarn irregularities or the very nature of a pattern stitch.

Many novice knitters create fabrics that are a little lumpy or bumpy—I did when I first started knitting! After many years of practice I have learned to control my tension and I am also fortunate to work with expert knitters who have perfected the evenness of their knitting. Sometimes all their knitted pieces need is a very light shot of steam, or even no blocking at all. That being said, I like knitted garments to look handknit and don't mind a little unevenness. Too much blocking, even when done well, can take away some of the inherent life in a knitted fabric.

When I began my career as a designer, I tried wet blocking, but as time went on, I experimented and found that steam, or no blocking at all, still gives a fine result if the rest of your assembly and finishing is good. When I give workshops on finishing, knitters are shocked when I say that I rarely block anything anymore, maybe with the sole exception of knitted lace fabrics. I truly spend very little time on blocking as a process—just a few minutes per sweater. I have found through experience that good seaming and well-done edges often create boundaries and

structure that make blocking unnecessary. However, beginning knitters or uneven knitters might still want to add some smoothness to their fabrics. And some stitch patterns, notably lace, require blocking to reveal the beauty of the fabric.

If you have used fibers that cannot be blocked and the pieces look dreadful, fear not. Even the ugliest-looking pieces can be structured to look great if they are prepared well. The pieces for a dress I designed in a bamboo/acrylic yarn looked like a limp pile of rags on my worktable. I was concerned, but as I seamed the garment and added edgings, the dress started to have shape. I also hung it on my dress form for a little while (I could have used a nice fat supportive wooden hanger) and it ended up looking as smooth as if I had steamed or wet-blocked it.

So, do not assume you must block a knitted piece. As you develop your assembly and edging skills, and even out the texture of your knitting, you will see it is not as necessary as it might seem. Believe in your own knitting—the grace and individuality of your fabric. Develop it and you will be rewarded!

▼ If you are unsure how your sweater pieces will react to blocking, for example if the yarn has a metallic component that might not respond well to heat, it is best to test an area of your swatch first.

▲When you plan to knit beads into a fabric that requires steaming, as this silk lace swatch did, be sure to test the steam on your beads first. If steam damages the beads, you will have to find an alternative.

Surfaces and Tools

You can spend as much or as little as you like on tools and surfaces for blocking. If you plan to do a lot of blocking, you can invest in specially made blocking boards, for example, or you can improvise with items you probably already have around the house.

Tools

IRONS AND STEAMERS

I am not fussy about irons—I have never owned an ultra-expensive one—but I do insist on a powerful shot of steam. A long cord is helpful, too, especially if you want to move around a very large piece that is pinned or carefully laid out. A dedicated hand-held steamer is perfect for blocking sweaters on a dress form.

T-PINS

I prefer to work with sturdy T-pins above all other types of pins for blocking. I tend to drop pins and needles on the floor while I'm working, and T-pins are easier to find than straight pins. T-pins are strong and do not bend, unlike dressmaker pins, and they have a wide, broad end, which is easy to hold and prevents the pins from slipping through knitted fabric. (See pages 24–25 for more on blocking lace with T-pins.)

LACE WIRES

I have actually never used lace wires, but they come highly recommended by those who do use them, so I suggest you try them if you like to knit lace. To use lace wires, you slip the wires through the edges of the lace piece to stretch it out and pin the wires down to your blocking surface.

GLOVE AND SOCK BLOCKERS

There are specially made forms for blocking gloves and socks. I have collected vintage wire and ceramic forms for gloves and wooden sock forms. I find them charming, but often they are better as collectibles and reminders of the past than for actual use.

Surfaces

PRE-MARKED BOARDS

Blocking boards come in different sizes and materials, including ones that can be folded for storage. Some are padded and covered with a heat-resistant fabric. The most useful aspect of blocking boards is that they are marked in a grid of one-inch blocks, which makes them very helpful for shaping pieces to size during wet-blocking and for opening up lace with T-pins.

CARDBOARD BOXES

While not quite as pretty as specially made blocking boards, sheets of cardboard are just as effective when opened up and placed on a table. I am not fussy about working with used cardboard boxes, as long as they are clean. When I need a large length of cardboard for a lace shawl, I simply overlap them. A little bumpy, but it works. I like that the boxes have fold lines—I use them to help me align pieces and measure! If when I am done they are a little buckled from contact with water or steam, I simply fold them up and put them in the recycling bin!

IRONING BOARD OR TABLE

Small pieces and items that just need a quick touch-up can be blocked on an ironing board, but for most jobs an ironing board is aggravatingly narrow. I prefer to cover a table or kitchen counter with a towel. My current apartment has a large granite kitchen counter that I can use for steaming, with or without a towel or sheet underneath.

RUG COVERED WITH A SHEET

For the duration of about three sweaters in my early career, I covered a rug with a sheet and pinned wet pieces, or pieces to be steamed, for blocking. If you are patient, have a good back, and can close the door against human and animal trespassers, this is a viable option.

DRESSMAKER'S FORM

If you want to block a sweater to shape and are fortunate enough to have a dressmaker's form, you can steam the garment on the form. Always allow pieces steamed on a dress form to dry thoroughly before removing.

Blocking Methods

Here are a few questions to ask yourself before you attempt any blocking method:

Are the fibers able to endure blocking, heat, steam, etc.? If the answer is no, skip the blocking and move on to assembly! Even if it is safe fiber-wise to block, do the pieces really need blocking? If not, don't bother! If blocking is safe and necessary, what is the least invasive blocking required? Less blocking is always better in my book. Besides, any time not spent blocking can be used for more knitting! Once you've asked yourself all of these questions and still want to block your pieces, the following methods are all you need to know.

CHEAT SHEET

Dress Form Substitute

If you don't have a dress form, you can roll up some clean paper towels or brown craft paper and insert them into the sweater to hold its shape.

Steaming

There are two kinds of steaming: I call them Shot o' Steam and Mega-Steam. One is a delicate refined whisper. The other, as its name implies, is a hot wet blast! Each has its place. For touch-ups and to even out surfaces, just use the Shot o' Steam method. For fabrics that require substantial smoothing-out, be more aggressive with the Mega-Steam method. But only do this if your fabric allows.

● SHOT O' STEAM

Lay the piece on a fabric-covered surface, shaped roughly to size. You don't need to pin it or stretch it unless you feel more comfortable securing it with a few T-pins. Hold iron an inch or so above the knitted piece and shoot steam toward it. Never press, never apply pressure and never touch the iron to the knitting. Flatten the fabric with your palms, gently. Quickly, while the piece is a little damp, pinch any cables, and tease any eyelets open with the tips of your fingers. Allow the piece to dry thoroughly before removing. This should be your go-to method. You can also use it along edges to even them.

When the sweater is done, I often like to give a slight shot of steam to seams, edgings and wool buttonholes to "set" them. I like to "set" a cable or any other textured pattern and give it the most texture possible, by steaming it slightly and pinching it to emphasize the relief. Even though we are admonished in the classic knitting texts to never steam ribbing, I always break this rule because I like to emphasize the depth of ribbing. To steam ribbing, I pat the ribbed area to condense it. Then I allow steam to permeate it, let it dry thoroughly and shake it out. It always emerges puffier and more pronounced and retains its shape better. Never press or flatten ribbing with heat or steam unless you want it to be pressed or flattened; the characteristic drawn-in quality of the ribbing will be lost.

● MEGA-STEAM

This is a heftier version of the above and again is reserved for those fibers that can take the heat. Prepare the knitted piece on the fabric surface, pinned slightly if necessary. Lay an 8- to 10-inch damp cotton or linen towel—never one with any synthetic content!—over the knitted piece. Working in sections, put the iron on a hot setting and touch it lightly to the damp cloth, allowing the large burst of steam to permeate the fabric below. Re-dampen the cloth and proceed to another section until the whole piece has been steamed in this manner. Again, while the piece is a little damp, pinch any cables and tease any eyelets open with the tips of your fingers. Allow the fabric to dry thoroughly before removing.

Wet Blocking

Wet blocking is not difficult, but it is a time-consuming process and takes up a lot of space. Don't bother with it unless you must. Wet blocking is necessary for fine-gauge lace (less-fine lace can often be steamed). It also works well for fluffing up wools, but so does steam.

When you wet-block, have a tape measure and your schematic at hand. Dip the pieces, one by one, into a small sink of water. Squeeze very gently to absorb water into the fibers. Then lift the wet piece onto a towel without stretching it, roll it up and squeeze to absorb excess water.

For lace shawls, have the blocking surface and T-pins ready. If you are not quite sure what the measurements will be, at least have a rough idea. Lay the shawl in place and spread from the center outward to stretch by hand as much as possible. For rectangular/square shapes, pin across the middle and then stretch evenly to each side, pinning as you go into an edge stitch. The edges get a little "pointy" where they are pinned, but you can take care of that later by steaming the points to even them out. If there are any scallops or pointed sections in the edging, pull them and pin to shape.

For lumpier sweater pieces that do not need severe blocking, pinning should not be necessary. Just unroll and pat pieces into shape, measuring and referring to your schematic. If the pieces seem big, and they often will when they are wet wool, pat them into their narrower dimensions, even if they bunch up or "ripple" a little. They will spring back to shape when they dry. You can place a fan to blow over the pieces to speed the process.

Wet Towel Blocking

A milder version of classic wet blocking, but almost as much work, is to lay a wet towel over a dry piece of knitting, pinned or unpinned. Leave it alone until the towel is bone-dry, and remove.

CHEAT SHEET

Using T-pins

When pinning into cardboard blocking surface, anchor the pins more firmly by placing the T-pins slanting away from the knitted fabric.

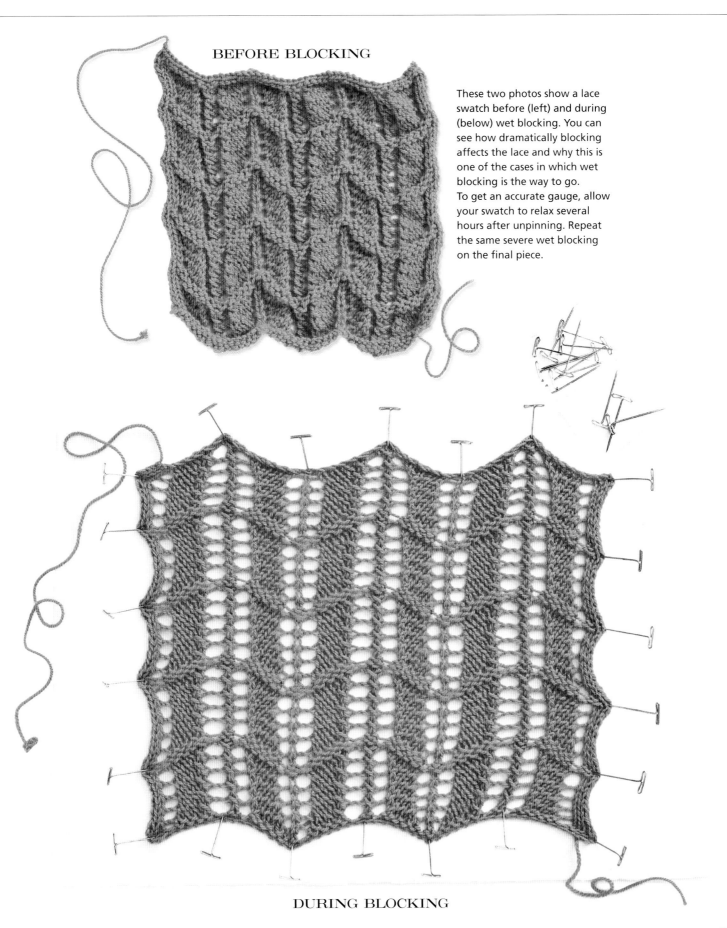

BEFORE BLOCKING

These two photos show a lace swatch before (left) and during (below) wet blocking. You can see how dramatically blocking affects the lace and why this is one of the cases in which wet blocking is the way to go.

To get an accurate gauge, allow your swatch to relax several hours after unpinning. Repeat the same severe wet blocking on the final piece.

DURING BLOCKING

LACE CASE STUDY
Two Scarves, One Pattern

Pattern Chunky Scarf
SEE PAGE 133

For these simple scarf projects, I wanted to contrast yarns of different weights, types of twist, and fiber. I knew both scarves would need some blocking, and I was curious what the different yarns would require.

Both scarves are worked in the same lace patterns but in two different yarns—one fine (pale blue) and one very heavy (purple). I chose to leave both ends untrimmed, and make that decision afterward— a finishing treat! The lightweight scarf is worked in a 3-ply 100-percent alpaca yarn with a soft sheen. I

chose to edge the scarf on each side with about one inch of garter edging, and the openwork lace patterns sit within this stabilizing edging. This fabric needed very little blocking: I lightly steamed the lace, spreading it a little with my fingers. I did steam the garter edgings very slightly, and I took special care not to stretch them. I applied no pressure to any part of the scarf: In fact, the iron never touched the fabric.

For the heavy scarf, worked in a bulky wool/alpaca blend, I felt the addition of garter stitch at the edges would be too heavy, so I added no edging at all, allowing the scarf to retain the natural curl of the stockinette stitch at the edges. I steamed the scarf, section by section, using a damp press cloth. This was not intended to flatten the fabric, but to both "full" the wool (make it become loftier and a little fuzzier) a tiny bit and open up the lace. I did not apply heavy pressure to the fabric, but I did touch the damp fabric of the press cloth lightly with my iron to send steam into the scarf beneath. Then I used my fingers and palms to flatten each section, allowing each to dry slightly as I proceeded.

In my mind, the ends cried out to be trimmed. I chose to add a triangular edging to both scarves—an idea that just came to me as I picked up along the first edge. In order to keep the join between the triangular sections and the main scarf as smooth as possible, without adding thickness along the join, I picked up into only the front strand of both the cast-on and bound-off edges. (See Chapter 4 for more on applying edgings.)

For the heavyweight scarf, I worked only a solid garter-stitch triangle, trimmed with a whimsical tassel (see page 96 for tassel how-tos)! I chose to incorporate more lace and a puffy leaf motif into the triangular edging of the fine-gauge scarf. Note that when I steamed this little leaf-unit, I pinched it with my fingers while it was still damp to help accentuate its 3-D quality.

The larger of these scarves has a wonderful heavy drape and a fuzzy quality that comes from a yarn that is not plied, only twisted. In contrast, the finer-gauge plied yarn has a crispness that lends a sharper quality to the patterns. You could use almost any yarn for these scarves, but when you make a substitution, be sure to ponder the qualities the yarn will impart to your project! I would love to try working the same pattern in mohair—perhaps two strands held together—or a brightly colored 100-percent silk or soft pima cotton. ■

When I studied the rectangular lace scarf pieces, before the decorative ends were added, I felt they would benefit from some blocking. I wanted to both open up the lace to show it to its advantage and to flatten the curling edges slightly.

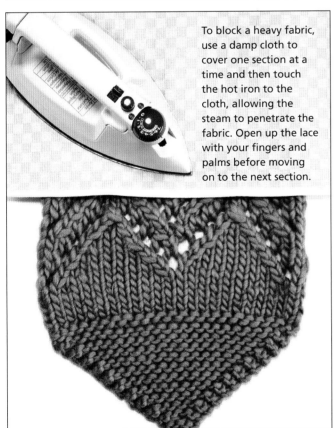

To block a heavy fabric, use a damp cloth to cover one section at a time and then touch the hot iron to the cloth, allowing the steam to penetrate the fabric. Open up the lace with your fingers and palms before moving on to the next section.

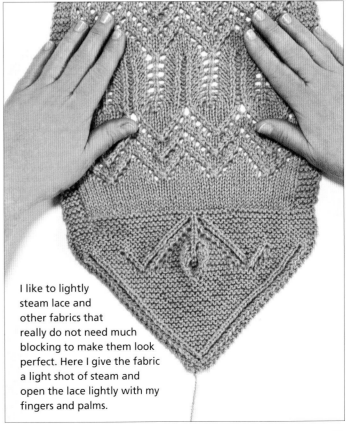

I like to lightly steam lace and other fabrics that really do not need much blocking to make them look perfect. Here I give the fabric a light shot of steam and open the lace lightly with my fingers and palms.

Pattern
Fine-Gauge Scarf
SEE PAGE 133

Yarn Smarts

Perhaps the most important factor to consider when finishing—before, during and after knitting—is yarn.

Yarn is the driving force behind every knitted project; every other aspect of a design is subservient to whatever yarn is being used. No two yarns are exactly alike. Although it's not common, even the same yarns from different dye lots can behave differently. So it is very important to be familiar with your yarn before you get to the final stages of your sweater.

Identify Your Yarn's Qualities

Yarn has inherent qualities that affect a garment and the finishing: Is the yarn drapey? Heavy? Springy? Yarn combines with pattern stitches to give a fabric certain characteristics that might affect your project. Is the fabric uneven? Does it draw in? Does it hang heavily?

General Guidelines for All Fibers

When choosing a method to block a project, I think it is most useful to follow the symbols on yarn labels for guidance. However, always err on the side of caution, and always check your blocking method on a swatch.
● If according to the ball band a yarn is washable, pieces made from it can be wet-blocked.
● Any natural fiber that is mixed with a synthetic fiber should be blocked according to the qualities of the synthetic, regardless of the percentage.
● When in doubt, test your swatch!

Wool

Wools of all kinds, for the most part, can be both wet-blocked and steamed. An exception to this rule: I am wary of steaming "superwash" wools (specially treated wools that can be machine-washed), because I have found that some—not all—lose a bit of luster and bounce when steamed.

Some wool yarns have a tendency to "full," which means that the yarn gets loftier and perhaps a little fuzzier when steamed, which can blur stitch definition. A step further makes certain wools "felt," which means that their fibers shrink and lock to form a dense fabric lacking in stretch (see pages 116–117 for more on felting). This tendency for some wools to full can be a real boon when you want a firm and solid fabric, and steaming helps to "set" patterns. I love using these kinds of wool to make the very best pompoms (see page 96). However, be careful not to full or felt unintentionally by blocking with too much heat, whether it be wet blocking or steaming your wool. As always—be sure to test your swatch.

Other Animal Fibers

Cashmere, alpaca, quiviut, mink and other fibers from animals other than sheep can have less bounce and springiness than wool, so be very careful when blocking them. They are also often mixed with other fibers in a yarn; be sure to study the labels carefully. A light shot of steam—tested first on the corner of a swatch—may be acceptable. If you do not like the look of the results—if the steam leaves the fabric limp or dry (what I call "cooked"!)—then count on perfect assembly, rather than blocking, to make the sweater look its best. Caution your dry cleaner, too, to avoid heat with any sweater you have had doubts about when you take it to be refreshed.

Plant Fibers

All plant fibers have their own characteristics, which are described below. When any are mixed with other fibers to create a yarn, consider the characteristics of both fibers when deciding how to block.

COTTON
100-percent cotton yarns can be wet-blocked or steamed.

RAYON AND VISCOSE
Rayon, a natural fiber, and viscose, its synthetic equivalent, should both be approached with care when it comes to heat and moisture. Check ball bands, and test on your swatch.

BAMBOO, HEMP AND SOY
Bamboo, hemp and soy are among the many strong and lustrous new plant fibers. Use care when they are blended and follow directions from the ball bands.

SILK
Silk yarns come in many types and in different textures, too. Silk as a fiber is very strong and can take heat. Since knitted silk fabrics tend to grow, be sure to spend some time with your swatch to see how it wears. Recheck your gauge and needle size before beginning a project.

LINEN
Linen is often combined with other fibers, and it imparts a cool, dry quality to a yarn. It is very strong and can be steamed and washed, and heat can be applied. A 100-percent linen yarn can be tricky (see pages 30–32), but the extra attention needed at the outset of a project is worth it. Skeins can be washed before swatching. Soften stiff and somewhat unyielding fabrics with washing and wear.

LIFE LESSON

Check Your Fiber Content!

Nowadays, I always test my yarns, but when I first began designing, I was not so careful. I once almost ruined a project: a long-sleeved dressy pullover. The yarn had been described to me as "silk," and I neglected to study the ball band to see that 30 percent of the fiber content was actually acrylic. The addition of the springy synthetic gave my knitted pieces a bouncy quality I liked. I steamed a sleeve to even out the texture and let it dry slightly. When I lifted the piece, it hung limply. There was no time to re-knit, and I winced as I revealed my mistake to the client. We decided that I should steam the other pieces, too, to give the sweater a uniform look. The client loved the sweater, but I was not happy at all; it was an entirely different design than I had planned. I vowed I would never again approach blocking and finishing without testing my yarns carefully.

Synthetics

If a yarn is synthetic or has a synthetic component—such as orlon, nylon, acrylic, acetate or viscose, to name a few—avoid heat or steaming fabric knit with it. Again, perfect assembly is the key to a beautiful sweater in these fibers.

Combining Yarns

If different yarns are mixed in a project, the results are not predictable. For instance, a tightly spun yarn mixed with a soft, loftier yarn may tighten up in the fabric after steaming, causing ripples or unevenness that cannot be eliminated. Be sure to test blocking on a swatch before making a project with mixed yarns.

Color Issues

When knitting colorwork projects in any fiber, you can check the yarns, especially reds, dark shades and black, for colorfastness, if you have any concerns. It is a good idea when working with a new or unfamiliar yarn, and it is easy to do. Wind a small bobbin of yarn, soak it thoroughly and roll it in a white paper towel. Let it sit a while and check if the dye bleeds into the paper. Do not wash or steam fabrics of more than one color if the yarns are not colorfast.

With bright yarns in any fiber, be careful that high heat does not dull their luster and depth. Natural dyes can be gorgeous and create subtle effects: Don't use extreme heat with them either.

Substituting Yarns

When substituting yarns, pay particular attention to the finishing instructions in the pattern. If there is any aspect of the garment that requires blocking or steaming, make sure your substitute can endure the treatment.

Breaking the Rules

I have a friend who is a very creative designer with an eye for the unexpected and a love for quirky effects. She has been known to heavily press all kinds of fabrics, including synthetics and rayons—really pressing with heat and weight on the iron. Often this results in unusual fabrics that can be dense, extra shiny, sometimes even slightly melted-looking. She designs with this aspect in mind.

So if you are daring, try this from time to time, even just as an experiment. Make an extra swatch and see what happens when heat is applied. It is a lesson in process and observation. What are the effects, and what can be done with this result?

CHEAT SHEET

Quick Test

You can test a yarn's ability to be steamed without even knitting a swatch. Just wrap the yarn around your hand a few times and then around the middle of the yarn loop to make a "butterfly." Steam the butterfly and see what happens. If the fibers go limp, avoid steaming the finished garment pieces.

A TALE OF TWO YARNS (and Two Tunics)

These two projects, each worked in yarns of vastly different fibers, surprised even a veteran knitter and designer like me with their results.

I had in my mind to work up two summer tunics in warm-weather yarns of the same weight and gauge to compare the finishing for two very different fibers. The yarns I chose for the two tunics were worked in the same patterns and had the same stitch gauge yet very different *row* gauges. And they could not have varied more from each other in the way they draped in the finished fabric.

The fabric of the blue tunic, knit in a soft bamboo-blend yarn, has a crisp stitch definition and a drapey "liquid" quality. It feels cool and refreshing. The yarn is soft and easy to knit and needed no preparation. The knitted lace fabric required no blocking or steaming whatsoever, even after seaming.

The yellow tunic was knit in a 100-percent linen yarn, which created a gorgeous and completely

The neckline edge of both sweaters is square and simple, with no shaping. I worked ridges of garter stitch on a stockinette stitch background, with mitered corners. I also used a simple garter-stitch edging to outline the armholes.

Pattern
Linen Tunic
SEE PAGE 134

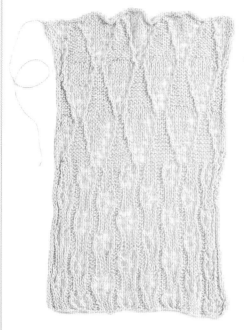

unique fabric that was vastly different from the bamboo-blend yarn. The yarn was challenging, but worth the preparation. Note that this garment has the same bust measurement and the exact same width as the blue tunic. This version is also knit to the same number of rows as the blue tunic, but you can see that the stiffer nature of the linen yarn elongates the patterns slightly. The hard edge of the linen yarn lends the tunic an entirely different drape: While the bamboo yarn has a clingy quality, the linen stands away from the body a little.

This linen yarn requires some special handling. Before knitting, the stiff wiry hanks were soaked in mild soapy water and dried before being wound into balls. Even after this soak, the yarn was slightly stiff. At bottom left you can see what an unblocked piece looked like, contrasted with one of the blue tunic pieces. After completing the front and back, before sewing the pieces together, I soaked them again for several hours, and then air-dried them. The fabric was softer, and I felt it was ready to seam and trim.

I was surprised at the stringlike quality of the linen yarn and how it made for a very open lacework, almost like netting! Judging from how each washing softens the fiber, I am sure that this is one of those garments that will bloom with age, and wear like iron. The garment has a lovely, slightly slinky feel; the fabric is cool to the touch and perfect for summer. What a rewarding and unusual project!

Note: I took care with the linen pieces when seaming not to pull the yarn too tightly along the side seams, to maintain the length of the pieces and avoid even the slightest "gathered" quality. The neckline was challenging: the bind-off row was stiff and very wide. I had to use a firm hand, and I picked up many fewer stitches than I expected to make the simple trim lie flat. ■

▲ Before knitting the tunics, I worked two large swatches to see how the patterns looked in different yarns. Although the stitch gauges were the same, the yellow linen swatch (shown here blocked) had a much more elongated row gauge than the blue swatch in a cotton/bamboo blend (shown unblocked).

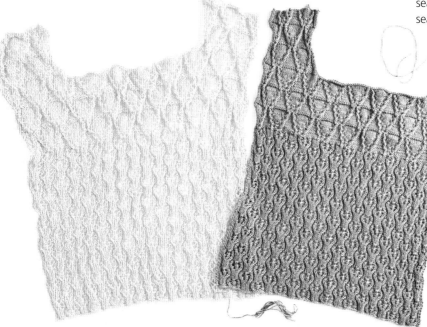

▲The knitted tunic pieces (shown here unblocked) had a very different feel. The yellow piece was a little stiff and clearly needed blocking. The blue piece was flat and supple and required no blocking at all.

CHEAT SHEET

On the Edge
I outlined the unconstructed armholes with a simple garter-stitch edging. However, you could easily substitute a different trim. A flat knit/purl pattern would work well, or you could knit a lace pattern for a longer length to create a cap-sleeve effect.

Pattern
Cotton/Bamboo
Tunic
SEE PAGE 134

Blocking Stitch Patterns

The yarn is not the only variable in deciding how to block a particular fabric. You also have to consider the stitch pattern. Here are some general rules about blocking various pattern stitches.

Always do to your swatch what you will do to the finished project to anticipate any problems and to see what the final fabric will look like, and, of course, to obtain the gauge of your knitting. Remember: If a certain pattern stitch, like the slip stitch patterns described below, needs blocking to look its best, do not use a fiber or yarn that cannot be blocked.

When I first began designing, I blocked my swatches severely. But experience proved that this was not always wise. I often blocked the life out of my swatch, and then the garment that followed had to be treated the same way to obtain the gauge.

Unless there is severe unevenness in a fabric, I use as little blocking as is necessary to give the piece an even, knitterly look. As I mentioned earlier, I do not want my pieces to look machine-knit either—too much blocking can have this effect.

Garter Stitch

Avoid pressing or blocking garter stitch patterns unless you want the fabric to lose all its life. Just let it be itself. If you do want to set a wool garter stitch, give it a shot of steam and let the fibers "full" a little.

Knit/Purl Patterns

A shot of steam is all these simple patterns might need. Never apply pressure with an iron to textured patterns unless you want the texture to be reduced. Press gently with the palms and fingertips.

Cables

I never wet-block cable patterns; I rely on steam and often pinch the cables to emphasize their texture.

Lace

In my mind, there are two kinds of knitted lace. The kind that needs to be severely blocked, as in shawl lace and fine-gauge lace pieces, and the kind that I call garment lace, worked in heavier-weight yarns in which the lace is as much texture as it is openwork. For garment lace, I simply steam to open up the patterns and give them a tease with my fingertips.

Slip-Stitch Patterns

Slip-stitch patterns, both color and solid, have a tendency to curl and widen. It is almost always necessary to block these fabrics to use them properly for garments. The pieces of the embellished cardigan shown on pages 126–131 needed steaming to get them to lie flat. I steamed my swatch for the project, and followed suit with the finished knitted pieces. Without doing this, the garment would have had a lumpy and untailored appearance. But if you desire an uncontrolled, untailored appearance, do not block these patterns!

Colorwork

Stranded colorwork most often needs a shot of steam to take away any surface irregularities and to keep the fabric from curling. Intarsia designs, those with large blocks of color, often need steaming to even out the joins between sections. Be sure to weave in all your ends before steaming intarsia. ■

▶ Stranded colorwork often needs to be blocked to even out the fabric. I prefer a light steaming, pressing the fabric with my fingers and palms to flatten slightly. Here you can see the difference before (left) and after (right) blocking. (The Fair Isle cardigan knit from this swatch is shown on pages 123–125.)

BEFORE BLOCKING

AFTER BLOCKING

CHAPTER 3

Seaming Seminar

As we learned in the last chapter, some yarns
defy blocking, so it is important to perfect your
assembly skills so your sweaters always look neat and
polished. Whether you sew traditional seams or join
by less conventional methods, assembly does
not have to be hard and should not be daunting.

In this chapter I'll present traditional and more
creative ways of joining pieces, as well as a
step-by-step approach to a project's assembly.

Three Simple Rules

There are several common myths about seaming—that it is difficult, that it is tedious and that seams should be invisible. None of these are true! Once you learn a few basic rules and some simple techniques, seaming can be a fairly easy and enjoyable process. Also, it is fun to be creative when joining pieces—sewing is not the only way to join pieces. Knitting, crocheting or embroidering them together are other options.

I made this old favorite sweater before I started adding seam stitches to my designs. You can see how sewing the reverse stockinette fabric to itself causes a deep, unattractive dent.

As I have learned over the years, seams need not be invisible—outline your seams and let them be a detail of your sweater!

In this chapter, I discuss a number of "rules" for seaming, but I don't want you to think that means it is rigid. Knowing that a process supports you, and having a vision as a guide, is the goal. Those who work with me know that I chuckle over mistakes and I always try to accommodate errors. Don't be rigid—just remember the helpful guidelines, test them, and know that in time your seaming will be just right. I learned these guidelines gradually, over a long period of time! Try to have a relaxed yet attentive approach to finishing—I do! Even though we want our work to look perfect, that takes time and experience.

As a beginning knitter, and even in the early years of being a professional designer, I used to struggle with seaming knitted pieces for sweater assembly. Each sweater presented its own challenges. I had to consider different fibers, different yarns—fine, heavy, textured, novelty—different pattern stitches, different garment types. And certain parts of a sweater, especially sleeve caps where a smooth curve is generally desired, were always challenging! I had to find a way to make this easier for myself. After years of learning, I came up with three simple rules to follow when assembling a sweater.

I almost never break these rules. Here is an overview of these rules and how they came to be:

Rule #1:
Seam Stitches Are a Finisher's Best Friend
Before beginning to knit a new project, always check to see if your pattern incorporates stitches at the edges that will make seaming easier. If not, add seam stitches to your pieces when you knit them.

I find sloppy or what I call "ragged" finishing in my designs unacceptable. As I've mentioned before, I love and honor the handmade nature of the knitted fabric and expect it to be a little bit uneven and charmingly imperfect! But to have a garment that is less than crisp in the seams and at the edges makes me cringe. Why work so hard on the knitting only to have the eye drawn to the poor finishing?

My most important red-alert about seaming came in the early days of my career; the difficulty I had with one particular sweater made me realize I needed to take more care with preparing for finishing.

I was sewing together an Austrian-inspired knitted jacket. The background fabric of the sweater was reverse stockinette stitch. As I sewed the purl stitches to the purl stitches in the reverse stockinette stitch pattern for the side seams, I hated the way the seam became "indented," or rolled inward. To make things harder, the yarn was a wool synthetic blend, so I knew I could not steam the seam to open it up without damaging the fabric.

When I started to sew the sleeve seams, I was even more appalled. I had worked my increases one stitch in from the edge, but as I seamed, the "indented" look was still there, and the increases were all too obvious. The seam had a very messy appearance where the edges met. I pulled the seam out many times, trying different ways to make it look better. First I attempted to sew a seam that was only a half stitch from each side, rather than one stitch. But this was also terribly uneven looking. Then I tried to sew further into the fabric of the sleeve, to avoid seeing the looped increases—now my sleeve was too narrow. By the time I was through, the seam looked even worse from having been redone so many times.

I eventually realized that seaming was not as much of a problem when I was working on smooth plain stockinette-stitch fabric as it was in the more textured reverse stockinette-stitch fabric. I had a eureka moment when I realized that all the issues could be solved—with almost any pattern stitch or yarn—if: 1) I added two stockinette stitches at the edges of my pieces, and 2) all increases and decreases were worked within the seam stitches. My seam could then be worked between these stitches. By doing these things, all my seams are outlined in a smooth yet inconspicuous way.

It is especially pretty to outline shaped areas with seam stitches. A fitted garment, with shaping at the waist, for example, always benefits from this kind of attention. In addition, the ugly indented look is avoided because stockinette stitch tends to push a little outward at the seam, whereas other textured patterns, such as reverse stockinette stitch, indent in the seam. These stitches can be worked on any seam to make sewing easier, not just at the side seams.

WHY TWO SEAM STITCHES?

One seam stitch is not enough! Through experimentation I have learned that you have to have two seam stitches to always have a smooth seam, without indentation. When you have two stitches at your edges, you can seam between them.

I now plan all my sweaters to accommodate these extra seam stitches. And you can do that too, almost all the time, regardless of the pattern you are using.

This solves other problems, too. If you are a knitter who usually works increases into the first and/or last stitch of a row, you know that this bumpy edge can be seamed to the inside, so that the jagged edge is not visible. But I am sure you see that the seam itself is often a little uneven. By incorporating two seam stitches and working increases next to them, the seam is accented and its line is smooth and even.

HOW TO ADD SEAM STITCHES

There are two things to consider when adding seam stitches, especially if you add two stitches to each side, as I do.

When seaming the body of a sweater, one stitch gets seamed to the inside and the other outlines the seam. Four stitches total remain on the outside of the garment, thus adding four stitches beyond the pattern stitches. In addition, if you add to the fronts of a cardigan to outline the edges, then pick up between, this number can jump to six extra stitches. (When adding stitches for picking up at the edges, rather than seaming, I refer to these as "edge stitches.")

When I first started incorporating seam stitches, I realized that if I added these stitches, they would contribute to the width of the sweater. I was adding eight stitches at the sides, total. Four of them would be seamed to the inside, so they were fine.

With finer yarns, an extra four or six stitches beyond the pattern stitches is a negligible amount and will not add considerably to the finished width of the garment. However, with a heavy yarn, the addition of these extra stitches can add an inch, or even two inches, to the finished measurement of your sweater.

So if you are concerned about adding extra width, see if you can subtract a stitch from the pattern stitch of your garment in order to add a seam stitch. With some pattern stitches, it is easy to lose one stitch of the pattern and change it to a plain stockinette-stitch seam stitch. Other times you will have to truncate a pattern, if possible.

EXCEPTIONS TO THE RULE

As with most rules, there are a few exceptions to this one. When I add seam stitches to an edge that I am

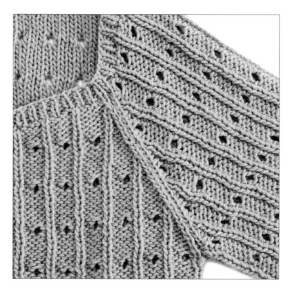

going to pick up into, I often incorporate only one edge stitch. Working the seam stitches in stockinette is not always ideal, such as when the fabric of the sweater has a tighter row gauge than stockinette stitch. This happens with many textured patterns that have denser than average row gauge. Stockinette stitch—our seam stitch pattern—often has a ratio of five stitches to seven rows; a denser pattern might have a row gauge with a ratio of five stitches to ten rows. If the row gauge of the seam stitches is looser than that of the main pattern, the "outline" stitch will be bubbly and not match the pattern next to it. In this case, I might add only one stockinette stitch as a seam stitch, and seam between the pattern and the single seam stitch. When seaming garter stitch, I do not add seam stitches.

◀ Here the raglan seam is outlined clearly and decoratively by the seam stitches.

◀ I avoided an ugly seam in this reverse stockinette stitch–based fabric by adding extra stitches that make seaming easier and both outline and highlight the seam.

This eyelet-rib tunic appeared in the Spring/Summer 2009 issue of *Vogue Knitting* magazine.

Tutorial
Where to Add Seam Stitches

Seam stitches are incorporated into a knitted project to make sewing pieces together easier. They are perhaps most useful along any vertical seam, such as body and sleeves, where increases or decreases for shaping can be worked next to them. I also border armhole edges with these seam stitches.

You have a choice of the final appearance of your seam, based on how many seam stitches you add to each piece, and in which part of the body of a sweater they are located. Here are some suggestions about how to vary the appearance of the seam based on seam stitches:

● Adding two seam stitches results in an outlined seam on the right side. When you seam *between* two stitches, one disappears to the inside, or wrong side, of the garment, and the other remains to be seen on the right side. When two like pieces are seamed, the resulting seam is "outlined" by two stitches.

● Raglan sweaters: Adding seam stitches to armhole edges and sleeve caps will outline the seam. Using more than two stitches can make this band that outlines the seam wider and bolder.

● Cap-sleeve sweaters: You can outline both the armhole edges and the edges of the adjoining cap. The outline of the stitches will disappear at the top of the cap where bind-offs occur.

● Vertical cardigan or neckline edges: For picking up along a front edge, add two or more stitches if you want the edging to have an "outline" stitch, or just one if you want the edging to emerge right out of the pattern of the piece. Adding seam stitches along a V-neck makes picking up stitches or seaming an edging much easier. To eliminate an outline stitch along a picked-up edge, add only one seam stitch and pick up next to it.

● If you want the ridge of a seam to be a detail on the right side of the sweater, work the two seam stitches on each piece on wrong-side rows. Seam to the right side.

Tutorial
Increasing and Decreasing Next to Seam Stitches

When working increases or decreases with seam stitches, you have to decide how they will be placed. Should you place them next to the seam stitches or work them into the stitches? What type of increase or decrease should you do? These decisions will affect the appearance of your knitting. Below I describe the increases and decreases I use most often with seam stitches.

PLACING INCREASES
I place the simplest increase next to my seam stitches. Here is how I commonly write the instructions for this type of increase:

Next (inc) row (RS) *K2 (St st seam sts), make 1, work in pat as est to last 2 sts, make 1, end k2 (St st seam sts). Working incs into pattern, continue to increase every... row, until . . .*

I almost always use a very innocuous increase—usually a backward loop (see page 161), which is a simple make one increase. I work increases into the pattern, maintaining the isolated seam stitches. For variety you can use other types of increases, maintaining the isolated seam stitches.

PLACING DECREASES
Decreases next to seam stitches offer more visual variety than increases. You can either decrease next to seam stitches or into them.

● Working the decrease into the seam stitches: I never work decreases into the first or last stitch of a row, but I do often work the second (inner) seam stitch into the decrease. This is how the knitting instructions would read for this action:

Next (dec) row (RS) *K1, ssk, work in pat as est to last 3 sts, end k2tog, k1.*
WS row (maintaining seam sts) *P2 (seam sts), work to last 2 sts, end p2 (seam sts).*

This kind of decrease has a more ridged effect than if you work the decreases next to the seam stitches. It also works nicely along raglan or armhole seams.

● Working the decrease next to the seam stitches: If you work the decreases next to the seam stitches, the seam will have a less raised appearance.

Next (dec) row (RS) *K2, dec 1 of choice (can be ssk or p2tog tbl), then work in pat as est to last 4 sts, end dec of choice (can be p2tog or k2tog), end k2.*
WS row (maintaining seam sts) *P2 (seam sts), work to last 2 sts, end p2 (seam sts).*

This allows the decreasing to be a detail—or not—next to the seam stitches!

Rule #2:
Check Your Pieces Before You Seam

As I mentioned in the last chapter, I always lay out my pieces and examine them before seaming. I spread them out flat and look closely at each piece one at a time and then in comparison with the other pieces.

These are the questions I ask myself as I review the pieces:

● Are all the body pieces the same length? Do they all correspond to my schematic drawing?

● For a cardigan, are both fronts the same shape and size?

● Do the sleeves match each other in size and shape?

● Do I want to seam or block any areas of a garment now—or after the assembly is complete?

● If I have not already, do I want to weave in the ends now, into the fabric? Or should I wait until later, and weave them into my seams?

● Is one side edge of a piece looser than the other? If the answer is yes, I make a note of the looser edge that will have an edging sewn or picked up along it so that extra attention can be paid to it.

I cannot emphasize this step enough. I always want an overview of the project, from both visual and measurement points of view. I look closely now to see if there are any errors I cannot accept. And at this stage I often lift and drape the fabric of the pieces in my hands to see how they move. It helps me "feel" what my seaming tension should be, and ponder what needle size I might want to use for edgings in the stages ahead.

Rule #3:
Seam with the Right Side Facing

I'm going make this point throughout this chapter, because it is so important: Always seam with the right side of the fabric facing you so you can see what the finished seam looks like as you go.

My fabric sewing and costume design background has provided me with a lot of inspiration for my designs—garment shapes, techniques and details. But when sewing by hand or by machine, I always seamed with the wrong side facing. For a long time, I assumed that sewing knitwear with the wrong side facing was also the way to go. I learned that there is a big difference. When you sew a seam in a sweater, you want to see what the seam looks like as you are working it. You don't want to turn the piece around and get an ugly surprise!

Seaming Basics

In the next few sections of this chapter, we'll look in depth at various seaming scenarios and the exact techniques needed. First, let's go over a few basics that will help make your sweater assembly easier in any situation.

Tips and Tricks

Using the right tools—in this case needles and yarn—will put you on the right foot toward perfect seaming.

SEWING NEEDLE SIZE

Choose your blunt tapestry needle to make seaming as easy as possible. A needle with a curved tip helps to dip under the "bars" between the seam stitches. For fine-gauge knits, use a small needle, not a bulky one; it will keep the seam stitches firm and close to one another.

YARN LENGTH

Sew with as long a strand as is comfortable for you. If the yarn is fuzzy and wears out as you sew, use a shorter length or a different yarn (see below). I often plan to have my strand end as I approach the armhole, a few inches below if possible, where I like to join a new long strand. Then I can flow into the sleeve cap or armhole join, a more demanding area, without adding another strand of seaming yarn again.

JOINING A NEW SEWING STRAND

If your sewing strand runs out or breaks, and is too short to sew with, leave the end hanging to the right side of the knitting, emerging from the top of the two bars between the seam stitches from which it emerges. Re-thread your needle and scoop under the same two bars between the seam stitches from which the short end is hanging. Leave an end of the new strand hanging on the right side.

Take both ends and tuck them to the wrong side of the fabric before resuming seaming with the new strand. You can weave these ends into the seam later. When you weave them in, do it so one goes up and the other goes down, to eliminate bulk all in one place on the seam.

WHICH YARN TO USE?

Whenever possible, I like to seam with the yarn used for the sweater, as I think it contributes to the uniform drape of the garment. But when a yarn is fuzzy or softly textured or loosely plied, the friction of seaming can easily cause it to break. If this happens, you can do one of two things:

1. For a loosely plied or loosely twisted yarn, roll the piece of seaming yarn with the palm of your hand on your thigh, holding the other end in your other hand. This will tighten the twist of the yarn before you thread it into the eye of the needle. Sometimes I lightly moisten the yarn to keep this twist, or I keep twisting it while sewing to keep it firm.

2. Use a different yarn to seam. Try to match weight and fiber content in a smoother, stronger yarn. If the pieces are soft and drapey, use a soft yarn. For a springy, bouncy fabric, choose a yarn that also has some elasticity to match.

Seaming Order

When you have your pieces examined (blocked if necessary), your tools lined up and your schematic at hand, set aside a time to start your finishing.

I *never* attempt any finishing when I am tired. I like to be fully able to focus—and enjoy the process! I like to do most of the seaming at the same time, so my tension in the sewing is the same. I might spend several sessions completing the sweater. I also like to do matching edges at the same time, so my tension is the same for both. This is the order I follow:

FOR A CAP-SLEEVE SWEATER
Step1 Sew front(s) to back at the shoulders.
Step 2 Sew side seams next in order to tame the shape of the garment, and prevent the pieces from waving around.
Step 3 Sew sleeve seams and set the sleeves aside (to prevent the extra weight of the sleeves from making finishing awkward).
Step 4 Work neckline and front edges.
Step 5 Attach buttons, zippers or any other closure elements or collar details.
Step 6 Finally, sew the sleeve caps into the armholes.

FOR A RAGLAN OR SADDLE-
SHOULDER SWEATER
For a garment in which the top of the sleeve forms part of the neckline edge, the front(s) and back have to be sewn to the sleeves so any edgings can be worked at the neckline edge. In this case, sleeve and side seams can be done before edgings.

FOR OTHER PROJECTS
You should seam in the order that makes things easiest for you. Less weight is better, so do not seam everything together unless necessary to complete the edgings or perform other finishing tasks.

There are many kinds of seams, and I have had a lot of experience with every kind. I can see why people are daunted—there are just so many different kinds of seams and they each require a different approach. Here are some of my favorite examples of basics that have served me well. In the projects at the end of this chapter, you will see some other ways of approaching seaming and joining.

Joining Shoulders

I am very opinionated about shoulder seams. All of the weight of a garment hangs from the shoulders, and good neckline fit is directly related to shoulder seams, so I always pay careful attention to this area of a sweater.

Shoulders should be seamed exactly to the width indicated on your schematic drawing. If shoulders are too wide or too narrow, the fit in the upper body will be affected: The sweater will have either a droopy look or a pinched appearance.

There are three basic ways to join front(s) to back at shoulder seams:
1. Seam the pieces together with right sides of the material facing.
2. Weave or graft "live" (not bound-off) stitches of fronts and back together. This technique is often called kitchener stitch.
3. Knit the pieces together with stitches for the front and back shoulders on separate needles, then bind them off, one at a time, with a third knitting needle. This technique is called three-needle bind-off.

I almost always prefer the seaming methods for shoulders, to ensure the strength of the shoulders, but I use the alternative methods on occasion if strength is not an issue and I want a different effect. I also like to seam shoulders with a firm hand, and the result is a strong seam that can support the weight of a garment. The sweater will also keep its shape longer.

Preparing Shoulders for Seaming

Bind off shoulders in steps if the pattern requires it. Even though I seam my shoulders firmly, I do not bind off firmly. I like the seam to be dictated by my sewing, not the bind-off row.

Shoulders are usually bound off in three (sometimes more) steps, resulting in an angle that more closely corresponds to the natural slope of the body's shoulder. Most patterns advise binding off stitches every two rows, either at the beginning of the right-side rows, or at the beginning of wrong-side rows, depending on which side of the piece you are approaching. Since you are seaming bound-off rows, there are no "seam stitches" to aid in seaming. Therefore, sewing with the right side facing is even more important, so you can see the seam as you complete it. When I sew, I use this little trick to match my stitches (see the blue stitches in the illustration at right): After the initial insertion of the sewing yarn, I always sew one stitch at a time from each piece. I envision the stitches as V-shaped. As I sew across the row, I always insert my needle into a V-shaped stitch, not an inverted V. The blue stitches in the illustration and the text that follows show how I stitch into the blue V-shaped stitches.

I do not usually do anything to eliminate the "stair-step" look that occurs when binding off the shoulders over the course of several rows. I think the seam is less strained if it is just bound off naturally with a small jag between rows. I like the extra few stitches to lend strength, and the extra bumps are there if I need a little extra material to grab onto. This is helpful when sewing on a reinforcing seam binding, tacking a lining or adding a shoulder pad.

Sewing Front(s) to Back at Shoulders

With right sides of the fabric facing, align the shoulders so that the edges butt together, one above and one below. (The bottom piece is referred to as the lower piece, and the piece at the top, is the upper piece; armhole edges are at the right.)

1. Upper piece: From the wrong side, insert needle into the center of the first stitch at the armhole edge and pull the strand through to the right side.

2. Lower piece: *Insert needle from right to left around the first whole stitch of the row—this stitch looks like a V—and pull strand through. Note that the needle goes under the two strands of the large part of the V (shown in blue in the illustration to the right).

3. Upper piece: Insert needle around the next whole stitch from right to left—this stitch looks like a V. The needle goes under the two strands of the skinny part of the V (shown in blue in the illustration). Pull the strand through firmly.

Repeat from *, tightening the strand to make it firm. At the end of the last piece, pull through half a stitch and tighten up to match shoulder width in the schematic. Lock both ends by taking an extra stitch in the ridge beneath the seam. Weave in the ends. If you come to a jog on the shoulder, slant your needle to move the seaming from one row up to another.

As with any area of a garment, I always seam with the right side of the fabric facing so I can see the way the seam looks as I sew it. Here the shoulder seam is partially sewn. This method allows me to match the ribs where they meet at the shoulder. I prefer a firm shoulder seam over a loose grafted one.

Grafting or Weaving Shoulders Together

When a garment is very lightweight and airy and I want a flowing, seamless effect, I sometimes employ weaving at the shoulders. When you graft stitches you are working with "live" stitches that are still on the needles.

Weave in all the ends, or tuck them to the wrong side to keep them out of the way of your work. Lay your pieces flat on your lap or on a table. Have stitches for each shoulder on separate needles, horizontally next to each other, one front and one back, points facing to the right in the same direction. Have a tapestry needle ready, threaded with a long strand of yarn (about five times the width of the shoulder).

Take one stitch from each needle alternately, as follows:

Step 1 On the front needle, insert needle as if to purl into first stitch, pull the yarn through the stitch, and leave the stitch on the needle.

Step 2 Rolling the back needle slightly away from you, insert the needle as if to knit on this needle, pull the yarn though the stitch, leaving the stitch on the needle.

Now repeat the following four steps to join the remaining stitches:

Step 1 On the front needle, insert the needle knit-wise into the first stitch, pull the yarn through and drop the stitch off the needle.

Step 2 On the front needle, insert the needle purl-wise into a new first stitch, pull the yarn through, leaving the stitch on the needle.

Step 3 On the back needle, insert the needle purlwise into the first stitch, pull the yarn through and drop the stitch off the needle.

Step 4 On the back needle, insert the needle knit-wise into the first stitch, pull the yarn through, leaving the stitch on the needle.

I often share this useful weaving "mantra" invented by my friend, expert knitter Pat Yankee, and it nicely condenses the last four steps above: "Knit off, purl on (front needle); purl off, knit on (back needle)."

Keep the tension in the grafting row the same as the tension in the stitches on the adjacent rows and as even as possible. Err on the side of being too loose; you can tighten the row later, stitch by stitch with the tip of a tapestry needle.

Grafting can be bit awkward until you get the hang of it, so if you want to practice before doing the real thing, make two small swatches and practice on them.

Knitting Shoulders Together (Three-Needle Bind-off)

I use this method of knitting together "live," unbound-off, stitches when I have less need for structure in light and/or small sweaters. This technique is slightly firmer than grafting. Place the shoulder stitches to be joined with their needles together, right sides of the fabrics facing each other, and the wrong side of the fabric facing you.

With a third needle, k2tog into one stitch from each needle; repeat. Pull the first stitch over the second to bind off one stitch. Then continue across the row until all stitches are joined.

Usually this is the most common join when the shoulders are not slanted, and the shoulder stitches are bound off at once, all on one row. However, it is possible to angle a shoulder by working short rows, keeping the stitches "live," and then work as above.

Special Shoulder Issues

If you follow the techniques outlined above, you should be confident to approach almost any shoulder-seaming scenario. Here are a couple of more unusual set-ups you might encounter.

DIFFERENT STITCH COUNTS

When the number of stitches differ from front to back (for example, when there is a cable on the front that is not duplicated on the back), you need to ease in the extra stitches while seaming.

If you are seaming, instead of matching stitch for stitch as you sew, take one and a half to two stitches for as many times as there are extra stitches, evenly across the section that has extra stitches.

If you are joining by knitting the pieces together, or grafting, decrease the number of stitches on the row before so that the pieces match. Then proceed.

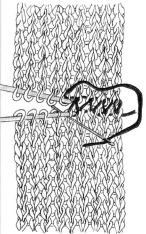

Grafting is easiest if done directly off the knitting needles. I prefer to first weave in the ends of the fabric pieces to the back to make the pieces very neat. Then I use a new strand to graft the pieces together.

Knitting together the shoulders of the cotton/bamboo tunic (see page 33). I also use this technique for the preppy vest on page 53.

REINFORCING SHOULDERS

Even if I take precautions to keep shoulders firm by sewing firmly, a very heavy coat or jacket sometimes requires a little more reinforcement in this area. I take a piece of firm seam binding (available at stores that sell sewing supplies), and sew it with sewing thread firmly to the width of the shoulder—and back neckline edge, too, if necessary. The inflexibility of the woven seam binding keeps these sections from stretching.

Vertical Seams

Vertical seams occur at the sides of a sweater (where front and back are joined), in sleeve seams, along raglan seams and in cap sleeves above lower armhole shaping.

If you leave a long "tail" of yarn at the end of your cast-on row, you can sew with it. Even if your "tail" is short, start the seam with it and the lower edge will be smoother.

Step 1 With right sides of the pieces facing, either in your lap or on a table, thread a tapestry needle with the "tail." Insert the needle on the other piece (non-tail piece) from under the cast-on row, and pull through.

Step 2 Separate the space between the two seam stitches on the tail side, and scoop your needle under the first single "bar" between the two lower stitches.

Step 3 *Return to the other side, and scoop your needle under two bars, on the other side, between the two edge stitches.

Repeat from * all the way up the seam, always scooping two bars. Remember: It is only at the very first stitch, the first time that you sew one side to the other, that you go under one bar.

Why sew with two bars at a time? Seaming two bars—or two rows at a time—is faster than sewing one row to another. And since the path of the yarn is longer, the seam has more elasticity.

Note that when you seam like this, one side is always one "bar" ahead of the other. When you do this, you are always going to be matching patterns and stripes accurately, from one piece to another.

Side Seams in the Body Pieces

When you get to the underarm, leave your sewing strand hanging, to be used to sew one side of the sleeve cap or the top of the sleeve.

Matching Rows and Patterns

If you start your seaming at the lower edge in the correct place, as described on the previous page, all of

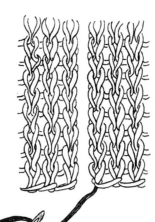

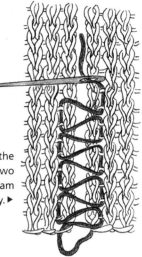

◄ Sewing a vertical seam: When joining two pieces vertically, I always use the "tail" or strand at the cast-on edge to avoid an extra end to weave in.

As you seam up the length of the pieces, scoop the needle around two bars on each side for a faster seam and to add elasticity. ►

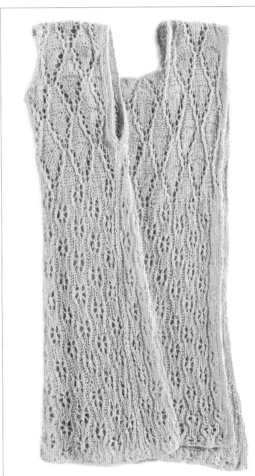

If you knit with a different tension at the beginning of right-side and wrong-side rows, the pieces might be different lengths. When this happens, tug a little as you seam to make sides match the correct length. Steam the seam to ease out any "gathered" effect. In the photo at left you can see the front and back lined up unevenly (on the right) and the sewn seam (on the left).

Every few stitches, tug very lightly on the sewing yarn. The seam itself should have the feel of the fabric around it—not tighter, not looser. If the seaming itself is tighter than the adjacent fabric, the fabric can droop or "bubble" around the seam. If the seam is too loose, the seam will be longer than the pieces themselves and might have a tendency to grow. Because you have the right side of the fabric facing, you can always see how your seam looks and adjust accordingly. Hold the piece up and see how it hangs, if you are not sure if your tension is right.

Even as an experienced seamer, sometimes I must rip out a seam that is tighter than the others—it happens. It helps to do all your seaming in one sitting so that the seams will have a similar tension.

This amount of attention might seem excessive, but in my workshops I often measure side seams in participants' sweaters and find that they can be as much as 1 to 2 inches shorter on one side than the another. This affects how the sweater hangs on the body and how it moves!

your patterns should line up, but if you do find yourself off by a row when you approach the section above a lower edge ribbing, or at a point where horizontal patterns meet, simply sew into one bar instead of two to make the match happen, then resume taking two bars at a time—no need to rip out the seam!

Armhole and Sleeve Seams

Since sleeve and armhole seams are also vertical seams, use the same technique when sewing them. Sew these just as you would the side seams of the body pieces. Do leave a long strand hanging at the top of the sleeve seam to help sew in the sleeve to the armhole. In the next section, we'll look at ways to attach different types of sleeve caps.

Sleeve Caps

When I began designing—and finishing—there was a dearth of specific information available about armholes and their details.

I read everything, eager to learn what would help me make well-put-together garments. I remember one book about "designer sweaters," which said that if your sleeve cap did not fit the armhole, then "ease in the excess fabric under the armpit so it will not show." I thought—my goodness! Why not make the sleeve cap *fit* correctly instead of having a lumpy armpit?! Here are a few hints I've since figured out to do just that.

Sewing the Lower Armholes Together

Always sew sleeve caps in from the lower armhole toward the shoulder, working one side at a time, or alternating both sides back and forth, sewing gradually. (The exception to this rule is for drop-shoulder sweaters, those with no sleeve caps—see pages 49–51 for seaming stitches to rows.)

Always sew this underarm section, from lower armhole to about 3 to 4 inches armhole depth, on both front and back, before sewing the upper cap.

I like to use the reserved strand from the end of the sleeve seam to go in one direction around the armhole, and the other reserved strand from the body side seam to go around the armhole in the other direction.

With right sides of the pieces facing, sew the bound-off edges of the sleeve armhole to the bound-off edges in body armhole, joining stitch to stitch. Then start to sew upward in the direction of the shoulder seam. When you reach the beginning of shaping on the sleeve, read the appropriate sections below.

Seaming Raglan-Style Sleeve Caps

The number of rows in a raglan sleeve cap should match the number of rows in the armhole of the body: This reflects a well-designed raglan. If your pattern does not have this feature, then you will have to "fudge" the fit of the cap into the armhole. Better still, adjust the knitting of the cap to get the correct number of rows so that seaming will make the cap correspond to the armhole.

When sewing a raglan cap to a raglan armhole, sew the underarm sections together as described above. Then sew the angled part of the raglan as for a vertical seam (see page 43), taking two bars at a time from each side until the pieces are joined.

Saddle-Shoulder Sweaters

These are similar to raglans but at the top of the cap there is a "strap" of fabric that extends to the neck. For this additional section, refer to the discussion of seaming stitches to rows on pages 49 to 51.

Seaming Cap-Style Sleeves

There is much more leeway for design in cap-style sleeves. A sleeve may be designed to fit exactly into the armhole. Or it may puff out at the upper cap. Or the sleeve may be pleated into the armhole.

In any case, the underarm of the sweater should match the underarm of the sleeve cap. It is *above* this area, at roughly 3 to 5 inches of armhole (or cap) depth, that easing should occur. See the workshop on the right for more information on seaming sleeve caps.

Sewing Caps Into Armholes

I use seam stitches at armhole edges and the sides of sleeve caps so that they can be easily sewn together.

Once the lower part of the armhole is connected, it is easier to sew in the cap. Tie a little marker at the center of the cap on its final bind-off row and match this with the shoulder seam. You can pin it or anchor it with another sewing needle. Sew a little bit from each side of the armhole, taking two bars at a time, until there is a section about 2 to 3 inches below the shoulder seam unconnected.

Sometimes it is most difficult to get a perfect fit in a smooth-fitting cap. Either the cap is too large and bubbles when you sew it in; or there does not seem to be enough fabric around the cap to fit the armhole.

This is a common occurrence and not necessarily an error of the pattern. It usually just reflects personal differences in row gauge. If your row gauge differs from the pattern, you may find your cap is either too high (looser row gauge) or too short (tighter row gauge). So if you encounter this situation, it might just be your uniqueness and is easily adjusted.

At this point you will see if your sleeve cap fits perfectly. If it does not, then try one of these tips:
- If cap is too large, unravel the bind-off row of the cap, rip down, and bind off (gradually, if necessary, over four rows) to the cap height that gives the best fit.
- If cap is too small, unravel the bind-off row of the cap, rip down, and work a few more rows until the cap height fits well. If it is necessary to rip down below your seaming to do this, rip out a few rows.

Note that any cap needs to have a little bit of ease, or else the armhole of the body will seem larger than the cap, and the cap will retreat into the armhole.

SLEEVE-CAP SEAMING
Eyelets & Cables Pullovers

Pattern Gathered-Sleeve Pullover

SEE PAGE 138

I know from my own early experience as a knitter, as well as from knitters who have attended my workshops, that sewing in sleeve caps can be a major challenge. I have learned a simple approach that helps enormously.

I set myself the challenge of designing two very different sweaters, using the same pattern stitches, each with a different kind of sleeve cap. To make things easy for myself — who doesn't like that?—I chose two stitch patterns that had the same number of stitches in their repeat. For all you budding designers, this is a way to easily make one pattern flow into another, without a

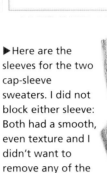

▶Here are the sleeves for the two cap-sleeve sweaters. I did not block either sleeve: Both had a smooth, even texture and I didn't want to remove any of the depth of pattern, either in the ribbed section or the lace.

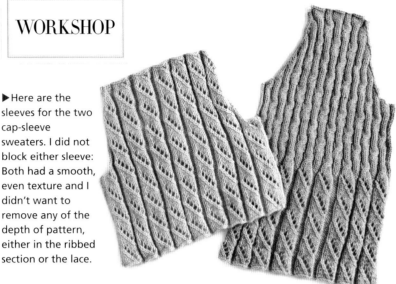

lot of fiddling with increases and decreases between sections. Despite having the same number of stitches, these patterns vary greatly in appearance: Contrast is what I wanted. As you can see, the rib and cable pattern forms a kind of allover check and has a firm texture. The other pattern is a series of lace panels, each divided by purl stitches, having a soft, open columnar effect. I incorporated stockinette stitches at all the edges, on all the pieces, including the armholes and sleeve caps, and this made sewing all the seams very easy.

My first stage of sewing a sleeve cap into the armhole is the same, both for the classic close-fitting cap (orchid pullover) and the puffed-sleeve cap (blue pullover), which has an almost pleated effect. To start, with right side facing, I began at the underarm, and I sewed about half of the front underarm to half of the cap. Then I repeated the same on the back. I marked the center of the upper cap to match it to the shoulder seam. Then I marked the center of each side of the cap, and the center of each side of the armhole.

I then sewed one side, matching markers and easing in any excess fabric in the cap. I continued over the shoulder, meeting the already-sewn section on the other side. This avoids having all of the sewing end at the shoulder seam, where I would have to weave in all my ends.

I *never* sew a sleeve cap flat on a table. A sleeve cap is three-dimensional: When I am sewing in a cap, I keep my hand inside the armhole to simulate the shoulder, and it helps me see the progress and the fit as I seam.

To finish the neckline on the orchid sweater, I picked up a large number of stitches along the neck edge, and worked only a few rows of k1, p1 ribbing. I bound off very firmly to avoid a flared ribbed edge.

Since these sweaters have wide scooped necklines, both front and back, I did not want the sweaters to slide off the shoulders. That look is fine with other kinds of sleeves, but a sleeve cap is designed to fit well along the armhole—and sweaters do stretch! To avoid stretch, I reinforced the back neckline of each sweater with a row of back-stitching along the ridge formed by the picked-up stitches, to keep it firm and assist the fit of the cap sleeves. To do this, I anchored my yarn at the shoulder seam. Then I ran my yarn through the back neck ridge, backstitching to lock the yarn every few stitches. I anchored the end at the other shoulder seam. I used the same yarn as I used to knit each sweater, but you can use a firmer one if necessary. ∎

FITTED SLEEVE

I always sew a sleeve cap to the armhole with the right side of the pieces facing. Since a sleeve cap is a three-dimensional part of the sweater, I hold my hand within the armhole and cap to fill it out as I sew. Here I have seamed the lower portion of the armhole, on both front and back. I match the marker at the center of the cap with the shoulder seam marker as I sew.

◀ Here the sleeve cap fits well, smoothly and evenly sewn to fit the armhole. The cap was eased in slightly as it was sewn in the upper portion of the armhole, and there was no excess puffiness. However, had the cap been too high to fit well, I would have pulled out a few rows at the top of the cap and bound off, then re-sewn the seam to fit better.

Pattern
Fitted-Sleeve
Pullover
SEE PAGE 136

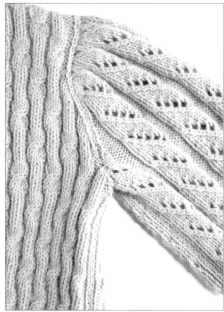

GATHERED SLEEVE

Here the sleeve cap is smoothly and evenly sewn with a pleated effect. The sleeve cap was gathered into the armhole in order to accommodate the extra fabric in the cap, and to create a slightly puffed effect.

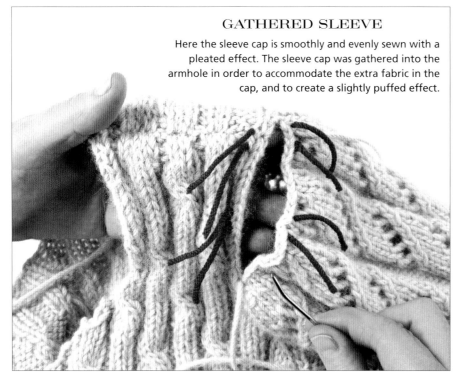

▲ Sewing the fullness of the cap of the blue sweater was a little more challenging as there was a great deal of extra width that had to be eased into the armhole. Again, the markers that I placed along the armhole edge, and on the cap, helped me to gather the fabric evenly for a good fit. I matched the markers as I sewed.

▶ I sewed a little organza "frill" inside the cap of this sleeve to help open up the pleats and enhance the puffed effect of the cap. To make it, I folded a 4-inch strip of organza in half, gathered it along the fold, and sewed the folded edge to the inner seam of the armhole, equally to either side of the shoulder seam.

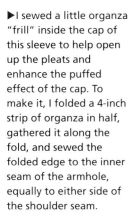

▲ The edging on this neckline is simply one repeat of the lace pattern from the sleeve. It has a slightly ribbed quality due to the purl stitches that separate the lace panels.

STITCHES MEET ROWS
Cabled Patchwork Scarf

Pattern
Cabled Patchwork Scarf
SEE PAGE 139

This scarf gives you practice in both picking up stitches along an edge, as well as joining edges that are very different.

My initial plan was to make this scarf from a series of different squares, for a truly patchwork effect. And you could do that, making a series of squares that have different cabled patterns. But I loved my first cabled square so much that I decided to repeat it over the length of the scarf.

I knit one square using a seed-textured "banjo"-style cable, divided by two-stitch ribs. I made the ribs at the edges of the square one stitch wider—three-stitch ribs—because I knew I would be picking up into these edges, as well as seaming along them. I wanted the look of the ribs to be uniform even after seaming.

Along the edge of my completed square, I picked up the stitches for another identical square. When done, this two-square section became my "unit" for the scarf. I made one more unit, then a single separate square to end the scarf in a symmetrical way.

I rarely block cabled patterns, but this fabric had a very ribbed quality. Since I wanted my scarf to lie flat, and I wanted each piece to be more square-ish in shape, I steamed each unit slightly to open it up. While the fabric was damp with steam, I slightly opened up the fabric with my fingers, taking care not to eliminate the texture of the cables.

After each unit dried thoroughly, I began to sew them together. I prepared the edges to be joined by marking the center and quarter length of each sides. As always, I align my pieces so that the right sides are facing me. I pinned the pieces together loosely, matching the markers.

When I sew a piece like this, I work outward from the center toward each edge, one half at a time: It ensures a more even join in a seam like this. I began sewing at the center, using one long strand, leaving a long end to sew the other side. I removed the pins as I came to them, and I used the markers to help me match the areas on each side as I approached them. On one side I inserted my needle between the first and second stitches of the outer rib (as in sewing a vertical seam). Then on the other side I took approximately one and a half stitches to match. When I reached the end, both pieces matched. I returned to the center and sewed outward to the other edge, using the strand that I had left hanging in the middle. When all the pieces were joined in this way, I wove in the ends, and steamed the seams slightly.

WORKSHOP

BEFORE STEAMING

A unit of the cabled scarf is made up of two identical squares. The second square is picked up along the edge of the first, so they are aligned in different directions. This very ribbed and drawn-in unit clearly needs a little blocking to make assembly of the scarf easier.

AFTER STEAMING

To prepare for seaming I steamed the units, stretching them slightly side to side to widen, and pinched the ribs and cables to maintain their depth.

When joining sides of pieces where "stitches meet rows" I like to start in the middle and work out toward each end separately. I always sew with the right side of pieces facing. I carefully match the pieces at their centers, and then place markers on each piece so I can match them as I sew. ▶

Although it was not really necessary, I chose to add a simple garter-stitch edging around my scarf. It capped off the squares and seemed to emphasize the undulating "wavy" effect. First I did a small test, picking up stitches over a short length to see how many were necessary. To emphasize the "wavy" effect, I picked up a few extra stitches along the bound-off and cast-on edges of the units than I did for the ribbed edges. I picked up along one long-side edge at a time, then worked the ends of the scarf last.

This kind of project is guaranteed to make you an expert in sewing and picking up stitches. And you can make the scarf as long as you like, by adding more units. You can used a heavier yarn to make a more shawl-like scarf. You could also choose to eliminate the garter stitch edging for a more unfinished, rough-edged effect. ■

I trimmed all four sides of the scarf in garter stitch to give it greater stability at the edges, but you may prefer to make the scarf without an edging.

CREATIVE JOINING VARIATIONS
Three Kids' Sweaters

Pattern
**Striped
Turtleneck**
SEE PAGE 142

◄ Start your seam as for the regular vertical seam: Thread your needle with the cast-on "tail" and insert it from the wrong side to the right side over and above the strands of the cast-on edge; pull through. *On the first side, take the needle under the "bump"; on the next side, take it under the bump, and, at the same time, under the strand above it. Continue from * up the seam.

Garter stitch is such a fun and easy pattern to knit, yet knitters often find it difficult to seam. Here I devised three easy kids' sweaters, each made in a basic rectangular approach. The shapes couldn't be simpler or more fun to knit. I used a different means of assembly for each sweater. The turtleneck pullover is sewn in the way I like best for garter stitch, the vest pieces are knit together with a three-needle bind-off, and the pullover with the embroidered flower pocket is crocheted together.

Each sweater has a different edging, too. The turtleneck has a ribbed collar. I also added a deep roll of reverse stockinette stitch on the lower sleeve, which I sewed to the wrong side to cover the edge, so that the sleeve could be worn down, or rolled up without a raw-edge look. The crocheted sweater has a simple single-crochet stitch (the only crochet I know!) around the neckline and all other edges as well. I used garter stitch as the trim on the vest—except for the little reverse stockinette stitch rolled edges on the little pocket flap.

I look for challenges as a designer, and it helps me to come up with new ideas and keep myself continually interested. These sweaters were no exception. How do you take simple shapes and transform them with finishing? Try it—it's fun. You could change the elements and make the sweaters in different ways: The pullover could feature pocket flaps, or the vest could be crocheted together. Or you could mix joining techniques in the same sweater! ∎

◄ Garter stitch might be the best fabric for kids' sweaters: It has a nice heft and it lies flat without any need to block. Here I chose a variety of shapes to allow me to explore a few different methods of joining.

Pattern
Preppy Vest
SEE PAGE 139

3-NEEDLE BIND-OFF

◄ To join the side seams of this garter-stitch sweater, I used the three-needle bind-off method. First, using a fine circular needle on each side, I picked up one stitch for every ridge along the side edges. Then I held both circular needles together and, starting at the lower edge, I knit one stitch from each needle together across the row, binding off at the same time. This makes a nice even ridge that accentuates the seam.

◄ Working a simple single crochet around edges and to join pieces is a nice non-knitterly way to join garter stitch, easy and fun to do. Again, just as with any other seaming, always have the right side of the material facing you so you can see the results and adjust if necessary.

SINGLE-CROCHET SEAM

Pattern
Crochet-Edge
Pullover
SEE PAGE 140

CHAPTER 4

EDGINGS
Intensive

In this chapter we'll look at the way I like to approach edgings. One of the most important aspects of finishing, edgings provide both structure and design detail. Decorative trims add contrast to a garment or dress up an otherwise plain design.

Working trim at the edge of a garment creates a firm outer boundary, in the same way that a seam creates structure within a sweater. And, in their most functional mode, edgings anchor buttons and other closures.

The Basic Approach
When I apply edgings and trims I like to follow a three-part decision process. Each part must be considered in relation to the others.

Step 1 Decide which edging to use. Each edging has its own qualities. Some are flat and firm. Ribbed trims draw in. Some trims, like ruffles, flare and are floppy and less structured. Patterns that are not traditional edging patterns, like lace or stranded or slip-stitch colorwork can be used, and all have unique qualities.

Step 2 Decide how the edging will be applied. Picked up and knit? Sewn on? Or added on by a more unusual method, such as embroidery or crochet?

Step 3 Examine how the edging will interact with the rest of the sweater. If you are following a pattern, the rules for trims and edgings are usually provided. But even then, you might be tempted to make changes. Perhaps in the past you have been frustrated with the numbers in patterns not working out for your particular tension, or your desired effect. Or, for a different look, you might want to choose an alternative edging.

Think Creatively!
Before you invest time in a pattern that gives generic numbers, you might want to test your own unique tension when applied to trims and edgings. And you also might want to personalize a design to change the edgings or other added-on details.

I like to assume all knitters are, or would benefit by being, creative thinkers! Patterns should provide an approach, a guideline, for creating a successful garment. In the case of my own designs, I love to think that knitters take them as starting points to which they add their own touches—changing lengths, working different edgings and incorporating details that contribute to the design.

Before deciding on trims, I often compare my knitted swatch to my knitted pieces when they are completed. If the fabric is softer and looser in the larger piece than in the swatch, I may change my mind about my original plans and incorporate a wider or firmer edging. Or the reverse: If the fabric seems

This is an example of a real "working swatch" that helps me visualize and test my finishing. I tried a variety of edgings on my swatch, picking up stitches along edges at different rates, and I even tested buttonholes. This kind of early planning makes the finishing on the sweater much easier.

stiffer than I expected, I may want the edgings to be equally firm. I am always examining my work and asking myself questions.

I find that even the simplest, most classic garment can be made extra-special by paying attention to the details. Altering the texture of a band, choosing a wonderful unique button, spacing buttons in an unusual way, adding a small pocket—any or all of these options can transform an ordinary project into something very special. In the next chapter, we'll go into more detail about these options.

Contrast vs. Neutrality

The easiest way to add detail to a knitted garment is with *contrast*. By changing colors in your garment, at edgings, bands and closures, you create visual variety.

Another way to add detail is to maintain color *neutrality* but add texture. In other words, by keeping all the details in one color, you can create a tone-on-tone look for your garment. To keep it from being boring, use a different yarn for an edging or collar than for the body of your project, or try a different stitch pattern. Use buttons that are the exact same color as the sweater.

Adding Edge Stitches

I always think about seam stitches when seaming, and I also think about adding stitches at edges to aid in picking up stitches for trims. As mentioned in the previous chapter, these edge stitches have to be added *before* your pieces are knitted. The stitches create different visual effects and influence the functionality of the trim, too. Here are some things to think about.

If I'm going to knit an edging that "grows" right out of the fabric of the body of the piece, I add only one edge stitch to the garment piece. I usually add one stockinette stitch (knit on right-side rows, purl on wrong-side rows). I pick up next to this stitch. With patterns that have a very dense row gauge (in other words, a pattern that has more than the usual number of rows such as with slip-stitch patterns), I often add one garter stitch. I also pick up next to this stitch, between the seam stitch and the pattern.

For an edging that I want to appear "outlined" on the right side of the fabric, I add two edge stitches and pick up between them. One edge stitch folds to the inside, and the inner edge stitch, closest to the pattern, shows on the right side of the piece between the pattern and edging.

For additional structure and to keep edges firm, I often like to create a tiny facinglike inner trim, created

▲There are two basic approaches to adding edgings and other details to a garment. A neutral way (left) is to maintain the same color scheme throughout. Alternately, you can contrast with the body of the sweater (right), using another color entirely for the edgings, or as accents.

Tutorial Gauging Your Edgings	Just as you measure for gauge in the body of a sweater, you can also measure for gauge in an edging, even a ribbing that has an elastic quality. Although it is not a commonly suggested technique, I check my gauge in edgings all the time and it is a big help.

Pick up over a small section on your swatch or the body of a piece, at least 6 inches, and work the edging as you would like it to appear in the finished piece. When you achieve your desired look, you can then measure this section and figure out the number of stitches per inch. Refer to your schematic, multiply the measurements by stitches per inch, and you have the number of stitches you need to pick up. If the edging has a multiple of stitches, round the number to the closest repeat.

by adding extra stitches that fold to the inside after the edge stitches are picked up. This lends structure to a front edge, with an extra two or three stitches folded to the inside.

For pullovers, it is best to work neckline edgings in the round whenever possible to avoid a seam that can make this crucial area of fit less elastic. However, if you do plan to seam a neckline edging, you need to add edge stitches to make your seaming neater and easier. If you are seaming a long turtleneck or cowl neck, you may have to reverse the seam so that it does not show when it folds over.

Picking Up Stitches

There are many things to consider when you pick up stitches to add an edging.

What needle size will work best with your yarn and pattern? What pattern will you choose to work at the edges? How do you know how many stitches to pick up along the edge? Are there challenging design details to think about? Let's work our way through these in the following sections, as you would when actually working on a project.

Mind the Gap!

When using a yarn that creates open spaces when you pick up into it, like linen or cotton, traditional techniques might fail you. You can thread a needle with a long strand of yarn and weave it in and out, on the wrong side, through the bars that lie flat between the picked-up stitches. Sure, it might seem like cheating, but it works!

Needle Size

My feeling about edgings is that they should be rich—not skimpy-looking! There is nothing worse than an edging that seems stretched, or thin, or as if there were not enough stitches picked up along the edge. And an edging should have a firm join to the main fabric, not be sloppy or loose.

You can use any needle size for edgings—depending on the effect you want. Edgings are often worked on smaller needles, one or two sizes smaller than the size used for the body of the garment. This ensures that the edging is firm. But this is also a rule meant to be broken. If you desire a softer look to your garment, or if your edging is to be decorative and not functional, you might want to try using the same size needle or even larger than you used for the body of the garment. However, if a sweater is to receive hard wear, I would suggest a smaller needle size.

Creating a Firm Join

For many knitters, one side of a knitted piece often tends to be looser than the other. Have you noticed

this in your own knitting? Take time to look at pieces when you have completed them. What happens when picking up on these edges? Notably—especially on necklines or cardigan fronts where it is most obvious—the picked-up row of stitches can be less firmly joined on the looser edge. Also, when using inflexible or non-springy yarns, the pick-up row can have a "holey" unconnected look.

As preparation in the knitted pieces, it is important to be careful to knit very firmly at the beginning of rows that will be edged. But I have found that even tugging a little extra at the start of these rows still leaves one edge looser than the other! There are two other things that can be done to avoid ugly joins. And these suggestions can be used for any edging. You can also use both techniques:

1. Pick up stitches along the edge with a *very* small needle, then switch to the larger needle after this pick-up row, as you work into the pattern.

2. On the first pattern row after the pick-up row, work into the back of each stitch.

Avoiding Holes

When picking up along shaped edges we often encounter areas where there are openings in the knitting that are looser or more open than we would like. The goal is always to make the join of an edging as firm as possible, so here are a couple of suggestions:

● When you encounter a hole or little opening, pick up into the spaces on either side rather than into the open space.

● Pick up more stitches than you will need and decrease the extra stitches on the first row of the edging.

● Along curves, such as at a neckline edge, pick up into the row below when there is a larger than average opening where bind offs occur. Gradually pick up closer to the bind-off row when the section firms.

How Many Stitches to Pick Up?

Sure, there are a few useful traditional guidelines for how many stitches to pick up along an edge for a given type of edging, but there are always exceptions to rules because all knitters do not knit alike, and the feel of individual fabrics varies. As I have mentioned before, I have discovered by working with many knitting assistants over the years that everyone has a unique tension as well as a unique "feel" or quality to their knitting. So not everyone will need to pick up the same number of stitches along a given edge. Rules are meant to be broken, depending on your yarn,

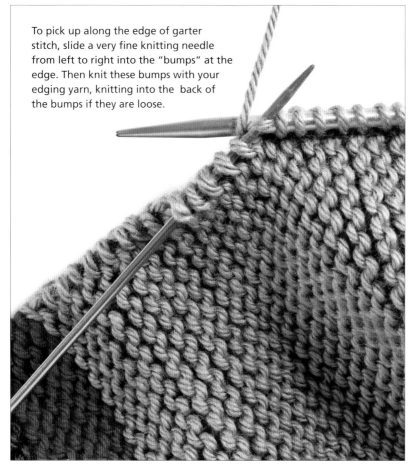

To pick up along the edge of garter stitch, slide a very fine knitting needle from left to right into the "bumps" at the edge. Then knit these bumps with your edging yarn, knitting into the back of the bumps if they are loose.

On a neckline, you might have to pick up along rows (below the shoulder) *and* across a bound-off edge (at the center of the neckline). Use a small needle and avoid picking up into "holes." I often pick up more stitches than I need and decrease them on the first row or round.

garment shape, needle size and the pattern stitch of the edging.

At this point you probably won't be surprised when I say that the only surefire way to know how many stitches to pick up is to make a test! There are two places you can do this. You can test an edging along the edge of your swatch, making sure that your swatch has the same edge stitches in place that the body of your garment has. You can also do a test along a small section of the piece you will be trimming.

With right side of your swatch (or small section of your garment) facing, and the yarn and needle size of your choice, pick up along a stretch of 6 to 8 inches. Work the edging over this small section to the desired width and bind off. Do everything to the edge you want to do for the finished garment. If you are satisfied, then repeat the process, the same ratio, on the longer edges of your sweater.

If you are unsatisfied, then try a different ratio of stitches to rows when picking up again, over a similar stretch.

▲ On this swatch I tested picking up ribbed stitches for a lapel. On the right, the stitches result in an edging that seems skimpy and drawn-in. On the left, I picked up a greater proportion of stitches, and the effect is fuller and more desirable.

Types of Edgings

My feeling is, and my experience shows, that any pattern can be used as an edging, but there are classic patterns that work well for any situation. The braver among you, with an eye for design and quirkiness, might explore other patterns than those I have listed here. The challenge of edgings is in their functionality. If an edging is purely decorative, anything goes. For stabilization of an edge and for creating buttonbands, these classic types will always serve you well.

Below are some of my go-to patterns for edgings. When picking up stitches for garter stitch or a knit/purl edging, I usually pick up two stitches for every three rows along the vertical edge. When working along a diagonal line, such as at a V-neckline, I often add an extra stitch regularly spaced—perhaps alternating two stitches every three rows with three stitches every four rows—so that there is no tightness along the angled edge.

Garter Stitch

This humble stitch should be everyone's favorite edging. It's easy, looks great, holds buttonholes beautifully, wears well and lies wonderfully flat. When a very narrow, innocuous edging is my choice, I always rely on garter stitch for its strength and ability to stabilize an edge without much width. I often work two ridges and bind off. If you want to work a buttonhole (see pages 85–88) in this very narrow edging, it is possible to do it on the first wrong-side row. Garter stitch can be altered with color and texture, while still keeping its characteristic ridges.

To knit garter stitch, just knit every row.

GARTER STITCH STRIPES

For smooth unbroken stripes, add a new color at the beginning of right-side rows and knit two rows. For broken stripes where the color is merged with the colors of adjacent stripes, add a new color at the beginning of wrong-side rows and knit two rows.

EXTENDED GARTER STITCH

In this variation, the garter ridges are separated by rows of stockinette stitch. I like the more open quality of this edging. Pick up on a right-side row to work this edging. Here is the pattern:

Row 1 (WS) Knit.
Row 2 Knit.
Rows 3–5 Purl.
Row 6 Knit.

Repeat these six rows for garter ridges that are divided by two rows of stockinette stitch.

Similarly, you can also work two ridges of garter stitch, divided by two rows of stockinette stitch, for thicker and slightly denser ridges.

SIDE-TO-SIDE GARTER STITCH

I adore this edging (I used it for the Fair Isle cardigan on page 123) and I often add another contrasting trim to it. It must be worked in a long strip and sewn to the edge of a piece. Then you can pick up along it in a matching or contrasting color and work another trim!

▶ On this colorful cardigan, the cuffs and neckline are worked in simple k1, p1 rib. The front bands, knit in different colors of garter stitch, contrast nicely.

◀ This design appeared in the Holiday 2009 issue of *Vogue Knitting* magazine.

Knit/Purl Patterns

There are many wonderfully textured knit/purl patterns that work well for edgings. They range from classic subtle texture to deep thick relief. These are a few of my favorites and the most reliable.

SEED STITCH

For a while I was utterly obsessed with seed stitch. It lies perfectly flat and has the most wonderfully pebbly surface that is exquisite in yarns with lots of bounce. It is worked over an odd number of stitches:

Row 1 P1 * k1, p1; rep from *.
Rep this row for seed stitch.

MOSS STITCH

This pattern is similar to seed stitch but has a more refined look. Since it has a four-row repeat, it is better suited to wider edgings. It is worked over an even number of stitches:

Rows 1 and 2 *K1, p1; rep from *.
Rows 3 and 4 *P1, k1, rep from *.
Rep rows 1–4 for moss stitch.

▲ This swatch has a very dense knit and purl textured rib. By working this rib at the bottom of my lace swatch I could test its elasticity and see how it compared gauge-wise to the other pattern.

▲ This cabled swatch has a flat textured pattern at the vertical edge and a wide flat ribbing at the lower edge. The edgings are very different, adding contrast to the design.

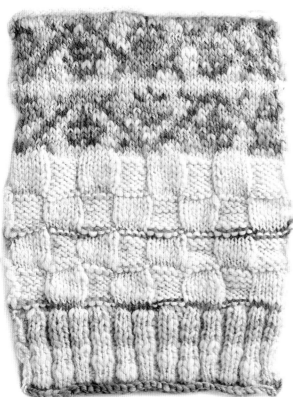

▲ The lower edge of this swatch is trimmed in a deep rib, which itself is trimmed with stockinette stitch that curls to the right side.

K2, P2 CHECK

I love all knit/purl checked patterns at edges because you can do a little decreasing to shape them without a jarring disruption of texture, and they also lie very flat. The k2, p2 check is very reliable and can be used at almost any width. Since it has a four-row repeat, it is better suited to wider edgings. It is worked over a multiple of four stitches:

Rows 1 and 2 *K2, p2; rep from *.
Rows 3 and 4 *P2, k2, rep from *.
Rep rows 1–4 for k2, p2 check.

▲ These two swatches feature textured checks at the edges.

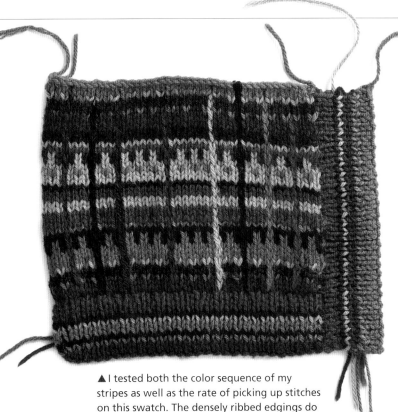

▲ I tested both the color sequence of my stripes as well as the rate of picking up stitches on this swatch. The densely ribbed edgings do not draw in, but lie very flat, and this was the effect I wanted to transfer to my sweater.

Ribbed Edgings

Probably the most classic of edgings, ribbed patterns help create shape in cuffs and waistbands. It's also one of the most versatile edgings. You can vary the number of stitches in the repeat to create more or less elasticity and incorporate other elements such as stripes and eyelets.

ELASTIC RIBS

There are all kinds of ribbings. Some draw in tightly like k1, p1 rib and k2, p2 rib. They keep their shape well and are best for areas that expect use.

The larger the number of stitches in each rib, the looser and less elastic the ribbing will be—in other words, a ribbing like k4, p4 rib will be more like a flat fabric, drawing in less than a ribbing with fewer stitches.

When I am knitting k1, p1 ribbing, I always want it to look rich and thick, with the ribs close and tight. I hate the look of a ribbed edging that is stretched to fit the length of the piece. When using a bouncy fiber, I often pick up one stitch for every row in the body; maybe five stitches for every six rows for a less elastic yarn. This often necessitates binding off very firmly with a smaller needle or requires decreasing along the bind-off row to keep the edging from flaring.

For looser ribbings, such as k2, p2 ribbing or any wider rib combination of knits and purls, aim to pick up a less dense ratio. Again, testing your edging is essential to get the proper ratio of stitches to rows so you can knit along on the actual edge without anxiety.

▲ This swatch tests a k1, p1 ribbing that is dense and flat, not stretched and strained. This rib is tipped with a contrasting color. I checked the look of my buttons by sewing them on the band.

◄ This swatch was worked to test a placket front that extended around a large hood: Testing the very deep flat k1, p1 rib on the right vertical edge allowed me to know exactly how many stitches I needed to pick up along all edges. The lower edge is a wide flat ribbing that does not draw in.

RIBS WITH EYELETS

Ribbed edgings that incorporate yarn overs tend to be less elastic as well and can be more ruffled, depending on how many stitches are picked up along the edge. For a ruffled effect, use a ribbing that does not draw in, a large needle and pick up one stitch for every row. You can increase a stitch every couple of rows (or more for wide ruffles) to make the ruffled effect more dramatic.

BRIOCHE OR FISHERMAN RIBS

Those ribs that have slip stitch elements, or have the action of knitting into the row below, actually tend to widen and are not for use where an elastic edging is desired. Be sure to test these kinds of ribs on your swatch.

Reverse Stockinette Roll

Early in my design career I became enamored of the reverse stockinette rolled edging. It is the simplest of all edgings and has a stabilizing effect. I see this edging as a boundary line, a simple and clean trim that works best on fabrics that are flat and uncurling, but I have used it in other places as well. It is worked over any number of stitches: Pick up on the RS, knit on the WS, purl on the RS and bind off in knit.

Slip-Stitch Patterns

Solid slip-stitch patterns are not great choices at edges, as they have a tendency to curl. The unblocked fabric of the embellished cardigan (see page 126) is a good example of this. However, I would not rule them out for uniquely textured collars, where looks and not function are the priority.

Colorwork

Fair Isle and other color patterns can be used at edges. Mosaic slip-stitch patterns that have a garter stitch foundation work rather well as edgings. However, stranded Fair Isle as an edging needs to be stabilized. A few ridges of garter stitch or a reverse stockinette stitch roll will prevent curling.

Cables

I generally prefer to knit cabled edgings separately and sew them. See page 75 for more about attaching cabled edgings.

Ruffles and Scalloped Trims

There are a number of ways to create a ruffled edging. Ruffled effects can vary greatly depending on your yarn, pattern stitch and needle size; testing the

▲ These two swatches were worked to test the qualities of two different lace ribs. The gray swatch, with an inner mitered corner, has a ribbed edging that lies even and flat and does not draw in. On the brick-colored swatch, extra stitches were deliberately worked to make the ribbing more of a ruffle, with a flared effect.

▲ This swatch features very easy reverse stockinette rolled edgings.

▲ When trying a new or unfamiliar pattern, it is best to work it first on your swatch. Here I tested a looped pattern that is not often used as an edging.

edging on your swatch will prove invaluable for saving time in the larger piece. Here are just a few suggestions.

● Pick up a lot of stitches along the edge and work in a plain pattern, like stockinette stitch, and increase regularly to achieve your desired effect.

● Pick up and work a ribbing, increasing in the purl ribs to flare the edging.

● Pick up a very large number of stitches, or increase to a large number on the first row, and work a lace pattern to your desired length. Steam the edging to open up the lace further.

● Try decorative patterns that have jagged or pointed edges. To find one that you like, refer to a good pattern dictionary. (I prefer those by Barbara Walker, as her editing is immaculate and her suggestions for pattern use are creative and interesting to read.)

Unusual Edgings

The edgings described above are the ones I turn to again and again, but there are many other options, including lace edgings, crocheted trims and more novel edgings, such as bobbles and looped edgings. There are several stitch dictionaries that focus exclusively on edgings and can provide myriad options. Just make sure the edging serves your garment well and is not just tacked on for the sake of having an edging. And remember, always test an edging on your swatch first!

Trimming the Trim!

I am a designer who likes detail—the more icing on the cake the better! One of my favorite ways to add extra detail to edgings is to knit an additional trim.

Reverse Stockinette Rolled Edging

A reverse stockinette rolled edging of three or four rows can be added to almost any edging. It utilizes the natural quality of rolling or curling that stockinette stitch naturally possesses, depending which side you choose.

● If the edging to which you want to add this trim is the same gauge, then work a single stockinette row (knit right side or purl wrong side) as an indenting divider row between the patterns.

● On the lower edge of a ribbing, it is necessary to have fewer stitches in the reverse stockinette roll, then increase to the number required for the ribbing, in order to ensure that the patterns achieve the same width. If you were to work the roll with the same number of stitches as the ribbing, it would bubble and waver. So, work two or three rows in reverse stockinette stitch, and then work a single stockinette row (knit on right side or purl on wrong side) as an indenting divider row, at the same time increasing to the number of stitches needed for the ribbing.

● To add a roll at the upper edge of a ribbing, you need to decrease stitches in order to ensure that the patterns achieve the same width. So after your ribbing is the desired length, work a single stockinette row (knit RS or purl WS) as an indenting divider row, at the same time decreasing to the number of stitches needed for the rolled edge.

Stockinette Stitch Rolled Edging

A rolled stockinette stitch edging of three or four rows can be worked the same as above. The difference? The reverse stockinette stitch roll has a purled surface and curls toward the wrong side of the edging. The stockinette stitch roll has the smooth side of the fabric curling toward the right side of the edging.

Garter Stitch Ridge

Garter stitch ridge can be added to any trim. For a clean break between patterns, work a single stockinette row as an indenting divider row. Then knit two rows and bind off. Or for a less bulky look, knit just one row and bind off.

Binding Off Edgings

I admit to being a minimalist when it comes to binding off. I like things to be easy, so I do not use fancy bind-off techniques

that require me to use a tapestry needle, or any sewing-type actions. You may do so, of course, and with nice detailed effects.

However, I do use one of several techniques to keep edgings supple and not too tight.

Bind-off on Wrong Side

Consider what the traditional bound-off edge looks like. When you bind off on a right side row, the edge has a "chained" look. If you like a bumpier edge, bind off on a wrong side row.

Decreased Bind-off

To restrain an edging so that it does not flare, as with a very densely ribbed edge, decrease at regular intervals. Test first on your swatch or a small area of the piece before binding off the whole edging.

▲ A few rows of stockinette stitch add interest to the ribbed edging on this swatch.

▲The ribbed edging on this swatch is also finished with reverse stockinette stitch.

Picot Bind-off

When an edging needs to be very loose—as with a lace shawl that will be severely blocked—or to add a frill of detail to a simple garter stitch, I use a "picot" bind off.

To try this technique on a bind-off row, work as follows: *Bind off 2 (or more stitches), then (yarn over, pull stitch over) twice (or 3 times) and then rep from *.

The little picot bumps work especially well as an accent on lace projects.

Edgings Along Different Parts of a Sweater

When you are preparing to add an edging to a knitted piece, study the work in your hands—what is it that the pieces do?

When picking up in different areas, with different shapes, the number of stitches picked up will vary from area to area. Really look at your pieces—will a choice of a single edging suit all the areas of your garment, or will you need to work different trim at different edges—based on desired look or function?

Often an edging needs to be shaped, increased or decreased to accommodate the shape of a piece. So when working a trim along a curved neckline, you need to make it curve! Think about these things ahead of time so that your choices about edgings are appropriate. Can an edging be decreased if necessary, without losing its good looks? For instance, if you need to decrease a pattern, can you transition into another rib or pattern?

Along Straight Edges

A straight edge is the easiest edge to approach! Pick up the same proportion along the entire edge. This applies to cast-on and bound-off edges, whether they be vertical front edges, or along the bottom of a garment, across a pocket opening or along the straight bound-off part of a neckline.

Angled Edges

If I am picking up along a vertical front edge, and then approach a V-neck shaping, I always pick up a slightly larger proportion of stitches along this angled edge than for a vertical edge. Consider geometry here! There is the same proportion of rows for a given length whether the edge is straight or angled, but the angled edge is longer. Think of a triangle in which a vertical edge is perpendicular to the lower edge and the opposite angled edge is longer.

Also, at the point on a cardigan front V-neckline, I often increase a stitch every other row. This is not strictly a "miter" (see below), but it expands the area that stretches around this outer bend in the road.

Curved Edges

Curved edges are a bit more challenging than straight edges, but with a little planning and a few techniques, they shouldn't cause any frustration.

NECKLINES AND ARMHOLES

How you pick up along a wide or deep curved neckline, depends on the kind of edge you encounter. An inner curve requires fewer stitches than a straight area or an outer curve. In fact, as you work your edging you may need to decrease a little if your pattern allows, or bind off with decreases in the curved areas, to keep the edging from flaring.

WIDE CURVED EDGES

When you have a long area that is curved, such as at a sweeping lower edge, consider that as the trim is worked, it must, by necessity of geometry, become wider. Either start with the larger number of stitches that will be required to keep the bind-off row from drawing in, or increase gradually as the edging gets longer. Ribbings are usually the best patterns to use at such edges.

Likewise, there may be occasions in which a wide stretch of edging needs to be narrowed. Do the reverse of the above. You can try to make your decreases an interesting detail or, if you prefer, keep them invisible. Refer to the sidebar at left for more tips about shaping edgings.

Tutorial: How to Shape an Edging

When you need to shape or narrow an edging, the best edging to work with is a ribbing.

● In a ribbed pattern, knit stitches alternate with purl stitches. If the increases to widen an edging, or decreases to narrow it, are added to a purl rib, the ribbing will keep its original look.
● If increases are placed within the knit ribs, the knit ribs will become larger and have a flared look, wider than its original appearance.
● If decreases are worked in the knit ribs, the ribs will narrow and the ribbing will also lose its original look.

Cardigan Edges

Which edge do you work first on a cardigan: front edges or neckline?

ROUND NECKLINE

With a round neckline, you have two options for edgings. You can do the neckline edging first, and then all your buttonholes will be in the front band. Or you can knit the front edgings first, and save the neckline for last. In this case you might want to put your top buttonhole in the neckline trim. Remember that the buttonhole on the neck edging, if you are using an elongated buttonhole, may face in a different direction than those in the front edging. For a mitered neckline, the neckline and front band will be knit in one piece, and the buttonholes will be worked into the front band.

V-NECKLINE

With a V-neckline, the edging is a continuation of the front edge. For extra detail, you can switch patterns in the knitting at the point where the V-neck starts.

Overlapping Trims

To overlap trims at an inner corner, such as at a V-neck or a bound-off front neckline, simply work your trim back and forth over the neckline and bind off at the desired length. First sew the outer trim to the outer neckline, or placket, edge. Then from the wrong side, sew the inner edge to the ridges formed by the picked-up stitches. (See the striped cardigan vest on page 73 for more tips on knitting plackets.)

Mitered Corners

Working a mitered trim around a corner is fun to do and the results are always rewarding. Mitering is one of my favorite corner treatments and I have used it in a wide variety of pattern stitches, from garter stitch to ribbing to stranded Fair Isle patterns.

Usually the shaping elements that form the corner detail, whether increases for outer corners or decreases for inner corners, are worked every other row; do this on right-side rows so you can see the result. Garter stitch or ribbed edgings will form a nice crisp right angle.

However, there is the occasion where the rate of increase or decrease does not make a clean right angle: This sometimes happens with stranded Fair Isle patterns, or some knit/purl patterns that have a less dense row gauge. In this case, you might have to work the shaping elements not only on every right-side row, but occasionally on a wrong-side row as well. As I always say, test first on your swatch!

THREE APPROACHES TO CARDIGAN EDGES

Always consider the order in which you will work your edgings so that you can decide on the look you would like to achieve. Here are just a few possibilities.

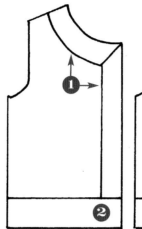 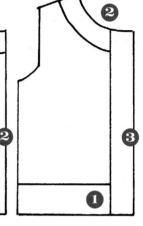

The neckline and front edge trim (1) are worked all at one time, with a decorative mitered corner. The lower edge trim (2) is picked up and worked last.

In this version, the lower edging (1) is knit in. Then the front band (2) is worked first and the neckline last (3).

This is similar to the middle example, with the lower edging (1) knit in, but the order of the neckline (2) and front edging (3) are reversed. This approach allows you to work all the buttonholes in the same band.

◄ In this swatch I wanted to test a ribbing for a wide neckline where I knew the collar would have to narrow gradually to fit well. I picked up stitches and worked in one ribbed pattern, then decreased into another ribbing to shape the band.

These swatches represent the two kinds of mitered corners. An "inner" mitered corner, the red swatch, can be worked on a square neckline edge, or wherever the edging needs to be decreased to form a 45-degree angle. An "outer" mitered corner is worked on an edging that goes around a corner and increases in size, such as in the orange swatch with the bold ribbed edging.

CHEAT SHEET

Swatch Test

To make an inner corner on your swatch to test your edging and mitering techniques, simply bind off at least 4 inches—wider if your edging is to be wide— and then work over the remaining stitches for at least 2 to 3 inches.

Here I am increasing one stitch with a backward loop before the stitches that were picked up in the corner. After knitting the two central stitches, I then increased again.

CENTER OF THE MITERED CORNER

The center of the mitered corner can be set up in basically two different ways: with central stitches or without. I like the look of one or more central stitches placed as a focal point at a miter, and I think they accentuate a corner in a most interesting way.

The central stitches of a mitered corner are most often worked in stockinette stitch (knit on right side, purl on wrong side). The center stitches can also be worked in garter stitch, but this is less common.

HOW TO WORK AN OUTER MITERED CORNER

For an outer mitered corner, the stitches are *increased* in the center of the corner. Pick up along the edge to the corner itself, then pick up the central stitches in the corner of the piece itself and mark them, then continue.

Work your wrong side row in pattern, purling the marked stitches.

On the next row, work in pattern to the marked stitches, then make one stitch, knit in the central marked stitches, make one, then continue.

There are two ways to increase, or make one, on either side of the center of the miter, each with a different effect.

1. A backward loop is easy (see page 161). You can slant it in opposite directions on either side of the central stitches for a mirror-image symmetrical effect. However, if you use a backward loop, you will not be able to work this stitch into the edging pattern until the next row.

2. If you prefer to work your increase into the pattern immediately, increase by lifting the divider strand and work the desired stitch (knit or purl) into the back of it,

Work to the desired length and bind off—but not without asking yourself which row makes your particular miter look best!

HOW TO WORK AN INNER MITERED CORNER

For an inner mitered corner, stitches are *decreased* from the center of the corner. The center of an inner corner miter itself can have central stitches as an outline, or no central stitch(es) at all. To have central stitches, pick up along the edge to the corner itself, then pick up the central stitches in the corner of the piece itself and mark them, then continue. Work your wrong-side row in pattern, purling the marked stitches. In the next row, work in pattern to the marked stitches, then, decrease on either side of the central stitches.

Different decreases give different effects: If you have two central stitches, you can work to one stitch before the central stitches, k2tog, then ssk in the second central stitch and the stitch that follows it. Or, for a more "jagged" effect in the central stitches, work to one stitch before the central stitches, ssk, then k2tog in the second central stitch and the stitch that follows it. To have more than two central stitches, your edging should be quite deep so that effect of the bold accent can be best seen.

If you have one central stitch, you can work a vertical double decrease that accentuates the miter's central axis: Work to one stitch before the central stitch of the miter, then slip two stitches from left to right (as if to k2tog), k1, then pass the two slipped stitches together over the knit stitch.

Lower Garment Edge

There are exceptions to the traditional approach of working the lower edge trim of the garment first, as part of the body piece(s). Although I think it is uncommon, I sometimes prefer to add lower edgings after a sweater is assembled. Often this allows me the surprise and delight of adding this important visual detail as a kind of dessert to my project. And there are functional reasons for waiting until the end, too, as I will describe below.

I also like the way a picked-up edging looks—with a slight indentation between the main fabric and the edging. As much as I like seams for structure in the body of a sweater, I often like the edging to be continuous around the lower edge. Ribbing is easy to seam and make it look continuous, but seaming some patterns creates an effect that doesn't flow.

There are times when you want a lower edging to merge into the body of a fabric, such as when a ribbing flows into a cabled pattern, sharing strands of the cable. In this case it would be undesirable—and impossible—to add an edging after the body was complete.

Sure, I always test edgings on my swatches to plan ahead. But sometimes there are two—or three!— patterns that I like equally. So now, after years of experience, I sometimes like to leave that crucial decision until the end. I have a particular interest in the boundaries of a sweater, and I do not always want to force myself to decide about that edging at the beginning.

It is also just fun and so easy to pick up into a cast-on row. Since I almost always use the long-tail method (see page 161) to cast on, the result is a nice evenly stranded edge that is easy to pick up into or sew onto.

On the next page are a few reasons to save the lower edge trim until the end:

▲ In this swatch, I picked up the stitches for the main section from the cable band, rather than sewing the band on. This is possible when the band is at the lower edge, and you are knitting upward; or when you are knitting a garment from the top down.

For most knitted edgings, you can use the same yarn as for the body of the sweater. There are, however, a few edgings that work best with finer yarns.

FOLDED BANDS

I like to work ribbed bands that are twice the depth of my desired edging and then fold them to the inside. This works nicely when working with a lighter-weight yarn at the edges. This also works well going around corners. Use a wide rib for the best effect—such as k3, p3 rib—and pick up extra stitches in the corner on the pick-up edge for the rib to be able to widen and stay flat as it rounds the corner.

At the end of the ribbing, you can bind off and sew the edge to the inside, along the ridge formed by the picked-up stitches. Or you can sew the edging down, stitch by stitch, which is nice when you want to retain a lot of elasticity at an edge, especially at necklines.

HEMS

I personally feel a hem in a knitted garment never looks right unless you use a lighter-weight yarn. Using the same yarn for the hem fabric creates an ugly bulge.

I like to add hems after pieces are completed and sewn together, picking up into the stitches along the cast-on edge. For the best preparation for hems, use a long-tail cast-on edge (see page 161).

Choose a yarn that is a slightly lighter weight than the main yarn. For instance, with a worsted-weight yarn, a DK-weight yarn would work well for the hem.

With right side facing, you can pick up into the back loops of each stitch along the cast-on edge—not including stitches that have been seamed. If you are working circularly, as with a skirt hem, knit every round. If you are working back and forth, purl the first row. Work in stockinette stitch to the desired length, then either bind off very loosely and sew the edge in place loosely as well, or sew each stitch separately on the wrong side, always taking care to sew into the same row on the main piece to keep the edge flat and unwavering.

NOTE This guideline for a hem is based on a stockinette stitch hem for a similar fabric. If the fabric to be hemmed draws in due to a firm pattern stitch, you might need to pick up fewer stitches for the hem, not one hem stitch for each cast-on stitch.

Again, testing on your swatch will save you time in figuring out how many stitches you'll need.

WHIMSY

Having an open mind when designing a sweater helps to make the process spontaneous—to some degree—and enjoyable. For the Fair Isle cardigan on page 123, I intended to work an edging at the lower edge, but when the time came, I decided I liked how it looked plain. The edgings added around the fronts and neckline and the cuffs provided enough visual interest, and I didn't want the sweater to be fussy.

SMOOTH, UNINTERRUPTED TRIM

Adding an edging around the lower edge after seaming creates an unbroken line and avoids having the seams continue right to the edge of the sweater.

AFTER BLOCKING

For the two lace scarves on page 26, I waited to add the edgings after blocking because I didn't want them to be affected by the blocking of the lace.

TO AID IN LINING

If you decide to sew a lining into a sweater, you might want to wait to add the edging at the same time as the lining so that you can tack the lining into the ridge formed by the picked-up stitches. ∎

The triangular edgings on the ends of these scarves (see page 26) were added after blocking.

MITERED MAGIC
Striped Tweed Cardigan Vest

Pattern
Striped Tweed
Cardigan
Vest
SEE PAGE 143

I have a penchant for sporty vests inspired by those that might have been worn in the 1920s. I love the long, slightly flared style that was so popular at the time. This vest design pays homage to these classics. I chose bright tweedy yarns and used stripes as a theme in both the main fabric and the picked-up edgings. Although the stripes make for a lively design, you could also knit this vest in a solid color. Or you could knit a solid vest body and work striped trims.

The most fun part of making this vest is in working the mitered corners and creating the placket in the back. I designed this vest to have four mitered corners in the striped garter stitch trim: Two are located at the front lower edges and two are at the lower back placket where the trims overlap. I seamed the pieces together in preparation for picking up along the edges. Since I had incorporated seam stitches on all the pieces, this made sewing the fronts to the back very easy. To create the mitered corners, I picked up stitches along the one front edge, lower edge and placket edge on one long circular needle and did the same on the second half.

The pattern (on page 143) gives the exact number of stitches to pick up along the edges, but since your tension might be a little different than mine, take the time to check a small section of trim along a short edge before picking up along the large stretch.

For the mitering at the corners, I picked up two central stitches in each corner: You could pick up just one if you like. You need to increase before and after these marked stitches. I find that a backward-loop increase (see page 161) works well. However, you may find it more to your liking to lift the strand before (and after) the marked stitch and knit into the back of it. Either way will work fine.

At the same time, if you like, test your buttonhole on your swatch. I used the Barbara Walker buttonhole (page 85) over six stitches since my buttons were so large. A smaller button would require a smaller hole.

When the trims were complete, I sewed the side edge of one trim to the top of the placket on the back. I then turned the piece to have the wrong side facing and sewed the side edge of the other trim to the ridge formed by seaming the first edge.

This is a great example of the power of an easy edging to transform a simple garment into something really special. ▪

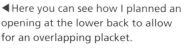

WORKSHOP

◀ Here you can see how I planned an opening at the lower back to allow for an overlapping placket.

CHEAT SHEET

Easy Stripes

To avoid a lot of ends while working the striped pattern, you can carry your yarns up the side of your knitting, twisting them at the start of right-side rows, to avoid having to weave in ends later. But if you prefer not to do this (I myself am not fond of having a lot of dangling balls of yarn getting in the way of my work), you can weave your ends in by twisting the cut end of the previous stripe with your working yarn over several stitches at the beginning of the next right-side row.

I had four large, ridged Bakelite buttons in my stash for a long time and when I held these red gems up to my swatch, I knew they would be the perfect accent for this vest.

◀ The placket has two layers. The side edge of the upper layer of trim was first sewn to the upper placket opening. Then the side edge of the under layer was sewn to the wrong side, to the ridge formed by sewing the upper trim.

Sewn-On Edges

Although I most often pick up stitches to create edgings, there are some cases in which it is better to knit the edging separately and sew it on.

My favorite edging to sew on at the fronts of cardigans is a band of k1, p1 rib, with an added edge stitch for seaming. I find that if I use a needle one or two sizes smaller than the body of my sweater—if it has an average stockinette stitch row gauge—then I can sew the ribbed trim row for row along the edge.

I like to knit the band as I sew in all instances so I can see how the band looks before I knit too long a piece, one that might be useless if it doesn't work. It's fun to sew as you go, too. If necessary, you can adjust your tension in both the knitting and the sewing.

When I use this ribbed band for a V-neck cardigan, I like to start on the buttonband side and sew it on—as I knit—all around the edge of the sweater until I reach the buttonhole side. Then I mark—or sew—my buttons on the finished side and resume knitting and sewing, working buttonholes to match the buttons as I sew on the last stretch to the lower edge.

The best thing to do if you are sewing on a band of another non-rib trim is to slightly stretch the edging as you sew. The band should be shorter than the edge you are applying it to. In this case, I might knit a longer stretch to see how the band "sits" on the front as I sew. I rarely pin the band in place. I prefer to "sew and see": After about 4 inches you can see a pattern of matching rows in the body to rows in the trim—once you know this rhythm, you can repeat it on the whole band. Of course, it is always useful to test this first on your swatch.

Cabled Edgings

Cabled edgings are usually knit separately and sewn on. They can be sewn on horizontally (as in a neckline) or at vertical edges for buttonhole- and button-bands. (It is fun to settle a button into a "dent" in the center of a cable—let the cable inspire the button placement!) If you try this, be sure to add seam stitches so the application will be easier, and work your cable on a needle one or two sizes smaller than what you used for the body of the sweater so that you can match the cable row for row as you sew. You might wonder why you wouldn't just knit the cable in as a part of the main piece? You could do that, but I like to sew it on separately because the seam gives structure and stability to the edge. The workshop that follows explores in more detail how to attach a cabled band. ■

SEWING A CABLED BAND
Cowl-Neck Pullover

**Pattern
Cowl-Neck
Pullover**
SEE PAGE 145

This design features several interesting finishing details. Most relevant to this discussion of edgings is the horizontal cable that is sewn on to the neckline. From there, stitches are picked up to knit an oversized cowl collar. I also designed the sweater to include a pocket facing that folds to the inside.

Many times you will see a design that features a horizontal cable where the cable must be sewn to an edge of a garment. This takes some planning to execute the seaming well. If you do the prep work, and you sew with the right side facing so you can see your

WORKSHOP

Here are the textured sweater front (left) and cabled band (above) that will be sewn on at the yoke of the sweater. The only blocking I deemed necessary for these flat, even pieces was a slight shot of steam to full the wool a little. The little extensions at the sides form the pocket facings that fold neatly to the inside, thanks to a slipped stitch along the side seam line.

When you have a little pocket facing like on this sweater it folds nicely to the inside along the slipped stitches. You can knit your pocket lining in a finer yarn from the inner facing, or you can attach a sewn fabric pocket to it.

seam, everything will work out easily. I first sewed my sleeves to the back and front at the raglan lines, then sewed the side and sleeve seams: This was easy do because I had incorporated those all-important seam stitches in my pattern.

As you can see in the photo on page 78, I joined the ends of the long cable into a ring, and then aligned it on a flat surface with the body pieces adjacent to it, as it would be sewn. I tied yarn markers evenly to each piece so that I could match the markers as I sewed. The edge of the body piece is often a little wider than the cable, in designs like this, so it helps to have the markers in place. I eased in the tiny bit of extra width as I sewed.

As with the patchwork scarf on page 49, this is an example of what I call "stitches meet rows." The rows of the cable are sewn to the stitches of the bound-off edge of the body pieces.

I knit the cowl collar on this sweater at the very end. For the collar to have a slight "rise," making the back of the collar a little bit higher than the front, I worked over the back neck stitches in short rows before picking up the full number of stitches around the front of the neckline. I also cast on a few extra stitches for a little overlap, which I later anchored with a pin. You could also add a button. No need for a buttonhole: Just attach the button by sewing through both layers of the edges of the collar. ■

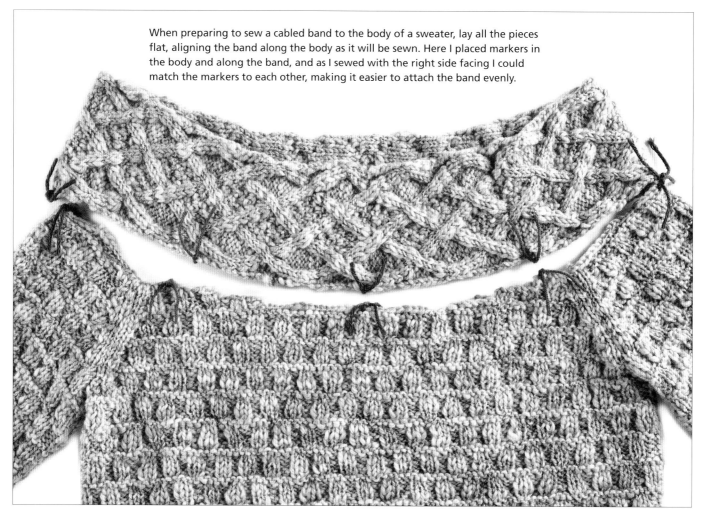

When preparing to sew a cabled band to the body of a sweater, lay all the pieces flat, aligning the band along the body as it will be sewn. Here I placed markers in the body and along the band, and as I sewed with the right side facing I could match the markers to each other, making it easier to attach the band evenly.

Here I knit a cabled band separately and picked up along it to knit the fronts and back for this zippered cardigan. (The cabled strips on the fronts are faux pockets.)

CHAPTER 5

Extra Credit
Buttons, Zippers,
Pockets & More

After a sweater is assembled and the edgings
  are in place, it's time to consider the little things
    that make a garment special. I am fanatical about
details. Often in the planning of a sweater when
  I think I am done, I deliberately ask myself, "Is there
anything else I can add that will make this piece more
visually interesting?" I try not to go overboard,
    but it's hard for me to restrain myself. After years
of finishing, I believe I have devised the best
      and easiest ways to work out the details.

Getting Closure

Although details are often meant to be decorative, I still always insist upon functionality and wearability. This is especially important when it comes to closures.

There are many ways to close a sweater, including buttons, zippers and ties, to name just a few! Sometimes I don't know which closure I'll use until the sweater is almost done; other times, it is the closure that actually inspires a design! As we all know, buttons come in a variety of sizes and styles. And the bands and borders that hold them and the holes that they slide into are all-important features to consider when finishing a sweater, or any other project that needs closure.

There are several questions to ask yourself when planning to use any type of closure:
● What kind of closure will you use?
● How many units of closure will you need?
● What kind of band, if any, are you applying to attach the closure? What kind of buttonhole will your button require?
● How will you join the button or closure onto the garment?

Following a process when making these decisions helps to give the best results—and it's fun!

Buttons

Buttons are a source of endless fascination to me. I troll for them online and I buy them in sewing stores. I covet vintage buttons, and I have been known to buy secondhand clothes in order to cut the buttons off! I never know where I'll find buttons.

Surely as a designer I use more buttons than most average knitters, but I still feel that everyone should have a stash of buttons on hand, both for inspiration and last-minute projects. And because buttons are so much fun to collect!

A few years ago, this urban-dweller—New England Yankee that I am —did not imagine that a road trip through the towering Cascade Mountains in Oregon would produce my ultimate button-buying event. In a tiny cowboy town, in a secondhand bookstore, of all places, I found the mother lode of vintage buttons. Here I spent $250 on hundreds of wood, ivory, plastic,

Bakelite, glass, jasper and metal buttons, in all shapes and sizes, most of which found their way onto sweaters over the course of several seasons. So much fun, like eating candy! Some days I wonder if I design just so I can use buttons!

Types of Buttons

There are many kinds of buttons available and they come in all shapes and sizes. Here is a review of them with knitted fabric in mind. Obviously buttons can be made of any material—ornate crystal to plastic to rustic pieces of twigs!

Make sure that the buttons you choose can be cleaned in the same way as the garment. If not, have a plan to remove them easily. Sew carefully so that the buttons can be cut away without damaging the band onto which they are sewn.

FLAT BUTTONS

For sweaters, the best buttons are those that have fairly large holes through which your yarn will easily pass. But for a more delicate look, you might want to use buttons that have smaller holes. As mentioned earlier, it is wise to have needles with very small eyes in your finishing toolkit. Sometimes it is necessary to use sewing thread and a sewing needle—see "Attaching Buttons" on the next page.

If the holes are big enough, yarn color and the way you sew through a button matters. Will you make an X or sew the button with an "equal sign"? Would a contrasting color yarn, different from your sweater add detail?

SHANK BUTTONS

Buttons with a shank, or a bump, on the back that holds a single hole are nice, but be careful of excess weight. If the shank is large and the band is thin, the button can hang awkwardly. So it is best to use a shank button when the band is firm, not flimsy. However, you can choose to work your button band

CHEAT SHEET

Use Your Schematic Drawing!

At this stage, I often study my schematic and sketch details on it to help me visualize what might add to, or personalize, my design. Where could I place a pocket? How would it look if I grouped my buttons along the band by twos or threes? You can also color in your schematic with colored pencils to check how contrast might work— I do! By drawing these details—in pencil so that they can be erased if I change my mind— I am testing the look of details before I get to them in real life.

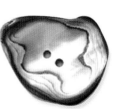

in a thicker pattern—or a different yarn—if you are fond of a particular shank button.

TOGGLE BUTTONS

Toggles are my current favorite buttons! We can all picture the traditional toggles made of wood in a predictable classic ridged pattern, but there are many other versions available in a variety of bullet and lozenge shapes. There are many interesting plastic and Bakelite toggle buttons. I have seen long skinny tubes and ridged barrel shapes. I recently bought toggles made from carved and smoothed tree branches with drilled holes.

Some toggle-shape buttons have a shank, but most of them have two large holes. A few I have used have only a ridge at the center around which you wrap the yarn as you sew, and for these you should form a yarn shank (see page 84 for directions).

A toggle button always requires a larger buttonhole than you would guess, in order for its long sides to slip in easily. Always do a test on your swatch to check the match between the toggle and the buttonhole.

Attaching Buttons

Traditional varieties of buttons have two or four holes for sewing, although I do have one huge, gorgeous mother-of-pearl button that has three large holes; I'm still waiting for the best place to use it!

NEEDLES AND YARN

The crucial quality of a button-sewing needle is that the eye be small enough to pass through the hole of the button and also large enough to be able to thread a piece of yarn. Often this proves a challenge. When threaded with yarn, often a needle that would have passed through the button with ease now gets stuck when the yarn in the needle meets the hole! That is why having a variety of needle sizes for sewing on buttons is essential. Search these needles out—collect these needles! Buy several of each kind, especially if you, like me, lose needles all the time!

I try to find a needle with a big eye that is thin enough to pass through the holes. Then I must separate the yarn into plies, if possible, and twist a ply or two tightly in order for it to pass through the holes. Often I will match a sewing thread to my yarn, and twist it by hand tightly with the smallest ply of the yarn possible. Then I can often get the twisted strand to pass through the small holes of the button.

If you divide your yarn's plies to make a smaller strand for sewing your buttons, try to keep at least two of the plies twisted, if possible, for extra strength.

▲ Buttons don't just belong on the front of a sweater! I sometimes like to design a sweater that buttons up the back. In this sweater, which appeared in the Spring/Summer 2010 issue of *Vogue Knitting* magazine, the little buttons nestle into a very firm, flat garter-stitch edgings. I used my favorite yarn-over buttonhole (see page 87).

◀ I often mix different buttons in the same project. Here I had some rich red vintage Bakelite buttons, but not enough of one kind to use for this intarsia sweater, so I alternated them along the band.

▲ This vibrant pullover appeared in a story about Brit-inspired designs in the Fall 2010 issue of *Vogue Knitting*.

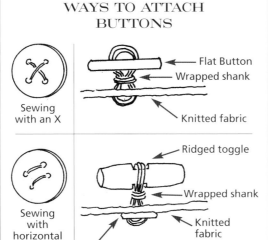

WAYS TO ATTACH BUTTONS

Sewing with an X

Flat Button
Wrapped shank
Knitted fabric

Sewing with horizontal bands

Ridged toggle
Wrapped shank
Knitted fabric
Anchor button on WS

Buttons can be sewn on in a variety of ways, taking into account the thickness of the fabric and the type of button.

Often a softly twisted yarn will split as you sew. Try this: Cut a length of the yarn; thread it into your needle. Then holding the needle in one hand, roll the thread in the direction of its twist on your thigh, to tighten the twist. When it is tight enough to hold together better, hold the loose end while you sew the yarn into the fabric to catch the twist so that it does not unwind again. As you sew, you may have to twist the needle to keep the strand firm if the yarn untwists as you sew.

You do not have to make a massive yarn join of button to band. If the yarn in the body of the sweater is not appropriate, of course you can use another yarn or a contrasting yarn for more detail.

In my mind, the best yarn for sewing buttons is a thin, smooth, strong, multi-plied yarn, like a merino sport-weight yarn.

MAKING A YARN SHANK

If the buttonhole band is extra thick, I sometimes sew the button on loosely so I can wrap the sewn strands between the button and buttonband to form a shank. This gives some extra room for the buttonhole to fit around the button itself, so there is no tightness or pulling. It also helps to reinforce the attachment.

When you sew on the button, place a tapestry needle between the button and the band to make a space. When you feel you have enough attaching stitches, then bring your needle to the space between the button and the band, wrap the long stitches a couple of times firmly, and then lock your stitch by sewing once through the shank and then to the wrong side of the band and lock stitch again. Proceed to the next button.

USING ANCHOR BUTTONS

I always have a variety of tiny lightweight buttons on hand to use as "anchor" buttons. I sew these on the wrong side of the button band as a support for the functional button, sewing them on at the same time. I often use a small, clear, flat plastic button as an anchor, one that virtually disappears on the back of the band. If you would like a more decorative button as an anchor, you can use a small colored or pearl button, like those made for baby clothes. Whatever you choose, be sure the anchor is lightweight—it just needs to provide support, not bulk or weight.

Use an anchor if a button is really heavy. Also, I use an anchor button when the button band is soft and will not hold a button well. The anchor button actually provides the stability that the band cannot—the band is sandwiched between the two buttons.

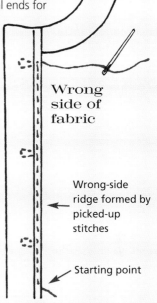

Tutorial
Sewing Buttons With One Long Strand

When sewing on buttons, I use this trick to keep the wrong side of the buttonband as neat as possible. My goal is to sew all the buttons with one long strand, with as few cut ends as possible. This also eliminates the need for weaving in individual ends for each button. I weave as I go and never cut the sewing strand.

1. Thread the needle with as long a piece of sewing yarn as you can manage. Of course, if there are only a couple of buttons, you can use a shorter length. If there are a lot of buttons you might have to change the strand at the halfway point. Tightly twist the sewing strand at the beginning and as you go along.

2. Referring to your schematic, mark the button band at each exact place where you want a button to be sewn with scrap yarn.

3. Starting at the lower edge of the button band, weave a length of about 1½" into the ridge formed by the picked-up stitches, planning to end opposite where the first button is to be sewn.

4. Enter the band itself with your needle to take a stitch exactly where you want the button to be sewn. This locks the strand.

5. Sew the button in place. Lock the button stitching in place by sewing into the band once.

6. Now that the button is sewn, weave the yarn back to the ridge formed by the picked-up stitches.

7. Without cutting the end, thread the yarn loosely through the ridge, stopping opposite where you want the next button to be.

Repeat Steps 4 through 7 to attach the remaining buttons. If you run out of yarn, simply re-thread the needle and start again. This method stops a lot of ends from popping out along the edge where there is a lot of use.

It's fun to see how many buttons you can sew with one piece of yarn! I always make a game of trying to guess the length of the strand I'll need.

Wrong side of fabric

Wrong-side ridge formed by picked-up stitches

Starting point

If your button has holes, it is best to use an anchor button with the same number of holes. Then you can just sew in and out. For a shank button, use a small two-hole anchor button.

How-to: First sew your decorative button in place on the band with one stitch, then insert your yarn to the wrong side, putting the needle tip into the hole on the anchor button, and pull the yarn through. Go through the other hole of the anchor button, pushing through the band and into the other hole on the decorative button. Continue until the join is firm.

Buttonholes

I have tried every knitted buttonhole known to needles over the years. I now choose from only three different ones. My favorite is the very first buttonhole I ever tried—why did I ever stray?—the one-row buttonhole from Barbara's Walker's essential *Second Treasury of Knitting Patterns.* The other is an eyelet buttonhole I devised when trying to make a buttonhole disappear into k1, p1 rib, probably something that other knitters have come up with as well. For some sweaters that do not have bands, I often prefer to cut and complete a buttonhole in knitted fabric after pieces are done.

These three methods suit most of my needs very well, and I share them with you here.

BUTTONHOLE SIZE

Most buttonholes need to be a little bit smaller than the width of the button. Knitted buttonholes stretch so it is better to have to force the button a little in the beginning, before growth happens! With long toggle buttons, sewn at the middle, the buttonhole needs to be a little more than half the length of the toggle. I suggest you test your buttonholes first on your swatch as I do. No surprises that way!

BARBARA WALKER'S SELF-REINFORCING ONE-ROW BUTTONHOLE

Barbara Walker has given hundreds of gifts to knitters in her many *Treasuries of Knitting Patterns,* but if her only gift were this buttonhole, I would still be grateful. Unlike other buttonholes, which must be completed on two rows, this one is completed all in one approach.

For a beginner, the number of steps and turning the work may be a little daunting at first. It was for me when I was just beginning to knit. But making this buttonhole is exceptionally easy—and rewarding!—especially after you have made a few. Practice on your swatch, working the buttonhole on ribbing, garter stitch (knit every row) and seed stitch.

Here, with permission from the Knitting Goddess herself, is the best buttonhole:

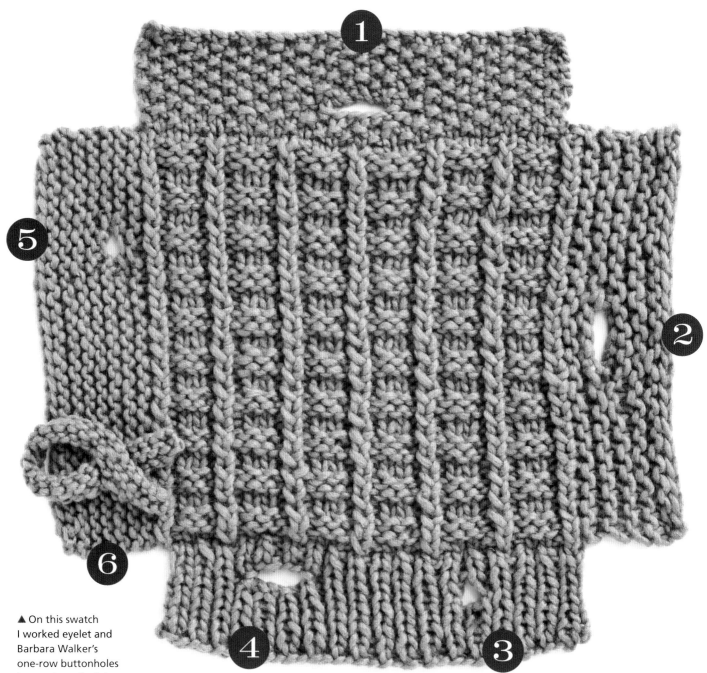

▲ On this swatch I worked eyelet and Barbara Walker's one-row buttonholes in a variety of edgings: 1) one-row buttonhole in seed stitch, 2) one-row buttonhole in garter stitch, 3) eyelet buttonhole in k1, p1 rib, 4) one-row buttonhole in k1, p1 rib, 5) eyelet buttonhole in garter stitch. I also created a toggle, or large button, loop out of L-cord (6).

Note that this buttonhole can be worked on any pattern stitch and also can be worked on either a right-side or a wrong-side row, although, as Barbara points out, this buttonhole is least visible in garter stitch, and blends into the ridges.

Step 1 Work the desired number of stitches before starting the buttonhole. I find it best to have at least three stitches—or more—before beginning the buttonhole. (When you try Step 5, below, you will see that you need two stitches to work the cable cast-on. If there are only two stitches, then your buttonhole will sit *very* close to the edge.)

Step 2 Bring yarn to the front of the work, then slip one stitch from the left-hand needle to the right-hand needle, pass yarn to the back of the work and drop it there. Just leave the yarn hanging until Step 5.

Step 3 Slip another stitch from the left-hand needle to the right-hand needle and pass the first stitch over it. Now one stitch is bound off. Repeat this step until the desired number of stitches for the buttonhole have been bound off.

Step 4 Slip the last bound-off stitch back to the left-hand needle. Turn the work.

Step 5 Pick up the hanging yarn that you dropped in

Step 2 and pass it between the needles to the back. Now, cast on the same number of stitches that were bound off for the buttonhole *plus one more,* using the cable cast-on method (see illustrations on page 161): *Insert the right-hand needle between the first and second stitches on the left-hand needle, wrap and pull through a loop, placing this loop onto the left-hand needle to serve as a new stitch; rep from *until the desired number of stitches have been cast on. Then, before placing the last loop on the left-hand needle, bring the yarn through to the front so the strand divides the next stitch and the next-to-last stitch. Turn the work again.

Step 6 You can do one of two things to complete the buttonhole, and each looks a little bit different. I use both of them, depending on what works best for the yarn in my hands and the pattern stitch of the band:

Slip the first stitch from the left-hand needle to the right-hand needle, then 1) pass the last, extra, cast-on stitch over it. This completes the buttonhole. Or you can 2) k2tog in the first two sets on the left-hand needle. This decreases the extra stitch and also completes the buttonhole.

DEBORAH'S SINGLE YARN OVER/DOUBLE DECREASE BUTTONHOLE

I like a buttonhole that disappears. This one practically does just that in a k1, p1 band and is especially good for the band that gets sewn onto a piece. But this one can also be used on garter stitch or any pattern.

The basic buttonhole:

Row 1 (either RS or WS) K2tog, yo, ssk.
Row 2 Work to yo and (k1, p1) into it.

This is essentially an eyelet. It is outlined on each side by a decrease that toughens it a little. If you want further reinforcement, you can take a very fine piece of yarn and a thin needle, and overcast stitch around it: I find that this is a good idea when using small buttons. For larger buttons it is usually not necessary.

To make this eyelet in a k1, p1 rib buttonhole band, cast on 11 sts.

Row 1 (RS) K2, p1, (k1, p1) 3 times, end k2.
Row 2 P2, k1, (p1, k1) 3 times, end p2.
Note If you cast on by the long-tail method, start with row 2 to create a smooth edge at the lower RS edge.
Work for desired length, end with a WS row.
Buttonhole row (RS) K2, p1, k1, p1, ssk, yo, p2tog, k2.
Row 2 P2, k1, (P1, k1) in eyelet, (p1, k1) 2x, end p2.
Tug firmly on the first and last stitch of every row to keep nice edges. Note that the eyelet is situated closer

to one side of the band—this is the side you should sew to the sweater piece. The rows begin with two stockinette stitches so that seaming is easier.

CUTTING A HORIZONTAL BUTTONHOLE

There are probably many ways to cut a buttonhole, and then bind it, but here is a description of my own process. It is less scary than you might think. Be of calm mind and have tools ready!

This works best for rather large buttonholes and with yarns that are not too slippery, such as wools. Mark the fabric in a space between two stitches where you want the buttonhole to be centered. Then count over toward the edge a stitch or two depending on how large the button is—this is the edge of the buttonhole where the button will sit (the button always slides to the front edge; it never sits at the center of the buttonhole).

With the right side facing, clip the marked space in

▼ In this swatch worked in a yarn with thick and thin texture, I show the various stages of cutting a horizontal buttonhole. From the bottom to the top: marking the location of the buttonhole, unraveling the yarn, slipping stitches to double-pointed needles, and the finished buttonhole.

Since buttons are such a delightful detail, you should display them to their best advantage. Placement of buttonholes is a big decision, at least in my mind. You need to consider three things:

1. Where on the band will the buttons be placed, from top and bottom? Whether I am sewing a band on vertically, or picking up stitches for a band along an edge, I prefer to work my buttonholes very close to the body, rather than at the center of the button band. Since buttons tend to pull with wear along the band, if you keep the buttonhole close to the sturdy edge of the band, the band does not bulge next to the button as much.

2. Will there be any unusual placement of the buttons, in clusters or varying sizes? A traditional rule is that buttonholes for women's garments are on the right front, and for men they fall on the left front. You may have a reason to alter this: After all, rules are meant to be broken. But for our purposes here, I will use the traditional placement to describe my preferences for when to work the buttonhole row itself.

3. Last but not least, and crucial in my mind, on what row will the buttonholes be placed? Think about it—it is always easier to start a buttonhole row at the neckline edge. In this way, the first buttonhole—most visually important and most functional—gets placed exactly where you want it, and you do it right out of the gate. If you start the buttonhole row at the lower edge, then by the time you reach the neckline edge, you could, as I often am, be a stitch off, and then the placement of this crucial buttonhole will be off, or you will have to rip out the row. If you are off a bit on the lower edge, it is not as big a deal.

For a woman's sweater, I often work the buttonhole row on the first row after the band's pick-up row. If the band is to be wider than 1½", or very wide, then I will opt to do the buttonhole row on the second or third wrong side row. For a man's sweater, the first right-side row is one row farther out toward the edge than for a woman's.

to the center, and unravel over the side where the button will sit. Then unravel over to the other side, the same distance. Top and bottom, loops will be revealed. Don't be nervous. Just let the stitches and loops sit. Bring the short yarn ends to the front of the work, the right side, so you can keep an eye on them.

With the right side facing, take two wooden or bamboo double-pointed needles, because they are not slippery, and slide one into the loops or stitches below, and one into the loops or stitches above. Allow the point of the needle to enter the adjacent stitch on either side, too.

Take a strand of yarn and with another dpn, bind off the stitches on the bottom needle, leaving an end of yarn hanging on either end. Turn the piece around and do the same thing on the top needle. If you need to twist a stitch or looplike stitch to make the edges firm, you can do that.

If the yarn you are using is slippery, you might want to try one of the other types of buttonholes. This one definitely works best with yarns that have some "grab" to them.

Handmade Buttons

There are times when a manufactured button is just not right for the design. Sometimes I want a button to match the garment exactly. Or I prefer to have the look of a yarn or fabric button. Here are two ways to do just that:

COVERED BUTTONS

On occasion I want a fabric button for contrast or for something out of the ordinary. There are a few ways to do this.

● Get a covered-button kit and use a woven fabric as directed.

● You can knit a small piece of stockinette stitch in a fine-gauge yarn, and gather it around a "base" button to cover it and sew the edges at the back. To stabilize the fabric if it is too stretchy, you can steam a small piece of iron-on fusible interfacing to the wrong side before applying it to the button.

● Felted fabric makes a nice easy-to-cut, non-raveling button covering.

If you cover a shank button, you can use the back of the "base" button to sew. If you use a button with holes, you can sew through the holes that are hidden by the fabric, either with matching or contrasting yarn, to add a bit of textural contrast.

CROCHETED RING BUTTONS

With a plastic or metal ring as a base, you can crochet around to fill in the circle, and then sew the button through the soft crocheted center.

Zippers

There are two reasons to use zippers—for function or looks. Or both! I fell in love with zippers early in my life—I fondly remember sewing a corduroy shift-style dress for myself when I was a teenager.

It had a marvelous ring-pull and the teeth were large, square, chunky bits of plastic. I wish I had that zipper today! I love glint of a metal zipper's teeth, and I adore zippers with pull-rings. After much practice, I have no fear of putting zippers in sweaters.

I have to admit that the first time I tried it, I was daunted by the prospect of sewing a zipper in a knitted fabric—and it was tricky! But I've experimented with a variety of applications over the years, and I've come up with a process that always works for me. If you follow my suggestions, you should find zippers easy to apply. You really don't have to be an experienced sewer to learn how to do it. True, working with sewing thread—not yarn—is required, but by choosing the right zipper, preparing your edge correctly and pinning carefully, your success is assured.

What Kind of Zipper to Use?

Not just any zipper will do for knitted projects. There are several variables to consider. You can apply a zipper to any knitted fabric, except perhaps the lightest lace-weight knitting. The best effect is when the zipper shares the same weight or is slightly lighter in feel than the fabric. Since the teeth of a zipper create stiffness along the line where the zipper is sewn, I prefer to sew the lightest zipper possible.

I remember when—and I show my age—zipper fabric was made of cotton. Nowadays, it is rare to find a cotton-based zipper; most zipper fabric is synthetic. Synthetic zippers are strong and often rather stiff, and with the addition of teeth, they do not share the draping quality of knits. If cotton-based zippers are available near you, grab them!

For garments that will open all the way, use what is called a separating zipper. Some separating zippers open from both the bottom and the top. Use a closed-bottom zipper for sweaters that open partially, for bags and for pocket openings.

In almost every case I prefer using zippers with metal teeth for knits. I like the way they look, but metal-teeth zippers are also a little bit slinkier and move more like knitted fabric. My second choice is zippers that have large plastic teeth—these are called

"molded plastic" zippers and also have pretty good flexibility, especially for heavier knits.

I have, on occasion, applied zippers with nylon-coil teeth, but when they are sewn to a knitted edge, they have a stiffness that tends to harden that edge. Nylon zippers tend to be very firm and just don't share the quality that most knits have.

There are many sizes of metal zippers available, with different teeth sizes. They are relatively inexpensive, so I suggest you buy a couple in different sizes and see what they look like, how they feel and the size of the zipper teeth. Also, you can choose the color of the zipper and often the style of zipper pull. What fun!

Where to Buy

I buy most of my metal zippers online from a professional zipper source (see Resources on page 160), and have them cut and finished to the correct length. It is actually very inexpensive and very efficient. You can shorten an existing zipper, but there are sources online that will create a zipper in the color you desire and the perfect length with the teeth size and pull of your liking. What more could you ask for? And your sweater deserves the perfect zip!

As with buttons, I am always on the lookout for special zippers. I browse through sewing-supply stores, searching out interesting plastic and metal zippers, both vintage and contemporary. I have even been known to save a wonderful zipper by ripping it out of a vintage garment.

If you do want to resurrect a zipper from a used garment, pick out the stitches carefully with a seam ripper. Then determine the fiber content of the fabric band and steam the edges of it appropriately to flatten them before applying the zipper to your garment.

How to Apply Zippers

As with most tasks, if you make the necessary preparations and approach zipper-sewing step by step, it's not as difficult as it might seem. The instructions below apply to an open garment that will have a separating zipper, or for a placket that will be open only at one end.

PREPARATION
Each edge that will have a zipper attached to it should have a small trim—either a garter ridge or a small reverse stockinette rolled edging. The garter ridge is my favorite if I want as much of the teeth to show as possible. For a slightly covered zipper front with a little more structure, I use the reverse stockinette stitch

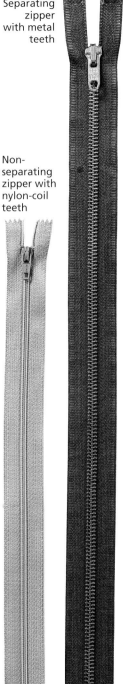

Separating zipper with metal teeth

Non-separating zipper with nylon-coil teeth

rolled edge on both sides. (See Chapter 4 for more on applying edgings and trims.)

The front trims on each side must be exactly the same length! This means that if you tend to knit more loosely along one side of your knitting, you will have to prepare the trim on the looser side so that it matches the other side exactly. You might, for example, have to pick up on the looser side with a smaller needle to draw in the edge slightly. After working the trim, steam the edges slightly, if the fiber allows, to even them out.

With few exceptions, a zipper should be sewn into a completed sweater. The front edges must be completed with neckline and lower edges finished, and ends woven in.

The zipper should be the exact same length as the front trimmed edges. If your zipper is longer, even by as little as ½ inch, the front of the sweater will not hang straight and will bulge slightly.

Once you have all of the above conditions met, you can sit down to apply the zipper.

PINNING AND SEWING

Work sitting down at a table when you the time and peace of mind to devote to the task. I have tried to sew a zipper—a task that requires attention—when I am fussy or tired, and it takes twice as long! If you are relaxed, it's fun!

You will need dressmaker's straight pins and a sewing needle. Your thread should match your sweater fabric: This may sound obvious, but I have made the mistake of sitting down with thread that matches my zipper instead of the sweater.

I like to place a piece of cardboard under the fabric to which I am applying the zipper. This allows me to keep the edges flat and prevents me from pinning into the under layer (usually the back of the sweater).

Again, check the zipper length with the zipper closed, matching it to both sides. If one side is off, you will have to bind off again to get the two sides to match.

With the zipper closed, pin one side at a time, pinning top and bottom first. The pins should be placed perpendicular to, or across, the zipper band—not along the band. The top of the band should be even with the stopper at the top of the zipper teeth. The bottom of the zipper hardware should be even with the bottom of the band. Next, pin the center of the zipper with the center of the band. Then pin the center of the remaining sections.

If there are knitted patterns in the fabric that need to match up on either side of the zipper, be sure that they match as you pin them to the zipper.

Thread the sewing needle and knot the end. Sew into the "dent" between the trim and the main fabric. Beginning at the bottom of the zipper, insert your needle from the wrong side to the right side, pull through, then insert the needle straight down into the knitted fabric about ¼ inch away and pull through to the wrong side, and repeat. I like to lock the lower and upper edges with a few extra sewn stitches, in the same place, before proceeding along the length.

Always insert the needle straight down into the knitted fabric and straight up from the underside of the tape. Never use a "running stitch" or take more than one stitch at a time. In this way the thread is always perpendicular to the fabric and zipper, and there will be no pulling. Every few inches, take an extra stitch on the zipper side to lock the stitches in place. When you reach the upper edge, fold the fabric tab above the teeth on a diagonal away from the zipper and sew it in place.

Repeat on the other side. Sew the other side of the zipper from the *same* direction, even though it might be easier to go in the opposite direction! It is my experience that if you sew the sides in different directions, the sides pull in slightly different directions and look awkward where they meet.

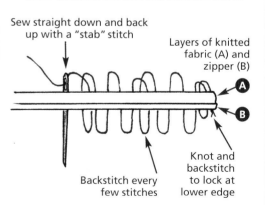

Sewing a Zipper

The line of hand-sewing should be done in the "dent" between the trim and the main fabric.

Sew straight down and back up with a "stab" stitch

Layers of knitted fabric (A) and zipper (B)

A

B

Knot and backstitch to lock at lower edge

Backstitch every few stitches

For a zipper to lie absolutely flat, it should be sewn by going straight down into the fabric with the needle, and straight back up. Although it might be easier to sew with multiple running stitches, they tend to cause pulling and unevenness. Always sew with the right side facing so you can see your work.

▲The sleeve of the zippered jacket shown on the next page. Always knit a narrow trim along the edges of an opening where a zipper will be attached. Here the lower sleeve is shown with trim alone and with the zipper pinned in place with long dressmaker pins. When you sew in the little dent between the trim and the main fabric, the seam is invisible.

▲The zipper is pinned in place with long dressmaker pins.

ZIP IT UP!
Fitted Colorblock Jacket

Pattern
Fitted
Colorblock
Jacket
SEE PAGE 147

▶ When sewn into a two-layer mock turtleneck, half of the ribbed collar folds over to the inside. The blue stripe on the inside provides a nice surprise of color.

I love zippers! And lots of them! I always encourage people in my workshops to try applying a zipper so they can see it is as easy as I describe. This jacket features zippers as its primary design feature. There are four of them: There is a vertical zip at each lower sleeve, a long one at the front edge that ends at a mock turtleneck that folds to the inside and one, sewn on horizontally, is actually a "faux" pocket.

I started the finishing on this sweater by testing my narrow knitted edging along one side of a lower sleeve opening. It took me two tries to get the edging to lie flat. Then when I knew the proportion of stitches per row, I knitted the edging on all the lower sleeve edges. To make it even easier, I sewed the zippers in by hand while the sleeves were flat, before the sleeves were seamed. (This is an exception to my usual rule of waiting until the garment is complete.)

Before sewing the body pieces together, I also worked the edging on the "pocket" opening on the upper left front. I pinned the tiny zipper in place and sewed it in the little dent between the trim and the main knitting.

Before I could attach the zipper to the front of the jacket, I had to assemble the sweater and work the collar. Since the collar was to fold over, for a double thickness, the zipper would extend only to the halfway mark of the collar.

After the collar was picked up and knit, I worked the edging, same as for the lower sleeves, along both front edges, including a little less than half of the collar. Since it takes a little length for the collar to fold over, the inside of the collar has to be a bit longer.

I then pinned the zipper in place and sewed it by hand. Next I folded the collar over and sewed the bound-off edge of the ribbing loosely to the ridge formed by the picked-up stitches. ▪

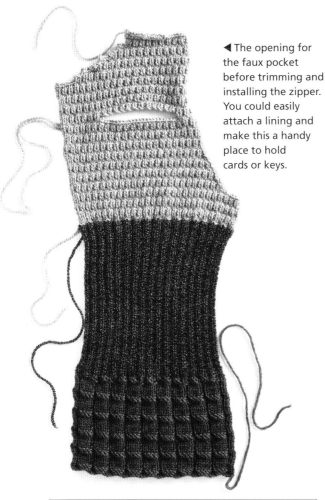

◀ The opening for the faux pocket before trimming and installing the zipper. You could easily attach a lining and make this a handy place to hold cards or keys.

A small zipper, custom-cut to fit this small pocket opening, is pinned in place. Here the opening is horizontal, unlike the lower sleeve, but the process for pinning and sewing is the same.

Embroidery

There are many ways to decorate a knitted fabric, and not all involve knitting! Simple embroidery stitches can easily transform a plain garment into something really special.

Use as small a needle as possible to make the path that your yarn passes through as small as possible. Sometimes stitching through, and splitting, the yarns in the knitted fabric helps hold the embroidery in place better than if you stitch through larger holes within or around stitches in the fabric. It's easiest to embroider with springy yarns that have a little "grab," and it's helpful to give the embroidered fabric a shot of steam to set the stitches in place, if the fibers allow.

Duplicate Stitch

Duplicate stitch, in which you cover a stitch with another yarn, is a way of working additional colors that would be difficult to do in the knitting itself. For example, in Fair Isle knitting you only knit with two colors in each row. If you want to add more colors, duplicate stitch is the way to do it. It is very easy to do and I use it often, especially in smaller projects where I want to perk up the patterning with dots of bright or bold color.

Duplicate stitch is also a way to mask errors in stranded colorwork. Before blocking or steaming, if you notice an error (again—it's always essential to check your pieces carefully before beginning your finishing!), you can work over the mistaken stitches with the correct color. Steaming will often totally merge the new yarn with the background.

For even more texture and color, add duplicate stitch to a solid-color fabric, then weave a strand of yarn in and out of the pattern you have created for even more texture and color.

Cross-Stitch Embroidery

Vintage maven that I am, I am always looking at the past for inspiration. I often see garments, both machine- and hand-knit, that feature cross-stitch. It is easy to do and is a nice, easy way to decorate plain fabric that cries out for a little detail. You could try mixing cross-stitch with Fair Isle to add a little more texture and detail. Embroider the Xs using the knitted fabric as a grid. You can embroider over a single stitch or over blocks of four stitches.

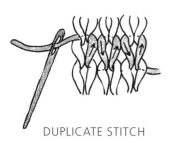

DUPLICATE STITCH

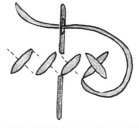

CROSS-STITCH EMBROIDERY

Chaining

You can chain lines on the top of any knitted fabric to create straight lines or free-form shapes. You can also chain vertical lines into striped knitted fabric to create a faux plaid look. I adore this technique and use it all the time. It requires preparation in the knitting: You must work a purled rib "channel" at intervals. For the most flexible fabric, make one chain stitch for every two rows, or two purl bars, and take care to work the chain stitches loosely. The chain stitch itself shares a flexibility that knitting has, and is a nice embroidery touch that, if well placed, will not stiffen the fabric very much. This technique is shown below.

To chain the lines, I always use a tapestry needle, but other knitters I know prefer a crochet hook. I like to weave in the ends at top and bottom of the plaid lines as I go—rather than wait until the end.

◄ This is a detail of a magnificent old Scandinavian sweater I bought for 25 cents at a yard sale many years ago, and it never ceases to inspire me. If you look closely, you will see that the base fabric was knit only in ivory and black. The red sections are embroidered completely in duplicate stitch. This exceptional effort, which was undoubtedly very time-consuming, is not one that many knitters would attempt, especially in a fine-gauge yarn.

CHAIN STITCH

▶ It's easy to create vertical lines on stripes to mimic woven plaid. Work purl ribs on a knit fabric, and then chain lines into the ribs, stitching over one purl stitch as is shown here. For a more elongated stitch, and a more quickly chained line, cover two purl stitches with one chain stitch. The cardigan in which this technique is used is shown on page 105.

Satin Stitch

Satin stitch completely covers an area of knitting and creates bold areas of color. It can be worked easily over any narrow area. For wider areas, it is useful to tack longer strands down, or instead work narrow areas next to each other. For satin stitch, I like to use a yarn that is springy and full enough to fill the area.

French Knots

A French knot is easy to make and lends a unique texture when used in groups or alone. It is best to use yarns that have some cling and grab. Smooth, shiny yarns won't attach to the knitted fabric as well. I often combine French knots with satin stitch.

Blanket Stitch

Blanket, or overcast, stitch is often used at the edges of knitted pieces. It works best, in my experience, when the fabric is very flat, or the edges have been trimmed to make the fabric stable. It lends a rustic look that emphasizes the handmade nature of a garment.

Running Stitch

A running stitch is simply sewing in a straight line, and is best worked vertically. Working it side-to-side, or even on the diagonal bias can restrict the stretch of knits. Use a fat yarn and a small needle.

SATIN STITCH

◀ Satin stitch can be worked over any narrow shape you can outline. For wider areas, it is useful to tack longer strands down; or intead work narrow adjacent areas next to each other to avoid this.

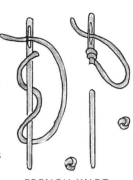

FRENCH KNOT

▲This swatch features traditional Scandinavian roses with satin stitch leaves and French knot buds.

▲ Sometimes just a running stitch in a contrasting color—the simplest of embroidery techniques—can really lend a lot of detail, as is does in this swatch worked to recall a classic denim jacket.

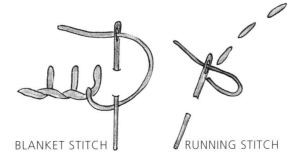

BLANKET STITCH   RUNNING STITCH

Making a Pompom

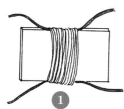

① Wrap a good amount of yarn around a piece of cardboard that is the desired width of your finished pompom plus about ½ inch. Run a strand of yarn under the yarn at the top and bottom edges of the cardboard.

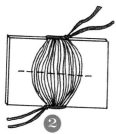

② Tie both sides *very* tightly, leaving long ends. Cut across the center of the strands on both sides of the cardboard. You now have two halves of a pompom.

③ Carefully tie the two halves together with the long ends, taking care not to catch any of the strands! Fluff up the pompom with your fingers. Arrange the long strands to one side and trim two of them, leaving two to attach to a cord.

④ Trim the pompom to a smaller size, clipping it into as even a ball as possible. Steam the pompom heavily with a wet towel and pinch the pompom into shape. Trim any long pieces.

▲ For this hat and mitten set from the Fall 2007 issue of *Vogue Knitting,* I created pairs of pompoms for the perfect "Winter Wonderland" ensemble. This set is actually an update of design that appeared in the magazine in 1986.

Pompoms, Tassels, Fringe & More

I love adding hanging things. And in my opinion, a perfectly made, thick, fluffy pompom is one of the great pleasures of the knitting life—even if it is not actually knitted!

Pompoms

Pompoms are my favorite detail for what I call "Winter Wonderland" knits. I love hanging pompoms from cords and ties and topping off a hat with a big one. My friend Margery says I make the best pompoms in the world. If that is true, it is because I adore them and take a lot of care to form them.

To create the densest, fluffiest pompoms, use a yarn that will full and fluff up with steaming. Using a stringy yarn will result in a limp pompom. If the yarn of your project is not suitable, then match the color with a more suitable yarn for better results. And use lots of yarn! Follow the steps shown at left to make your own perfect pompom.

Tassels

A tassel is sort of a cross between fringe and a pompom. To create a tassel you also wrap yarn around a piece of cardboard that is the length you want your tassel to be plus ½ inch. The more yarn you use and the shorter the strands, the fatter the tassel will be. Follow the steps at lower left to create a terrific tassel.

Fringe

A row of fringe on the edges of a scarf or along the bottom edge of a sweater can be a whimsical design

Making a Tassel

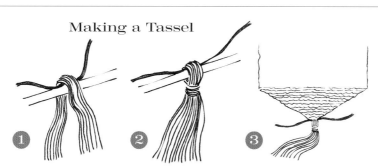

1. Wrap yarn around the cardboard and slide a separate piece of yarn under the strand at one side. Cut the wrapped yarn on the other side. Drape the strands over a knitting needle. **2.** Take a few of the strands and wrap them around the hanging strands close to the needle. **3.** Attach the tassel to your garment with the free strand of yarn.

▲ This large-scale tassel matches the large scale of the scarf (see page 26), and draws attention to the triangular end of the piece. This tassel is fat and full because the yarn is big and bouncy.

element. To create fringe, take a piece of cardboard that is the length you want the fringe to be, plus an inch or two. Wrap yarn around the cardboard several times and cut on one side only. Refer to the drawings at right to attach the fringe to your knitting. Experiment to see which side of the finished loop you want to be seen. On a scarf this does not matter, as both sides are visible, but on a garment sometimes one side is prettier than the other.

Braids

One of my favorite trims is made by braiding together multiple strands of yarns. To do this, I divide strands of yarn into three groups, then sew them at one end. I stick this end in the drawer of my desk and braid the yarn. When I have the desired length, I lock the yarn in place by tying or sewing the ends, then cutting. You can also make a very long braid and then cut shorter lengths after locking the strands in place.

I sew this braided trim along edges, or sometimes on the fabric itself as a "false" cable, a visual joke of sorts. You can tuck the ends around to the wrong side of the fabric, or let the yarn ends hang free like pigtails. How fun! For more variety, use different colors in each strand section, or vary the kind of yarn in each strand.

Belts and Straps

Any knitted pattern that lies flat can be used to make a belt. My favorite pattern stitch for straps and belts is the most basic k1, p1 rib. Any rib would work, but a thick wide one, slipped into a narrow buckle, makes a belt that flares in a most attractive way.

Two stockinette edge stitches on either side of any belt pattern make the edges turn in slightly and lie flat. You can also use two garter stitches on either side, especially if the fabric—like a slip-stitch pattern—has a tight row gauge!

Work your belt pattern to your desired length plus 2 to 3 inches extra for the fold-over into the buckle. (Remember that a belt worn over a sweater has to be longer than your waist measurement to accomodate the extra bulk.) A knitted belt will stretch, so check the length of the belt as you knit it. I often narrow the final tip slightly by decreasing gradually at each side, until I have only one or two stitches left, then cut the yarn and pull through.

Here is a belt pattern that works nicely for many weights of yarn. Add or subtract an even number of stitches to vary it. Use a smallish needle for a trim, classic belt, or a larger one for a softer, less structured, sashlike belt.

Cast on 11 stitches for the end that joins to the center of the buckle and work toward the point.
Next row (RS) K2, p1, (k1, p1) 3 times.
Next row (WS) Knit the knit sts and purl the purl sts as they appear.
Rep these 2 rows until belt is your desired length to the pointed end, end with a WS row.
Work belt point:
Next row (RS) K1, ssk, rib to last 3 sts, k2tog, k1.
Next row P2, rib to last 2 sts, p2.
Rep last 2 rows 2 times more.
Next row K1, SK2P, k1.
Cut yarn and thread through rem 3 sts. Weave end to back and neaten the tip. Steam the belt and sew the cast-on edge around the bar of the belt buckle.
Optional side belt loops (make 2) Cast on 13 sts. Bind off. Sew to each side of the garment.
Choose a belt buckle with a center bar and without a prong—if there is a prong, remove it. A double thickness of your belt material will pass through the opening in the buckle, so be sure you have one large enough to accommodate it.

Cords

Knitted cords can be used to attach pompoms to a garment, become ties for a hat, or be threaded through eyelets to create a drawstring. There are several ways to make cords.

I-CORD

The most popular knitted cord by far is Elizabeth Zimmermann's I-cord, and most knitters have made one at some time or other. The I-cord is a three-stitch tube that is most easily knitted on double pointed needles. It is a beautiful tube, juicy and thick. It is probably the most perfect cord. To make an I-cord, cast on three stitches, knit one row and (without turning the work), slip the stitches back to the beginning of the row. Repeat until the cord is the desired length, then bind off.

LAZY CORD (L-CORD)

I am often too lazy to knit I-cord, or if it is too thick for my needs, I make another simpler cord. This favorite cord of mine is thin and lies flat. It is the soul of simplicity. Use a smallish needle for a dense cord. Use a larger needle for a more open, lacy cord.

Cast on a lot of stitches. Bind them off on the next row. Weave in the ends with as small a needle as possible—or use them to tie a tassel. Stretch and steam, flattening the cord with pressure if you like and as much as your fiber allows.

Making a Fringe

1 Insert a crochet hook into the knitted fabric, grab the strands in the middle with the hook and pull through the knitted fabric.

2 Pull the cut ends through the loop with the crochet hook.

3 The finished fringe.

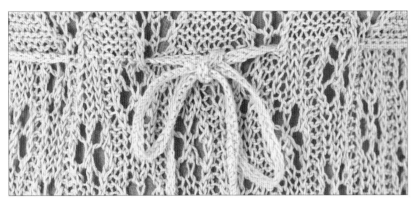

▲ Drawstring made from my favorite L-cord (tunic appears on page 30).

These two hats both feature woolly pompoms and decorative cords. The ivory tweed hat (featured on the cover of the Winter 2010 issue of *Vogue Knitting*) has easy L-cord strands. The cord on the red hat is twisted and has a ropelike quality.

For a slightly thicker cord, cast on a lot of stitches and purl or knit one row. Your cord will look a little different depending on whether you knit or purl. Bind off in purl or knit. Stretch, then steam.

To figure out how many stitches to cast on, cast on what you think will give you about 4 to 6 inches worth of stitches. Work a mini cord to calculate the number of stitches per inch, and test the look of the final cord by steaming. Multiply the stitches per inch by the approximate desired length. Add about 20 stitches, then cast on that number of stitches.

TWISTED CORD

A twisted cord is not technically knitted but it is often used in knitted pieces. Measure out a piece of yarn four to five times as long as you would like the cord to be. Loop the yarn so it is arranged in four parallel strands of the same length.

Knot the end of the yarn that has the two free ends and slip about one inch of this end into a drawer. Put a pencil through the looped end and stand far enough away from the drawer so the lengths of yarn are taut. Using the pencil as a holder, twist the strands together until they form a firm spiral.

Hold the pencil end firmly with your right hand. With your left hand, pinch the taut cord at the halfway point. Bring your right hand close to the yarn end in the drawer and, at the same time, pull firmly with the left hand to keep both halves of the twisted strand taut. With your right hand, grab the end that is in the drawer and remove it. Let go with your left hand and allow the strands to twist around each other. Fasten the two ends together and pull to even out the cord.

Collars, Cuffs & Cowls
Adding on extra pieces to a sweater or project is one of my favorite ways to increase detail, warmth and/or drama.

They need not be a part of the original pattern: You can make your own personally designed additions to any sweater.

Some of these details do not have to be attached permanently. They can be buttoned or tied on or they can sit separately on a garment, like a large cowl knitted in the same yarn as a sweater. I recently saw a Carole Lombard comedy from the 1930s, which featured fabulous clothes. As two women chat in one scene, the heroine's friend helps her to attach some cuffs to her lower sleeves with pins, then fold the cuffs up to hide the attachment. I filed this beautiful moment away in my mind and will use this inspiration at some time, maybe to design a set of removable collar and cuffs, perhaps using snaps or buttons.

Collars

Collars come in all shapes and sizes. They can be narrow and prim, fluttery and seductive, or huge and cozy. Collar edges can butt together or their ends can overlap. Stitches for collars can be picked up, or collars can be knitted separately and sewn on. Once you start thinking about collars, you will see inspiration everywhere in garments of all kinds.

A plain, unshaped rectangle is woefully inadequate for a collar. As I will describe below, the neckline edge, where the collar meets the back neck, is best if curved. And the pointed tips can be shaped slightly as well so that the collar sits better around the neck.

ATTACHING COLLARS

There are several ways to join a collar to the neckline of a knitted garment. Consider which method best suits your type of collar.

Since the ridge formed by the row where stitches are picked up can be visible where a collar is attached, I like it to appear as neat as possible, or be hidden if possible. A visible ridge may not even be an issue, but I like to consider it. Similarly, if you sew on a collar, consider how the ridge formed by sewing will present itself—to the right side or the wrong side.

PICKING UP STITCHES

When you pick up stitches along a neck edge, you have to decide whether you want to pick up with the right side facing or wrong side facing, or a combination of the two.

When you pick up from the right side, the ridge formed by the picked-up stitches is to the inside of the sweater. This works best with small collars where the join can be seen, and those where the collar will not be open, revealing the ridge. When you pick up from the wrong side, the ridge formed by the picked-up stitches will be visible on the outside of the sweater. This works best with large collars that will fold over and cover the ridge, for the neatest appearance. If a collar is to be worn open with the pick-up row visible, then it's best if the ridge is not seen.

In some cases I pick up the front sections of the collar stitches from the right side, and the back neck with the wrong side facing. This alters the way the picked-up row is seen in each section.

SEWING ON A COLLAR

My favorite way to sew on a collar is a two-part process that makes the job easier. It also adds a little detail to the neckline where the collar joins the body of the sweater.

Step 1 Edge the neckline with a ridge of reverse stockinette stitch. Pick up the necessary stitches to edge the neckline, knit the wrong side, purl the right side, then bind off on the wrong side in knit.

Step 2 With the right side of the collar facing, and the wrong side of the neckline edge facing, pin the collar in place, butting the curved edge along the ridge formed by the picked up stitches. Sew the collar fairly loosely to the ridge beneath the rolled trim.

In this method, the trim adds firmness to the neckline edge, so the collar can sit loosely and naturally, without a tight and binding join.

In order to make sewing on this collar (see page 105) easier, and at the same time add detail and color to the neckline edge, I first worked a small roll of reverse stockinette stitch. Then I pinned the collar in place at the base of this trim and sewed the collar to the ridge formed by the picked-up stitches.

SHAPING THE NECKLINE EDGE OF A COLLAR

Something I learned in my early years of sewing theater costumes is that collars fit best when they have a "rise" at the lower back neck: This allows the back of the collar to sit a little higher than the front and eliminates any pulling or awkwardness as the collar encircles the neckline edge. If your pattern does not include this "rise" at the back neck, and you desire the best fit, you might want to add it.

If you are picking up stitches for a collar along an edge, you can short row over the back neck area to create a little extra crescent of fabric before working back and forth over all the stitches to complete the collar.

If you are knitting the collar separately to be sewn on, then work this shaping at the end of the collar, which is easier than at the beginning. For small collars, this extra area can be about one to two inches in height, such as in the plaid collar shown on the previous page. I also worked the "rise" on this plaid collar in garter stitch to give this area a firmness that would not collapse at the back neck.

If your collar is very large and dramatic, such as the blue shawl collar shown below, the rise might be four to five inches in height.

SHAPING THE POINTS OF A COLLAR

When knitting your collar, shape the points both for detail and so that they spread nicely without straining.

It is easiest to plan this shaping if you are knitting a

collar from picked-up stitches along a neckline edge. After your short-rowing is completed for the "rise" at the back neck, simply increase at the beginning and end of approximately every fourth row until the collar length is reached, then bind off.

A little more planning is necessary for this collar-tip shaping if you are knitting a collar separately from the outer edge to the neckline edge. First, figure out how many stitches are necessary for the collar neckline edge. Then add extra stitches for the shaping at the tips, figuring that they will be eliminated gradually as decreases are worked approximately every fourth row. When the neckline edge is reached, you will bind off gradually for the shaping of the "rise" of the collar.

For a collar that overlaps at the front edges, add at least 2 inches, and maybe up to 8 for a dramatic overlap. I often like to play around with a piece of fabric, in a similar weight, to decide the shape of a collar before planning how to knit it. This works well for helping determine how much fabric is needed.

Cowls

Cowls can be knit as simple tubes or scarflike rectangles, or be shaped like a collar to have a rise that extends at the back neck for drama. Or they can be pointed or peaked like a cowboy's bandanna. Like collars, cowls can be knit separately and sewn on, or you can pick up stitches to knit the cowl. Working a cowl as a separate unit, to sit on top of the neckline

This sweater features a ribbed section at the base of the cabled band that allows the sewn-on collar to stand slightly higher in the back and drape more naturally to the front of the garment.

▲The ribbing of this very large collar was short-rowed across the back neck to create a rise that allows the collar to stand slightly higher in the back.

This shawl-collar sweater appeared in a story about knits inspired by the Southwest in the Fall 2010 issue of *Vogue Knitting.* ▶

▲The cowl in this design from *Vogue Knitting*'s Winter 2006/2007 features a cable pattern that echoes the cables in the body of the sweater.

of a sweater or be buttoned or tied to it, creates a convertible, multifunctional garment.

Hoods

There are many kinds of hoods, from the simplest rectangular shape to curvy head-and-neck-hugging versions. Hoods can be sewn to a neckline, or buttoned onto the neckline edge. One thing to remember with a hood is that when it is not being worn, it lies across the shoulders and back so that the wrong side of the fabric shows, as well as any seams in the hood. Also, with front-opening garments, the wrong side of the front edges and part of the inner neckline edge will show when the hood is down. So make your join—whether it is picked up or sewn—as neat as possible.

Cuffs

Cuffs are just little collars for sleeves—as well as for mittens, gloves and even hats. They can be knit in or added on. Remember that a cuff has to face in the opposite direction from the piece it is attached to: In this way both sleeve and cuff will have the right side facing when the cuff is folded up.

Knit your sleeve ½ to 1 inch shorter than you want the finished sleeve to be so that the cuff can roll out from the lower edge and make up the length. Be sure the cuff is long enough to both roll up and make up the extra sleeve length. The thicker the cuff, the more length you will need for it to fold over neatly.

To add a cuff at the lower edge of a sleeve (or anywhere for that matter), pick up the stitches for it from the wrong side of your sleeve; the ridge formed by the picked-up stitches will be enclosed and hidden by the cuff as it folds up over it.

For a short, close-fitting cuff, pick up just enough stitches for the same width as the lower edge. Work straight and bind off at the desired length. For a longer cuff—gauntlet style or flared—you might want to widen the cuff as you knit.

The potential for adding detail is endless. Your cuff can have an edging that matches the main sweater, and it's also fun to make a cuff that has buttons, just like a little cardigan!

◀In this photo of a design from the Fall 2007 issue of *Vogue Knitting*, you can see that when the hood is worn down, the wrong side of the front placket as well as the join of the hood to the body is visible. When this is the case, be sure the finishing is neat and well considered.

Tutorial Short-Row Shaping	Short-rowing is a technique in which you knit over only some of the stitches on a row (often over several rows) to form a lozenge of knitting, then resume knitting over the entire row again.

You can use this technique to expand an area of knitting, such as at the back neck of a collar; to add length within a piece for someone who might have an extra-broad back; to form horizontal dressmaker darts to accommodate the bust in a close-fitting garment; to make ruffles or to create shaping in accessories.

Short-rowing works best with simple pattern stitches so you do not interrupt the overall pattern. It works fine in simple stockinette stitch and most ribbed patterns.

To avoid a hole between the short row and its unworked neighboring stitches, you must "wrap" an adjacent, unworked turning stitch on the first row, then work this strand together with the stitch that surrounds it on the return row, or any row where you encounter a wrapped stitch.

These fold-up cuffs feature satin stitch and French knots to embellish the rose patterning. Also note how the sleeve folds naturally on the reverse stockinette ridge.

Pockets

Pockets are a detail that might be a part of the pattern you are following, or they might be an extra that you add—and they always have the potential to personalize the design and make it more functional. There are several kinds of pockets. Learn how to plan, make and attach all of them and you will add valuable skills to your knitting repertoire.

My Three Favorite Pockets

Here are the three pockets I use the most. One sits invisibly in the side seam of a sweater, lined in woven fabric or knitted fabric. The second is a patch pocket that can go anywhere. The last is a vertical slit pocket that has a trimmed opening, lined in either woven or knitted fabric.

SIDE SEAM POCKETS

The side seam pocket with a fold-in facing is so easy and can be adapted to any sweater pattern that has a side seam. The knit-in facing folds naturally to the

inside of the sweater. I learned this pocket years ago from my designer friends, sisters Carla Scott and Mari Lynn Patrick, when I did freelance work at the offices of *Vogue Knitting* in the early part of my career as a designer. It is such a simple idea, and so utterly perfect. I remember how delighted I was to learn it, and I have used it so often!

This concept is extremely variable. You can make the facing itself be as large as a pocket (by casting on more than the five stitches suggested below). Or, once a small facing is made, and the side seam of the sweater is sewn, you can either **1)** sew on a fabric pocket, or **2)** pick up along the edge of the facing and knit a pocket. I often use a lighter-weight yarn for less bulk, and a contrasting color adds a nice detail. I like to shape the picked-up pocket so that it curves and droops into the body of the sweater.

Here is how to work two pocket facings, one on each side: On your back piece, work even in pattern, with two stockinette seam stitches at the sides; end with a wrong-side row at the desired point of the pocket placement. Cast on for pocket facings.

Next row (RS) Using the backward-loop cast-on, cast on 5 stitches, k1 (the first edge stitch), then slip the second seam stitch with yarn in back, work to last 2

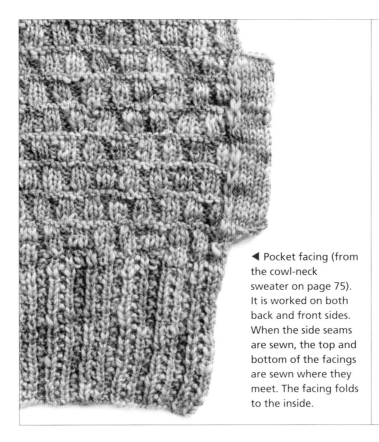

◄ Pocket facing (from the cowl-neck sweater on page 75). It is worked on both back and front sides. When the side seams are sewn, the top and bottom of the facings are sewn where they meet. The facing folds to the inside.

▲ The finished pocket. The facing folds naturally to the inside along a slipped stitch line of stitches at the side seam. Inside, the pocket lining is picked up along the edge of the facing.

stitches, slip 1 stitch with yarn in back, k1 (the last seam stitch), then cast on 5 sts with backward loops—10 stitches have been added.

Next row (WS) P7, work to last 7 sts, end p7.

Next row (RS) K6, sl 1 wyib, work to last 7 sts, sl 1 wyib, end k6.

Repeat the last 2 rows until pocket depth is around 6 inches or as deep as you desire, then end with a wrong-side row.

Bind off 5 stitches at the beginning of the next 2 rows—10 stitches have been decreased.

Work the remainder of the piece, with two stockinette seam stitches at the sides. Repeat this on the matching front(s).

When you seam the back to front at sides, join the bottom of the facings together where they meet.

To make a fabric lining, see my instructions for linings on page 114. Here is how to knit a pocket lining along the edge of the sewn facing: With double-pointed needles, pick up stitches around the pocket facing. Mark a couple of stitches at the top of the facing and at the bottom too. Work in rounds of knit (or purl according to taste)—and at the same time, decrease one stitch before and after the top marked stitches; at the same time, increase one stitch before and after the lower marked stitches, every other round to slant the pocket. When the pocket is long enough for your taste, put half the stitches on two needles so that the pocket is flat along the increase and decrease lines. Then bind off the lower edge stitches of the pocket together with the three-needle bind-off method (see page 42), or weave the stitches together.

PATCH POCKETS

Patch pockets offer endless possibilities. They can be square, rounded, gathered or embellished! They can be knit in the same pattern as your sweater or contrast with it. How about making the pocket the focus of an otherwise plain garment? Why not design your initial swatch to become a pocket for your project?

You can knit a patch pocket separately, trim it and sew three sides onto the sweater. However, it's easier to pick up the lower edge stitches into the knitted fabric itself, work the pocket upward and just sew the two sides. This type of pocket looks a little more refined than a completely sewn-on patch pocket.

To pick up and knit a patch pocket, first plot your pocket on your schematic. Then, measuring your sweater piece, mark the row where the lower pocket will be, and also mark the width of the lower edge of the pocket.

With right side facing and holding the yarn strand beneath the fabric, poke your needle into a stitch, pull through a loop and place it on the needle. Pick up the desired number of stitches for your pocket. On the first row back, make a single edge stitch on each side for seaming, either by making a backward loop onto the needle, or working into the front and back of the first and last stitch. This extra stitch should be free from the picked-up edge, as it will get seamed.

Depending on the yarn, and size of the needle, or if the pocket is far away from the edge of a piece, sometimes I find it easier to pull through the loops for the pocket stitches with a crochet hook and place them on the knitting needle.

Work your pocket to the desired length and work any edging as desired. Steam the pocket lightly if the fiber allows. Starting at the lower edge, sew the pocket to the body of the sweater, keeping an even line. If the fabric is thick, you can use one half stitch as a seam.

If your pocket has more stitches gaugewise than the fabric beneath it (if, for example, it has a cable on it), pick up one stitch for each stitch in the body, and then increase to the necessary stitches on the first row.

SLIT POCKETS

A slit pocket can be horizontal, angled or vertical. Any type will add lovely detail to any garment.

For a horizontal pocket opening, bind off stitches where you want a pocket to be, then cast them on again in the next row; proceed with the knitting. Or make a giant one-row buttonhole (page 85), working

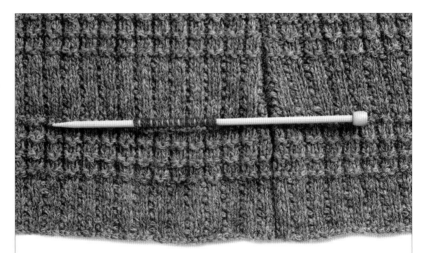

To avoid having to sew the lower edge of a patch pocket, pick up the stitches into the piece, plus an edge stitch on either side. Work the pocket, leaving only the sides to sew. The finished sweater is shown on page 105.

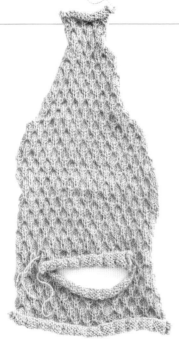

▲ This unfinished pocket opening (from the cardigan shown on page 126) features a bound-off edge at the front and a small 1"-deep pocket facing at the back, added on the next row, to replace the bound-off stitches.

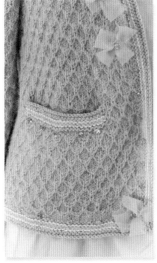

▲ The completed pocket opening is trimmed with striped garter stitch, sewn-on beads and handmade silk organdy fabric flowers.

Inside the jacket is the free-hanging silk pocket lining, made from a rectangle sewn at the sides.

▲ This little flap, edged in a roll of reverse stockinette stitch, is a faux pocket—there is no pocket underneath (although you could add one!). A button adds an extra touch of color and texture. (The vest is shown on page 53.)

it as wide as the pocket. After the knitting is complete, you can pick up and knit a pocket from the upper cast-on row, to hang from, or be attached to, the wrong side of the sweater. Then add an edging on the lower bound-off row. Or add your edging first and then sew a fabric pocket for less bulk.

A vertical pocket opening is a good choice if you want to add a zipper. Mark the spot on your row where you want the pocket opening to begin. Knit to that point; join a second ball of yarn and work to the end. Work back and forth with separate balls of yarn. When the opening is deep enough, work across a row with one strand to close the pocket. Add trim for buttons or to apply a zipper. Then add a pocket to the wrong side, by sewing a patch pocket or a free hanging knitted or fabric pocket.

An angled pocket opening might look difficult, but it's not. Again, plot your opening on the schematic. Mark the spot on your row where you want the pocket opening to begin. Knit to that point; join a second ball of yarn and work to the end. Work your wrong-side row with both balls.

Work the right side row as follows: For a left-slanting pocket opening, increase a stitch on one section and decrease on the next; or for a right-slanting pocket opening, decrease a stitch on first section and increase one on the next. Repeat this row every second or fourth row, depending on the angle you would like.

When the opening is deep enough, work across a row with one strand to close the pocket. After the piece is done, edge the pocket and make a lining, either a knitted inner patch pocket or a free hanging fabric pocket.

For a knit-in pocket lining do this: As you begin the slanted decrease for the front edge of the pocket, with the second strand of yarn, cast on enough stitches for a pocket on the back side, which will be attached under the slanted edge. When the slanted edge is deep enough, bind off the pocket stitches, and work across the entire body piece with one strand to close the opening. The pocket opening and pocket lining are complete! Sew the lining to the wrong side when the piece is finished.

False Pockets

Sometimes a pocket is just a visual detail. A fun moment of trompe l'oeil. The easiest way to create a false pocket is to create an opening, pick up and knit trim along it and then sew it closed! Or simply pick up at your chosen spot and work an edging into the fabric. To really fool the eye, leave one edge of your trim open or close with a button through both layers.

ALL THE TRIMMINGS
Plaid Accents Cardigan

Pattern
Plaid Accents
Cardigan
SEE PAGE 150

This jacket features a multitude of finishing issues. First of all, something unusual happened. After the pieces were knit, I decided I liked the "wrong" side of the fabric better. I had planned to feature the nubby side, the one with the more reverse stockinette look to it, but when I saw the larger pieces, I decided I liked the smoother more refined look of the other side! It was a real finishing "surprise."

Since I had added seam stitches to make the seaming easier, I had a choice: I could have my seams fall to the outside of the sweater as a detail, or I could seam them inside, which would mean I would have to seam on the reverse stockinette, or purl side, of the

▲ I tried something new in this design. After knitting a solid-color buttonhole band, I decided it was too plain and knit a striped one to play up the plaid accents.

seam stitches. I decided for the more refined look—no visible seams—since the cardigan would have enough detail already.

I loved the color range of the yarns, and I wanted a tweedy, traditional look to the sweater—a refined "Lady of the Manor" look, with plaid accents. So after the pieces were knit, I worked deep cuffs at the lower sleeves, with the vertical lines embroidered in afterward to form the plaid pattern.

The patch pocket also features plaid detailing and is closed with a button detail that matches the buttons on the button band. The loop is an L-cord (page 97).▶

Flip-Flopping

Note that if you decide to use the original side of the fabric—the one that is written in the pattern as the right side (instead of the "wrong" side as shown here)— your front pieces will be reversed in shape from the sweater in the photo, and the buttonhole band will be on the opposite side. You won't, however, have to make any changes in your finishing: You will still work the same band and sew it to the front in the same way. It will just be on the right sweater front, instead of the left.

The collar was worked separately, with shaping at the points as well as a flat and firm garter stitch "rise" at the back neck to ensure the collar would fit well. I wanted the join of the collar to be as invisible as possible, so I picked up stitches around the entire neckline and worked a ridge of reverse stockinette. You can see in the photo on page 99 how I pinned the collar and sewed its bound-off edge to the ridge formed by the picked-up stitches from the ridge. This is an easy way to join a collar, and the ridge lends some extra detail as well.

For more plaid detail, I picked up stitches for the pocket right into the fabric and knitted them upward. It was easy to seam the pocket, with right side facing, to the sweater because of the vertical lines in the pattern: I just followed one of the lines.

I used my favorite sewn-on ribbed band for this sweater, incorporating the yarn-over buttonhole (see page 87) that works so well in a ribbing. The band, knit on a smaller needle, has the same number of rows as the front edge, so I just knit a section and sewed it on, matching two bars in the band for every two bars at the edge. How easy is that?

However, after I first knit the band, I made a big change. In a solid color, the band looked flat and uninteresting. I always scrutinze a sweater in its final stages, asking myself if everything looks as good as it can; in this case, the solid color bands did nothing for me, so I tried something I had never done before. I worked the ribbed bands in sections of color, different from band to band and without a repeating color pattern. I was happy: This random look contrasts with the regular patterning of the plaid and lends the sweater an ever-so-slightly quirky detail.

There was another unexpected finishing detail: Because the sweater fronts overlapped, the buttons would have to be sewn to the main knitted fabric, not the other band. With right side facing, I used a crochet hook to make a firm vertical chain opposite the line of buttonholes. I sewed the buttons onto this chain. I could have used anchor buttons alone on the wrong side when sewing on the buttons, but the firm foundation of the chained line reinforced the fabric.

After you knit this sweater you will have an impressive array of techniques in your finishing repertoire! ■

These deep cuffs were knit from the lower edge of the sleeve. The vertical plaid lines were chained in afterward.

CHAPTER 6

Continuing Education

Special Finishing

This chapter is about the more unique aspects of finishing that I have explored and enjoyed in my own designs. Not all of them are knitterly. Some involve incorporating interesting details, and others make use of sewing skills, like adding linings. I also give solutions for what to do if a sweater doesn't fit, and we'll explore more extreme finishing techniques such as felting, repurposing knitted garments and, that most daring of techniques, the steek. I hope you'll be inspired to approach finishing in less traditional ways.

Alterations: When Good Sweaters Go Bad

Who has not made a sweater that didn't fit? It's an all-too-common dilemma. It can happen when you don't get the gauge, or when you mistake the amount of ease or the weight of the fabric. Often a sweater like this is just set aside, never worn. It's sad—and a big waste of time and money!

I don't want to make light of alteration—it is often a daunting job to fix a sweater that is not right. However, since yarn can be expensive and your knitting time is valuable, I think it is better to try to make a knitted garment fit than throw it away. Sure, in many cases, ripping out is the best solution for a garment that is way off base. But when a great deal of time and effort has been expended, sometimes it is worth trying to "make it work."

There are many ways a sweater can go wrong. Widthwise, a sweater can be too narrow—perhaps the most common issue!—or much too large. Maybe the body or the sleeves are just too long. Sometimes a sweater would look better if it were more—or less—fitted!

If you have read the preceding chapters, you will know how to examine and prepare your pieces. Some of the techniques I have already mentioned, such as blocking and seaming, can be put to use.

The most important thing to know when beginning an alteration is to be absolutely sure what size you want the altered sweater to measure! There is no point in making even more errors. Take time to alter your original schematic, or make a new one, to reflect the revised corrected measurements. If you aren't quite sure, compare the measurements with a sweater that fits you well, in the same weight knitted material.

When you have a challenging project that needs to be altered, put it in a basket with all the tools and supplies you'll need to fix it. Keep it neatly isolated from other projects until a very relaxed time comes along when you can give it your full attention. Don't start something like this when you are tired!

One way to feel more confident about alterations is to share the project with a friend. You'll both learn!

When a Sweater Is Too Small

I always feel that a too-small sweater is easier to alter than one that is too big. You might also consider these methods for keeping a favorite child's sweater alive for another year of wear.

BLOCKING

I am very reluctant to use blocking as a method to enlarge pieces. Often the fabric springs back to its original size anyway, and at the same time a severe blocking can take the life out of a knitted fabric.

Only if your fiber allows and only if you need to add just a tiny bit of width, consider blocking your pieces by wet-blocking. However, do not force this blocking, or you'll risk ruining the drape of your fabric.

ADDING ON

On a cardigan, if just the body is too small, perhaps you can add wider front bands to give the necessary width. Consider a neat little double-breasted front section, which is easy to add and contributes additional detail.

Perhaps the best way to add to a much-too-small garment's width is to add a section to each side as I did with the sleeve shown on the opposite page. There are two ways to do this:

1. Knit some strips in the yarn and to the same number of rows and sew to each side of the garment.
2. Pick up stitches to the width of the seam area and knit the extra width outward, then sew the bound-off edge of the piece to the other side. The drawback—or benefit, depending on how you look at it—is that the knitting in the extra pieces will go in the opposite direction of the body knitting.

Generally speaking, if you add width to the body, you should also add width to the sleeves, either by adding a strip, or knitting a gusset, a small pie-shaped section that is the same width as the piece added to the corresponding side of the body.

If you need to add only to your sleeve, often the extra fabric can be eased into the armhole without adding extra width to the body.

If the lower body of the garment fits well, adding a diamond-shaped gusset to the armhole area of the garment will expand the bust width. To check this before doing it, you can experiment by opening up the sleeve and side seams in the armhole area alone to see how extra ease affects the fit. If you find this works, then with the help of a friend, measure how wide the diamond of space is. Knit a gusset to mimic this shape, adding seam stitches of course. Sew the gusset into place.

There are decorative options for adding pieces. For the most invisible join, choose a similar pattern or an

▲ When a piece is too small, it's possible to add another piece to enlarge it. I deliberately made this sleeve narrow so I could demonstrate adding a cable strip to enlarge it. Here the piece for the sleeve shows a different side of the fabric than I actually used—I preferred the wrong side for the finished jacket.

▲ The finished sleeve with the extra strip sewn in.

innocuous one, but for whimsy, use contrasting color or bold texture. Cabled strips, as for the sleeves on the asymmetrical cardigan with plaid accents on page 105 (the sleeve is shown above) are a natural choice for narrow—or even wide—additions. Add stripes or texture—anything that appeals to you.

When the Sweater Is Too Big
Removing width is actually a more challenging alteration than adding width, but it can be done.

SEAMING IN EXCESS
Seaming pieces farther in from the edge is the most obvious solution for getting rid of width in a too-large sweater. In a simple dropped-shoulder garment this might work best.

CHANGING GARMENT SHAPE
If you were to take away extra fabric in almost every seam in a garment, it would have a lot of bulky seams, creating just another kind of poor fit. In a

111

garment with more sophisticated shaping, especially in the armhole area, my suggestion would be to rip all the pieces—front and back and sleeve caps—down to the armhole and rework the sweater to make a simpler garment shape. A dropped shoulder, for example, is more suited to a garment that is oversized and can drape rather than fit closely.

CUTTING

Just as you can create a steek (see page 123) to make a planned opening in a sweater, you can also use steek techniques to eliminate width in a sweater that is too big. For instance, you could mark your desired width, machine knit next to the revised seamline, then narrow the body by cutting. You could cut—or re-knit the armhole areas—to make a smaller size.

I have also used cutting to shape a neckline that was too small. I worked a lace dress in a very fine gauge yarn, and the neckline was just too prim—not dramatic enough for my taste. I did not want to rip out the shoulder seams or rip out the very complex lace, so I decided to cut. I marked my preferred neckline on the sweater with yarn, then sewed next to the marker yarn with a slightly zigzag machine stitch in order to make the neckline area a little more stretchy than it would have been if I had used a straight machine-stitch. I picked up my edging next to the machine stitching. It was a very successful alteration.

Creating More Elasticity

Often a fiber will not impart the necessary cling to a ribbed area that you would like. If you want the waistline area of a ribbed garment to be closer to the body, weave elastic thread as support on the wrong side after the garment is complete.

With the wrong side facing, firmly lock or tie the covered elastic thread to a side seam or to the ridge formed by the picked-up stitches along a cardigan front. Then with a tapestry needle, weave the thread through the prominent ribs of the area that you want to be more fitted, going entirely around the whole sweater, to attach the thread firmly at the beginning again. Repeat this step about ½ inch away, above and below, for as many rows as is necessary to give the area the narrower effect you want. Often you need not add too many rows; a little encouragement is sometimes all a ribbed pattern needs. Do not pull the thread too tightly—it needs very little tautness to do its job.

Here's another useful tip for areas needing more elasticity: You can work a line of single crochet along

the wrong side of a fabric to gather an edge or a ribbing that has lost its oomph. Chain loosely along a horizontal line in the knitting, inserting the hook into an occasional "bump" on the wrong side. This technique works well under the bustline of a sweater to gather gently without working any complex shaping in the sweater itself.

When a Sweater Is Too Long

When a sweater is too long, you can get rid of the extra length by removing a strip of extra knitting. Then you can either re-knit a new lower edge, working downward, or you can reattach the former edging after some length has been removed from it; this obviously works best if the patterning is not too complex.

If your garment is seamed, open up the seams first. If you used the strand at the cast-on edge to seam, start to open the seam above the area you want to shorten. This way you will not cut the crucial seaming yarn at the lower edge and mess up your cast-on row, especially if you want to reattach the lower edging in a higher place.

Because of the structure of knits, it is almost impossible to unravel from the bottom up. Therefore, it's better to clip and unravel a row as for a cut buttonhole (see page 87). Here's how:

Step 1 With the right side facing and the lower edge of the piece facing up, clip a thread at the center of the row where you have decided to shorten.

Step 2 Unravel the yarn to one side and slip the loops onto a long circular needle as a holder. When you get to the end of the row, leave the strand hanging.

Step 3 Repeat in the opposite direction from the center to the other side.

Step 4 At the beginning and end of this "wrong direction" row, you will have the loops at the tops of the stitches. You can either:

a) Knit downward, working into the back of the loops on the first row to tighten them, in a new, different pattern; you will not be going in the correct direction to continue the original pattern.

b) Or use grafting (see page 42) on a portion of the section you removed after shortening, if your pattern stitch allows.

When a Sweater Is Too Short

If you have a plain lower edge, it is easy to lengthen a sweater by picking up and knitting a trim from it. But if there is an edging, you might want to remove it and work a different pattern, and new edging, using the techniques described in the section above.

Incorporating Other Fabrics

Coming from a sewing background, I love woven and machine-made fabrics of all kinds, and over the years I have happily incorporated many into my sweater designs.

I have made pockets and other details, like collars and cuffs, out of contrasting woven materials. I have also knit the body pieces of a garment and attached woven sleeves.

Woven fabrics can be used as trims, edges, plackets or bands. Or woven fabrics can be made into pieces of a sweater. There is a tradition of adding woven sleeves to knitted sweaters in parts of Scandinavia, so the idea is grounded in history! If you want a truly couture touch you might make a lining for a sweater with a lightweight luxury fabric; I like to use the most featherweight silk I can find.

I also love ribbons, tapes and other woven trims and look for ways to use those, too, as trim and in the place of knitted cords. You can sew trims onto the surface of a sweater, or weave them through a pattern stitch.

Working With Other Fabrics

Using manufactured fabrics might require sewing skills, but don't let that intimidate you. For those less experienced in this world of fabrics, there are some basic characteristics to consider. Woven fabrics have much less "give," or stretch, than knit fabrics, except perhaps when cut on the bias, the diagonal line, instead of the straight of the grain. Most cut fabric unravels, so you'll need to hem the edges to avoid that. I cut the trim for the embellished cardigan on page 126 from silk organdy, a crisp lightweight fabric; because I cut the strips on the bias, not the straight of the grain, the edging did not have as great a tendency to unravel. If you want a very different look at your neckline edge, cut a length of bias fabric and use it as trim around the edge.

The possibilities for using fabrics are endless. If you have never considered this aspect of finishing before, you might be surprised at what ideas can emerge when you start to think about it.

Matching fibers from a sweater in your fabric is not necessary. Of course, mixing wool fabric with wool yarns produces a strong seasonal mix for fall or winter, but even that is a rule made to be broken. You could just as easily mix silk and wool, or silk and cotton for other interesting combinations of fiber and texture.

Types of Fabrics

A trip to the fabric store can be a creative jolt to a knitter, and the entry into a new set of skills. Even if you come away with only a handful of buttons, you might find it very interesting to see what there is in the fabric marketplace.

Just seeing what kinds of fabrics exist is inspiring, and it can stimulate an idea that can make a sweater one of a kind. It is hard to browse for fabrics online unless you are very experienced and are familiar with a range of fabrics and their qualities. It is much easier to witness and feel fabrics first-hand in a store, so that you can match texture, consider exact weight and coordinate colors. For fabrics that are more standard and familiar to you, online stores offer variety that might not be available to you locally.

MACHINE-KNIT FABRICS

Machine knits range from those that resemble handknits to others that are highly textured, to very fine-gauge tricots used for T-shirts.

Purists may not agree with me, but I find it fun to combine a machine-knit fabric with a hand-knit one. It need not be "Clash of the Titans" but rather a curious visual statement. The nice thing about it is that they share a similar stretch!

WOVEN FABRICS

Silk is a versatile, strong fabric that has both luxurious and functional qualities. I love the lustrous finish of so many silks: They tend to glow. Many have a crisp, papery quality that could provide a stunning contrast with knitwear. They are perfect for draped collars and trims of all sorts. My favorites are sheer, crisp organdy and lustrous, slightly nubby dupioni silk.

Don't forget to consider more everyday fabrics like light cotton lawn, sturdy denim or checked denim for summer accents. Lighter-weight cotton lawn or voile can mimic silk.

LACE

Machine-made lace, either off the fabric bolt or the trim reel, tends to combine well with knits. Often lace fabrics are very lightweight and also have considerable stretch as well as a lot of surface texture.

I love the idea of using lace as an outer layer for a knitted piece: See how lace can be used to cover knitted fabric, as in the photo on page 114.

I have always thought that a lightweight machine-knit lace would make a marvelous lining for a simple sweater—a secret detail glimpsed only occasionally when worn.

VINTAGE FABRICS

Occasionally I will run across a marvelous piece of fabric or a garment from the past that I am tempted to include in a hand-knit design. Recently I purchased a tissue-thin Pucci-like silk tricot blouse from the 1960s that I would love to use as a lining. I have a wonderful handwoven vintage tablecloth, embossed with multicolor "floats" across the fabric; I like to imagine incorporating this into a colorful cotton summer sweater. Take a look in your closet or local thrift shop or vintage store for a wonderful source of fabrics to work into your knits.

ODDITIES

You can find sequined fabrics, tulle and netting for ballerina accents and fabrics that mimic animal fur. All of these specialty fabrics immediately conjure up design ideas!

Creating Linings

An obvious way to incorporate another fabric into a knitted piece is as a lining. Use your knitted pieces as a pattern and follow these general guidelines.

Step 1 Pin your body pieces along the grain on a piece of lightweight fabric: This means that the center of the pieces should be parallel to the selvage edge of the fabric, which is usually a denser weave than the rest of the piece.

Step 2 Mark ½ inch, or more, as seam allowance around each piece and at the same time, mark the lining to be 2 inches longer at the hem edges.

Step 3 Cut the lining pieces. Cut two sleeves at the same time through a double thickness of lining material.

Step 4 Join your lining pieces by hand or by machine. (If you sew by hand you will have a real couture garment!)

Step 5 Turn the hem and all edges, pin if necessary to keep from shifting, and press up ½ inch. Then turn up about 1¾ to 2 inches so that the lining will be just a hair shorter than the sweater.

Step 6 Insert the lining into your sweater, wrong side of sweater facing the wrong side of the lining, and pin in place. Check fit.

Step 7 Sew the lining along the edges. If your sweater has a knitted edging, then the lining can be sewn to the ridge formed by the picked-up stitches on the wrong side. I like to leave the hems free for movement, not sewn down, and tack along the side and sleeve seams to keep the lining from shifting

These basic steps can be followed to create linings for cardigans, jackets, hats, bags and other knitted projects.

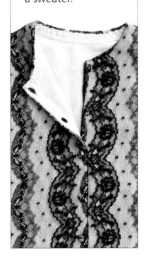

This unusual sweater from my vintage garment collection demonstrates the opposite of the concept of lining: The right side of the sweater has been covered with a lace fabric. Even the buttons have been covered. Although the base sweater was machine-knit, you could also do this with a handknit sweater, or parts of a sweater.

WORKSHOP

SUPER-SIMPLE LININGS
Swatch Purse

One of my favorite swatches made many years ago features a polar bear, a motif of my own design. It's fun to repurpose a favorite swatch—it could be used as a pocket or as a decorative patch on a larger piece. This diminutive swatch called out to me to be made into a little purse.

Using the same yarn as my swatch, I picked up stitches along the lower edge of the swatch and knit in the opposite direction to make the back side of the purse. I then added a garter stitch trim to the top of the front and back. I seamed the sides, including the upper edging.

I like to use T-shirt material for the linings of pieces that do not need to slide on and off (like a sweater sleeve). A lining made from this kind of fabric tends to cling to the outer knitted piece very nicely—good for a purse in which you do not want a lot of shifting between the layers. I cut the lining for this purse from the lower sleeve of an old but clean tissue-weight cotton T-shirt—new life for the shirt and the little swatch.

I searched through my stash for a perfect button and found one that is reminiscent of the brilliant sun in a frozen terrain. I made a loop out of L-cord (see page 97) to close the top.

Surely you must have a favorite swatch—and a less-than-perfect T-shirt—to make a cute little purse for yourself or as a gift. ∎

Polar Bear Motif Chart

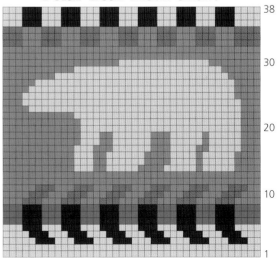

40 sts

①

Pick up stitches along the lower edge to knit a back section. Pick up along the top to knit the trim.

②

Sew the sides, including the trim. Make an L-cord loop and attach it to the back. Sew a button on the front.

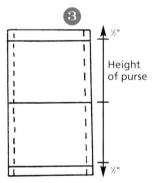

③

½"

Height of purse

½"

Cut a lining out of lightweight material to the measurements shown.

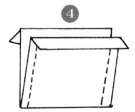

④

Sew the sides of the lining together. Insert the lining into the purse with wrong sides facing. Sew the top of the lining to the ridge formed by the trim on the inside.

I made this purse from an old favorite swatch I knit years ago from a fine-gauge qiviut (musk-ox) yarn. Why not give a new life to one—or two—of your own swatches?

Here the purse is turned inside out to show the bright red lining.
I like to use cotton tricot, the same material that T-shirts are made of, to line bags.
It is soft, and it clings softly to the knitted fabric.

BEFORE

AFTER

◄ These two swatches show the textural difference between felted fabric (left) and knitted garter stitch fabric before felting (above). The felted one has lost most surface definition.

Felting

Felting is a process in which a fabric knit with wool fibers—or other animal fibers—responds to heat, water and abrasion and shrinks into a dense, thick fabric that lacks stretch. It is really a finishing process of the greatest extreme in which the fabric undergoes the most dramatic transformation.

Felting has become very popular in the knitting community and is used for bags, hats, slippers, rugs and more. I became interested in felting in the 1980s when I discovered a shop in New York City that featured traditional Bavarian felted jackets and vests, decorated with coin buttons and feathers, with contrasting trim. At the time, I had never seen these classic garments, and they inspired me to design a whole line of Bavarian-inspired felted sweaters. My favorite yarn was a Shetland wool that is no longer available, but since then I have used other yarns and blends successfully to create felted designs.

Since no two yarns shrink to the same degree, the rules for felting are by necessity fairly general. As

unreliable as the process can be, I have learned that there are ways to make felted projects turn out close to perfect. Here are some guidelines to follow and pitfalls to watch out for when felting knitted fabrics.

Choosing a Felted Project

Ideal projects for novice felters are those that don't require an exact finished measurement. In other words—if it shrinks too much, the project will still be fine. Rugs and very simple bags fit this category. And these kinds of projects let you find a yarn that is reliable and fun to work with for future projects. If you are felting a knitted garment, it is best to avoid seams, as they might felt to a lesser or greater degree than the main fabric of the piece. Whenever possible, work pieces in the round, or back and forth on a circular needle for cardigans.

Yarns for Felting

One hundred percent animal fibers are best for felting. Avoid yarns that contain synthetic fibers. If you are not interested in experimenting, use a yarn that has been recommended for felting. Since yarns felt at different rates, it is not wise to mix yarns of mixed fibers in a single project unless you want a variety of shapes and textures.

Swatching

As with any knitted project, it is important to make a test swatch for the greatest success in predicting gauge. You need to put your swatch through the same felting process as you plan for your project, to have the "before" and "after" gauges. Larger pieces often tend to felt differently than smaller pieces. I have found that the larger the swatch, the more reliable the felted gauge will be.

I also work the same edging or trim on my swatch as I plan for the body of the projected piece. This allows me to control the edges, which, without trim, can often be wavy and uncontrolled. Even a small ridge of reverse stockinette stitch, my favorite edging for felted pieces, holds edges in place.

Pattern Stitches for Felting

As long as your yarn felts, any pattern stitch worked with it will felt. Those patterns with texture, however, might be wasted; felting will eliminate most texture and will often blur into a soft, fuzzy mass.

Fair Isle, stripes or intarsia are all good choices, as they will keep their color definition. Embroidery will felt into the fabric if you use the same yarn or another that felts, which may or may not be the effect you want. Check for colorfastness in any project that combines colors.

I prefer garter stitch (knit every row on straight needles; knit one row, purl one row on circulars) for the greatest reliabililty for garments; its thick, uncurling fabric felts well, and it is easy to trim—pick up one stitch for every ridge in the main fabric.

Garment Types for Felting

I suggest working with simple garment shapes to start. Although I have had success making more tailored garments, even those with knit-in collars and cuffs, it is best to get familiar with how a yarn felts first before designing or planning something very complex. For cardigans and jackets, I recommend planning a generous overlap at the fronts. This will allow some room for adjusting fit in case the garment felts a little too much or not enough. I did this with the felted vest on the next page.

Preparing and Finishing Details

When working a garment, plan to make your openings for pockets and buttonholes before felting. To avoid having the edges of a pocket buckle or felt at a different rate than the surrounding area, I like to first trim the side that will be visible, then I like to sew the pocket opening closed with some smooth non-felting yarn that I can remove after the felting is done. This way there is no pulling on the opening during the felting process, which might alter its shape.

After the garment is felted, if any of the edges have flared slightly, or have lost their shape, you can thread a piece of the original yarn within the thickness of the edge itself, drawing it in slightly, and locking it to hold in place. A really strong shot of steam, with a damp press cloth, will lock this sewing thread in place and hold your edge in nicely.

Pocket linings should be knit in afterward so the layers don't felt in an odd way during the process.

How to Felt

Follow these steps for successful felting:

Step 1 Knit a large swatch—preferably at least 8 by 8 inches. Work your chosen edging.

Step 2 Set your washing machine to "warm." If you set the temperature to "hot," your piece might felt too quickly and, I find, too harshly, resulting in a dense, immovable fabric. I prefer to work more slowly.

Step 3 Set the agitation to "normal." Add some gentle soap to slacken the fibers, and if you live in an

▲ There are lots of finishing details on this felted jacket I designed for the Fall/Winter 1985 issue of *Vogue Knitting.* The diagonal pocket flaps and shaped cuffs, as well as the shawl collar and color blocking add zip to the otherwise plain, boxy shape.

◀ This is the large swatch I used to test all the details of the felted jacket above. The entire swatch was felted to check the process and the gauge for the jacket it preceded.

area with hard water, add a ½ cup or so of baking soda to soften the water.

Step 4 Add a small towel—one that will not lose fibers that will cling to the felted piece—and run the swatch through the cycle, checking occasionally to see if the swatch has reached its desired consistency.

Step 5 Run through the cycle, stopping every five minutes or so to examine your swatch for signs of felting, and to decide if it is time to take it out. Try to keep track of the amount of time that passes. A piece will often felt when it goes through a rinse cycle of a different temperature. Be alert these junctures.

Step 6 When you remove your swatch, allow it to dry on a flat surface covered with a towel. Take your gauge from this felted swatch.

Follow the same steps for your project pieces, keeping in mind that they might not felt at the same rate as the smaller swatch. It is a good idea to check your pieces often when they are in the washing machine. When you check a piece, you may find it has stretched to a scary extreme before it shrinks and felts. Other times, with a different yarn, a piece may shrink and felt almost immediately. Be prepared! Felting is an unpredictable, but very rewarding, process.

▲ When felting, I use a smooth yarn that will not shrink to close the pocket openings before putting the piece in the washer. This eliminates any pulling that might distort the opening. Above you can see the remnants of a smooth ribbon yarn I used to close this slanted opening.

FELTING FUN
Asian-Inspired Vest

▲ The unfelted vest is worked in one piece, in garter stitch, with buttonholes and pocket opening. The extensions at the armholes and the trim are added before the felting process. I chose a wide overlap for the front of this design to accommodate any unexpected shrinking that might occur.

I take as much care—and enjoyment—in the invisible details of a project as in the visible. For the inside of the felted vest, I chose a beautiful, smooth black button to serve as an anchor for the big, black toggle on the right side. And my pocket lining, knit in the same contrasting color as the trim, is a little surprise of color.

A felted project is all about finishing, right from the beginning. For this vest, I wanted a soft, flexible fabric, and one that would felt to a reliable gauge. Close-to-perfect gauge is not so important with accessories or smaller projects, but for a garment it is essential. I also wanted to devise a garment that had some room for adjustment: An overlapping front would give me that built-in ease. I like a felted garment to have some detail, since the fabric lacks some of the surface texture of traditional knitted patterns, so I added an edging in a contrasting color.

Before felting, I sewed the shoulder seams loosely to mimic the feel of the fabric. I trimmed all the edges first, picking up one stitch for every ridge along each edge, and along the pocket opening. To avoid having my pocket edges pull out of shape during the felting, I sewed it loosely closed with a smooth piece of non-shrinking cotton that I knew would not felt, and which I could remove later.

On page 116 you can see what my swatch for this project looked like before and after felting. The photo at left shows the knitted vest before felting. During the felting process, I watched my pieces carefully, checking their progress every few minutes. When I took the vest out of the washer, I held my breath as I measured the pieces. Even though I felted many garments over the years, it is always a nerve-wracking process. To my relief, the vest was very close to the gauge I achieved by felting my swatch—a testament to doing the prep work up front.

When the sweater was complete, I used a little of the original yarn to stabilize the back neck, which had stretched a bit, and sewed on some wooden toggles I had been saving for just such a project like this.

I was pleased with the fit, but if it had been tight or loose, this style of front opening could have given me an inch or so of wiggle room, by simply moving the buttons. This is something to think about for your next felted garment.

A simple shape, like this boxy vest, is safer for felting than a more fitted garment, especially if you are new to the technique. As you gain more experience with felting, you can try more complex shaping and be assured of success. ■

Pattern
Asian-Inspired
Vest

SEE PAGE 153

Tutorial
Shaping Mittens, Fingers, Thumbs and Toes

Who doesn't love small projects? Socks, mittens and gloves are some of the most fun—and fastest—projects to knit. But just because they are quick to knit doesn't mean you should speed past the finishing process.

CHEAT SHEET

Be Size Wise

Mittens can be cute if they are a little bit big, but there is nothing worse than a floppy large glove that does not hug the hand. When you are knitting for yourself, it's easy to try on a mitten or glove and check the fit as you knit. When you are knitting mittens or gloves as a gift, it's useful to trace the recipient's hand to have a record of widths and finger lengths. You can even use it as a kind of schematic to keep notes.

There are many ways to shape the tips of accessories that are worked in the round, like mitten tops, socks, thumbs and fingers. Since this is often a challenging part of finishing, here are some hints to make it easier.

ROUNDED MITTENS AND TOES

For a more rounded top at the tips of mittens and the toe ends of socks, decrease gradually at the sides, both front and back, over an inch or so before the final length is reached, leaving a few live stitches on each side. Slip the remaining stitches for both the front half and the back half to double-pointed needles. For the smoothest finish, graft the front and back stitches together (see page 42). Although it is possible to join these stitches together, with the wrong side facing, with 3-needle bind off, this method creates a less flexible join and a ridge that might make socks less comfortable.

POINTED MITTENS

For a pointed top at the tips of mittens, work with an odd number of stitches for both front and back. When you are 2 to 3 inches away from your desired length, begin to decrease gradually at the sides, both front and back; decrease every round or every other round, depending on how sharp an angle you want for the top. Continue until there are no stitches left. Cut and weave the remaining strand into the wrong side of the fabric.

The same concept works for pointed tips of thumbs and fingers, with the decreases worked at the sides for a more flattened tip. When you are about ½ inch away from the desired length of your finger or thumb, decrease every round, or every other round, until two stitches remain. Again, cut and weave the remaining strand into the wrong side of the fabric.

ROUNDED FINGERTIPS AND THUMBS

For the best look, start to decrease rapidly about ¼ inch before each fingertip. Try on the mittens or gloves and make sure the base of the thumb or each finger fits the hand correctly. Divide your stitches evenly if you want symmetrical decreases. For example, 15 stitches divided evenly on three needles allows two decreases on each needle on one round, followed by a round without decreases, then one more decrease round. At this point, cut a long strand and carefully thread the strand through the remaining stitches, tightening them as much as you can. If the tip has a pointed look, weave the end to the wrong side and pull the tip inward. Steam, if possible.

Because less-resilient yarns do not full when steamed, you need to knit the fingertips and thumbs more firmly. It helps to change to smaller needles on the last couple of rounds.

With very fine yarns and more stitches to work with, decreases can become a design feature. You can even work the decreases all in one direction to give the tips of the fingers a spiral effect.

ROUNDED TOP
Live stitches to be grafted together

POINTED TOP
Mitten top and thumb shaped to a point

EVERYTHING OLD IS NEW AGAIN
Upcycled Bucket Bag

Enthusiasm for recycling and eco-friendly crafts has inspired a surge in interest in repurposing vintage garments. I feel so at home with this concept: In fact, I was "upcycling" decades before it became a new "green" word.

Since we were kids, my sister Regina and I have always been interested in old clothing, from all eras. When we were in high school and college, we could still easily find inexpensive items from the 1930s and '40s; today many of those now-rare clothes cost a fortune. We both collect vintage clothing and textiles of various sorts, and we love to study old clothes in vintage stores and online shops.

I started collecting old Swedish machine-knit sweaters when I was in my teens. Even before I was a serious knitter, the strong patterning and marvelously blended colors attracted me. I have them in Nordic blues, forest greens and browns, various combinations of bright shades, and the most luscious berry reds. I decided to take one I no longer wear and give it a new life—a special kind of finishing that merges past and present, and for me, combines memories and my skills.

I designed a bucket-style bag that merged my old Fair Isle–style machine-knit sweater with some new knitting of my own. I love the "bucket bag" form for knitted bags because the gathered top, often made of soft or pleated leather or vinyl, translates perfectly to knitted ribbing.

I pondered how to make the bottom of my bag firm so that it would stand up. Should I use a cardboard disk for the bottom, or a plastic plate? Then I thought of a gallon-size plastic water bottle, which would not only flatten the bottom of the bag, but also give some structure to the lower section. And it adds another element of recycling! My only question was how I would make it stay inside. I had an idea that just might work, so I knit a long L-cord (see page 97) and punched holes around the top edge of the plastic piece.

I made a paper pattern out of the bottom of the bottle, adding a ½-inch seam allowance to all sides, and then pinned this piece to an opened up sleeve. I sewed around the edge with my sewing machine set on a medium zigzag stitch, then cut the piece outside the machine sewing. A kind of steek technique (see page 123) to prevent unraveling.

Then out of the larger body of the sweater, I machine-stitched two tall rectangles the same width as the lower square, cut them out and seamed them (with right sides facing to create a tube. I hand-sewed the bottom to this tube.

I inserted the cut plastic jug into the bag and threaded the L-cord through the holes I had punched to connect the fabric to the base—it worked like a charm!

I edged the raw top of the tube with a single-strand ridge of reverse stockinette, just as I did at the end of the sleeve on the child's turtleneck on page 52, to cover the cut edge.

I knit a ribbed fabric, double strand, from the tubular part, picking up 4 inches down from the covered edge. The extra 4 inches of sweater material folded to the inside to give the upper part of the bag some body. At the halfway mark on my ribbing, I made a row of eyelets, then continued to my desired length. I made another L-cord, this time double strand, to thread through the eyelets.

I found a tissue-weight T-shirt in a deep purple and matched the size of my knitted pieces to make a lining (see page 114), which I inserted inside with the wrong sides of the bag and lining facing. I sewed it in place. I can't wait to make more bags in other colors, using other sweaters. If you have a loosely knit sweater, you could even felt it before cutting it. The possibilities are endless! ■

MATERIALS

- Clean plastic 1-gallon milk or water bottle
- Scissors
- Hole punch
- Adult-size sweater of firm texture to cut pieces for bag
- 2 or 3 balls of matching yarn in sport

gauge (I used several shades of Brown Sheep *Nature Spun*)
- Circular needle and straight needles in sizes to match your yarn
- Wooden buckle
- Cotton tricot fabric (for lining)

I have been collecting these vintage Scandinavian machine-knit wool sweaters since high school. I have them in many colors. They are very densely knit and perfect for transforming into other projects.

UPCYCLED BUCKET BAG STEP BY STEP

1. Cut the bottom from a plastic gallon bottle and punch holes at regular intervals around the edge.

2. Cut the sweater seams as shown and open flat.

3. After machine-stitching around them to reinforce, cut out one A (bottom) piece and two (B) side pieces.

4. Sew the sides of the two B pieces together to create a tube. Sew A to the bottom of the tube.

5. Insert the plastic liner inside the tube and weave an L-cord through the holes and fabric. Lock the ends of the cord inside.

6. Work an edging to cover the raw edges. Pick up 4 inches down from the covered edge and knit 2 to 3 inches of ribbing, followed by an eyelet row. The extra fabric above the pick-up row will fold to the inside.

7. Complete the ribbing to the desired height. Attach a buckle to the side. Knit a cable band with edge stitches. Thread the pointed end through the buckle and attach the cable at the sides. Thread another L-cord through the eyelets.

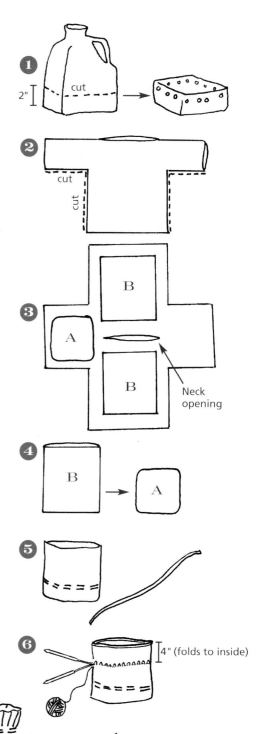

FEARLESS STEEKS
Fair Isle Cardigan

**Pattern
Fair Isle
Cardigan**
SEE PAGE 155

When knitting a garment in a Fair Isle (two-color stranded) pattern, some knitters prefer to knit in the round rather than back and forth to avoid purl rows. If you knit a cardigan circularly, you can cut the fabric to create the front opening and armholes. These cuts are called steeks. A steek can be a challenging, somewhat daring, technique, but as a seasoned finisher, I no longer cringe when I cut a steek. This design features several to give you plenty of practice. I incorporated steeks at the front edge, the armholes and the caps of the sleeves so that I could knit the pieces in the round.

When you work a steek, it is helpful to work it in a simple pattern that contrasts with the main fabric of the sweater to make it stand out. My steeks for this sweater were worked in a simple 1/1 checkerboard of color, with solid lines along the sides.

I chose the colors for the stranded colorwork to contrast boldly. For the two background colors, I picked a citrusy chartreuse and a pale slate. For the patterning itself, I chose berry shades. Against the light, bright background these colors really popped.

Since I like to sew sleeves into armholes for the structure of this seam, I did not work my sleeves to be part of the body of the sweater. I had two choices: I could either knit the sleeve cap circularly with a steek or work in the round to the armhole and then work the cap back and forth. The two options are shown on the next page. It is really a matter of taste which way you choose to knit your cap. For such a small piece of knitting, some knitters might find a steek in a cap not worth the effort.

To keep the fabric from unraveling, you should reinforce the steeks by sewing a straight line down the middle to cut along and two lines on either side. I almost always use a sewing machine for reinforcing steeks, but with the small size of the cap, I chose to sew the stitch-locking lines by hand. This could be done on any steek: Just use a sewing needle and sewing thread and, using very small hand stitches, back stitching frequently, you can achieve the same effect and not have to drag out the sewing machine. It is a couture touch.

After I reinforced and cut the steeks, it was time to work the trim at the edges. I tested the number of stitches to be picked up along the front edges of the sweater by first working the trim at the lower sleeve. I wanted to edge the front with a ruffle of some sort. At first I thought I would use a lace pattern (you could!), but after experimenting on the lower sleeve, I decided I preferred a flared edge worked in seed stitch. I thought this same trim might also accent the fronts in an interesting way. For the trim, I used all the "berry" colors for a dark accent to the brighter main pieces. After testing the trim on the lower sleeve, I picked up a similar proportion along the front edges and back neck.

Along a regular un-steeked edge, I would almost always pick up one stitch in from the edge. But when

▶For the pieces of the Fair Isle sweater (shown unblocked here), I added steeks at the front edge, the sleeve cap and at the armholes so I could work all the pieces in the round. I worked the steeks in a small 1/1 checkerboard pattern and outlined the steek on the front edges to make picking up stitches later easier.

picking up along a cut steek, it is necessary to pick up several stitches in from the cut edge, along the stitches added for the steek itself. These extra steek stitches fold nicely to the inside after the edging is picked up and worked.

After comparing the gauge of the lower sleeve trim, I noted that it would work out well if I picked up one stitch for every row along the front edges. Knitting the first row on the wrong side and at the same time working in seed stitch, I increased a few stitches along the angled V-neck edges only. Instead of working more increases to make the trim ruffle, I changed at roughly the halfway point to a larger needle, which did the trick.

I added little ties below the bust, made with L-cord (see page 97) and anchored by buttons, and a belt at the back in simple striped garter stitch, with a wooden buckle. To neaten the inner edges, I sewed the cut steeks loosely to the strands of the pattern beneath. With so much detail in the sweater, I decided I liked the raw lower edge unadorned. All it needed was a shot of steam. ▪

▶Here are two different ways of working a sleeve cap in a circularly knit sweater. The sleeve on the left has a steek for the cap above the initial armhole shaping. The one on the right is worked back and forth above the armhole. (Both sleeves are shown unblocked.)

I usually outline the edge of the steek with a solid unpatterned line to make it easier to pick up the stitches for an edging after it is cut. Here you can see the stitches for the cardigan's trim picked up along a solid line.

▲ If you do not have a sewing machine, you can reinforce any steek, on any part of a sweater with hand-sewing. Mark the steek in the same way, and sew in the same places. Take small stitches and backstitch often to lock the line of sewing. Here I did the sewing for the small sleeve cap steek by hand; the stitches are exaggerated slightly in size for this photo.

▲This is a close-up of what the machine-sewn reinforcing stitches look like on the wrong side of the fabric.

Here you can see my cut into the steek at the front edge of the cardigan. The cut goes right up the center of the steek. On the folded-back wrong side, you can easily see the machine-sewn reinforcing stitches.

CUSTOM COUTURE
Embellished Cardigan

Pattern
Embellished
Cardigan
SEE PAGE 158

When I want to design a sweater that really stands out from the ordinary, something luxe and one-of-a-kind, I often incorporate unusual elements. For this sweater I was inspired by some wonderful Swarovski crystals that reminded me of champagne. They defined my color choices.

I had also recently seen a woven jacket that had a rough-edged fabric trim, cut on the bias. I wanted to explore the idea of a bias fabric trim, but one that was more delicate. I bought some sample silk fabrics and silk ribbons online to experiment with. I fell in love with a silk organdy, a fabric both crisp and delicate, which I thought would be lovely at the edges of a sweater. I discovered that this organdy had very little tendency to fray when cut on the bias, so it occurred to me that I might be able embroider with narrow strips. My design mind met my finishing mind and I was at work!

When designing—and preparing for finishing— I like my swatch to dictate what I will do in the sweater. The swatch is my testing ground; it tells me what I need to know. You can see from my original swatch on page 128 that I played with a few ideas: I settled on a yarn and knitted pattern, I added a layered bias-cut trim at the edges, I sewed on crystals, and I also embroidered some loopy flowers with narrow bias-cut strips.

In the end, as much as I liked my swatch, I abandoned the notion of the embroidery because I thought a mass of it might disfigure my fabric, and I intended to have a mass of flowers! Instead, I decided to make the flowers separately and sew them on.

You can see in the photos that the pieces for the sweater looked very unshapely, with edges that were not well defined, all because of the nature of the slightly textured slip-stitch pattern I chose. To block, I steamed all the pieces very lightly, with the right side of the fabric facing; I did not allow the iron to touch the pieces, nor did I stretch the pieces at all (they were knitted perfectly to gauge) as I flattened them slightly with my palms.

I sewed the pieces together with the aid of the seam stitches I had incorporated into the pattern. I knit a simple edging that would not compete

Assembling your materials can be a real inspiration before diving into the finishing steps of a challenging project. Here I have everything I'll need.

KNITTING NEEDLES

TAPESTRY NEEDLES

SCISSORS

PINS

SWAROVSKI CRYSTALS

T-PINS

COTTON THREAD

YARN

SEWING NEEDLE

RULER

SILK ORGANDY

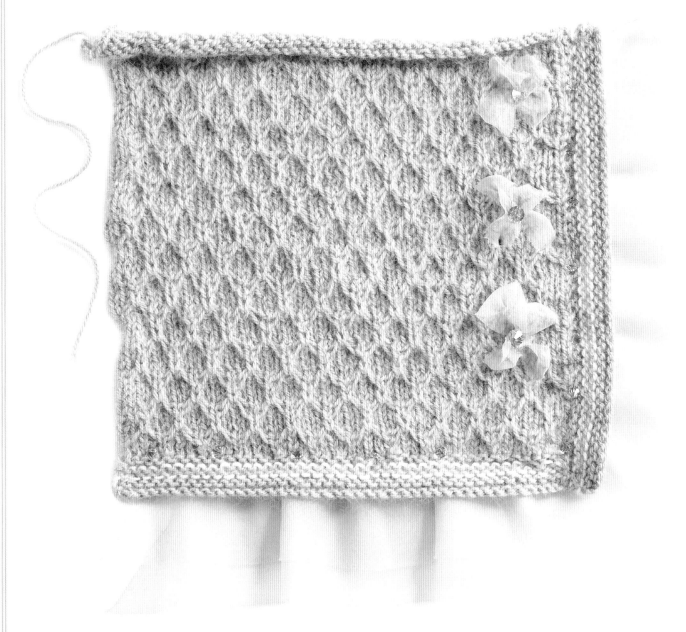

▲ I'm glad I took the time to test my ideas on my swatch. I learned that many of my original plans had to be tweaked. In this swatch, I embroidered the flowers with the bias strips; this less-than-successful attempt led me to decide to make the flowers separately and sew them on.

with the bias trim. All of the wiggly edges disappeared into the seaming, and the sweater had a crisp and neat look that belied the look of the original pieces. I knit an edging on the pocket opening, then made a little silk pocket lining, which I sewed to the inner knit-in facing, and to the ridge along the wrong side of the trim (see page 104).

The most demanding finishing of this sweater was the cutting and sewing of the fabric edgings (see page 130). I cut the fabric, after laying it out carefully on a wide, flat surface and marking the lines lightly with pencil. I love to sew by hand, so sewing the bias

bands together and locking the layers in place, in one long strip, was fun for me. I pinned the bands loosely along the lower sleeve and sewed the piece in place. Then after the experience of this smaller area, I pinned the bands in one long strip around the entire edge of the cardigan, extending it to the desired length beyond the knitted trim. I allowed some ease as I pinned, so the bands would flutter and ruffle slightly, and not be stretched or strained in appearance. When pinning around corners I allowed the bands to gather slightly so they would not pull. I used a lot of pins! I tried the sweater on my dress form, and finding that

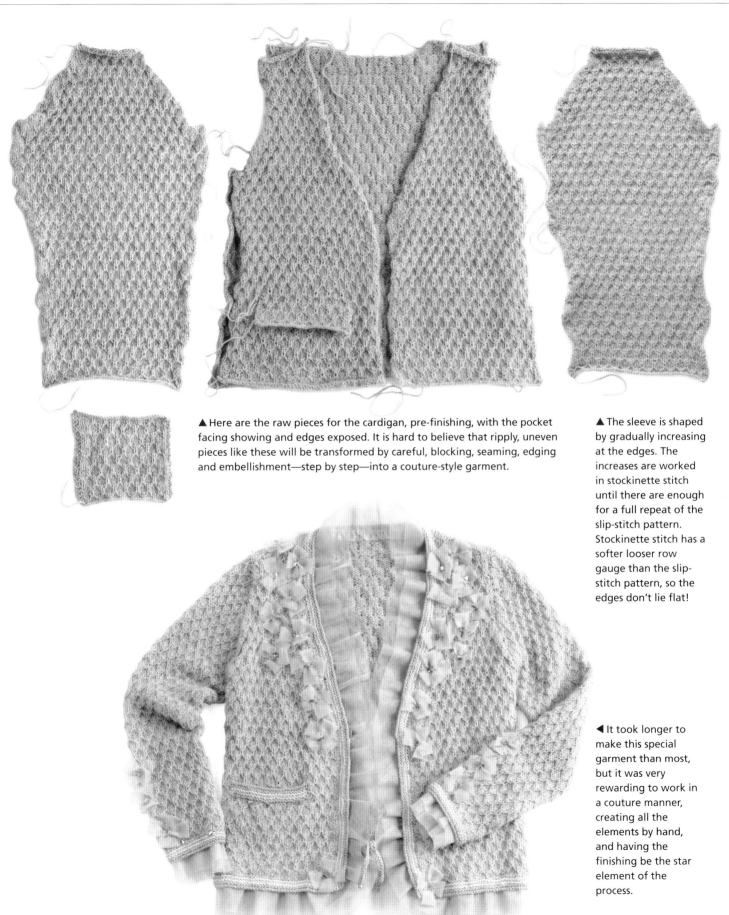

▲ Here are the raw pieces for the cardigan, pre-finishing, with the pocket facing showing and edges exposed. It is hard to believe that ripply, uneven pieces like these will be transformed by careful, blocking, seaming, edging and embellishment—step by step—into a couture-style garment.

▲ The sleeve is shaped by gradually increasing at the edges. The increases are worked in stockinette stitch until there are enough for a full repeat of the slip-stitch pattern. Stockinette stitch has a softer looser row gauge than the slip-stitch pattern, so the edges don't lie flat!

◄ It took longer to make this special garment than most, but it was very rewarding to work in a couture manner, creating all the elements by hand, and having the finishing be the star element of the process.

Tutorial
Making Fabric Edgings

To make the ruffled edgings out of the silk organza fabric, I cut the strips on the bias, layered them and gathered them slightly before pinning and sewing them to the final garment. Make one ruffle long enough to edge the fronts and bottom edges of your cardigan and two shorter ruffles for the cuffs.

CUTTING AND JOINING BIAS STRIPS

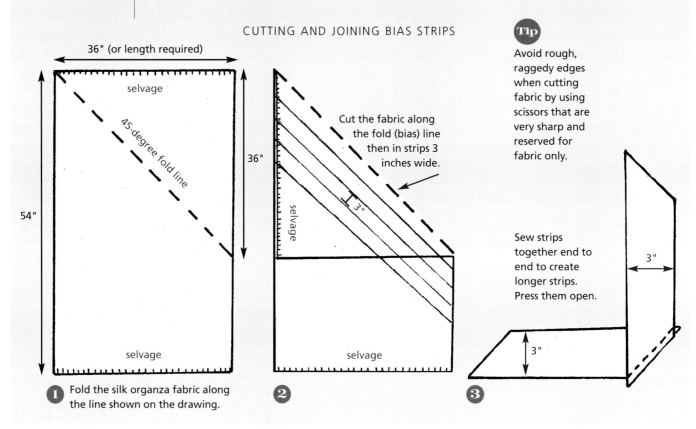

36" (or length required)

selvage

45-degree fold line

54"

36"

selvage

selvage

selvage

1 Fold the silk organza fabric along the line shown on the drawing.

Cut the fabric along the fold (bias) line then in strips 3 inches wide.

3"

2

Tip

Avoid rough, raggedy edges when cutting fabric by using scissors that are very sharp and reserved for fabric only.

Sew strips together end to end to create longer strips. Press them open.

3"

3"

3

MAKING A DOUBLE-LAYER RUFFLE

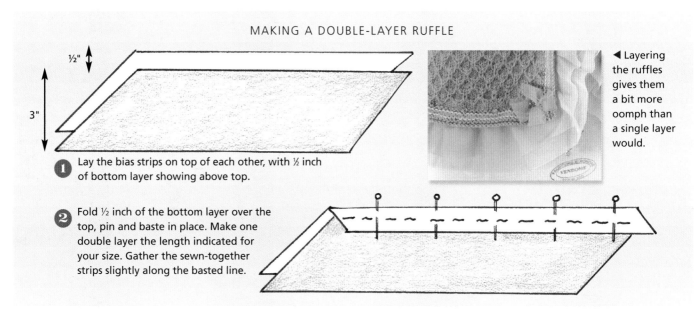

½"

3"

1 Lay the bias strips on top of each other, with ½ inch of bottom layer showing above top.

2 Fold ½ inch of the bottom layer over the top, pin and baste in place. Make one double layer the length indicated for your size. Gather the sewn-together strips slightly along the basted line.

◀ Layering the ruffles gives them a bit more oomph than a single layer would.

the trim was fine, I sewed it on by hand to the wrong side, attaching it to the ridge formed by the picked-up stitches of the knitted trim.

Using sewing thread and needle, my sister Regina and I spent a happy Saturday morning making the little flowers. Later that day, I sewed all the flowers to the jacket with a sewing needle and thread, and also sewed a line of beads around the sleeve cap, attaching them along the seam. I also added a line of beads in the little dent formed where the knitted trim met the body pieces, and along the pocket trim, too.

As a final couture touch, I made two short lengths of L-cord, added a sparkly crystal to one end of each and attached these little ties to the inside of the sweater to hold the front edges closed.

This special sweater was not difficult at all to make, just time-consuming—but a delight—to finish. By working methodically, in stages, the sweater came together with ease. Since I spend so much time knitting, it was a rare treat to incorporate some other fabrics and unusual techniques into a project.

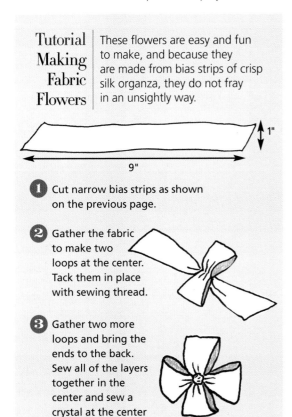

Tutorial Making Fabric Flowers These flowers are easy and fun to make, and because they are made from bias strips of crisp silk organza, they do not fray in an unsightly way.

1" 9"

1 Cut narrow bias strips as shown on the previous page.

2 Gather the fabric to make two loops at the center. Tack them in place with sewing thread.

3 Gather two more loops and bring the ends to the back. Sew all of the layers together in the center and sew a crystal at the center of each flower.

Final Note on Finishing

I might love finishing more than any knitter around. I see myself, as I often mention in my workshops, in the long tradition of people who make clothing by hand. I want to be fully involved in every aspect of every garment I make.

You can imagine my delight when I was hired as a stylist in the 1990s for a book about couture clothing. I was able to get up close and see the work of some of my favorite twentieth-century designers in the collections at the Metropolitan Museum of Art in New York: Schiaparelli, Dior, Balenciaga and Vionnet, to name a few. Talk about finishing! Those magnificent garments were all about finishing. I feel that by taking care when putting together a knitted garment, we transcend even our own beloved craft, joining the long tradition of wonderful garment makers.

If there is one piece of advice I hope you will take away from this book, it is that it is essential to really look at what you are doing in the finishing process. Study your pieces before and during finishing, keep the right side of the fabric to the front while you are working and examine your finished garment carefully to see if you have done everything you can to make it the best garment possible.

Remember also that rules are made to be broken. You can decide to change things at any stage of the game, just as I decided, at the last minute, to use the "wrong" side of the knitted fabric as the right side in the plaid accents cardigan (page 105). Years of experience finishing knitted garments have taught me what works best for me, but don't be afraid to tweak my techniques and experiment to find what works best for *you*.

Through careful attention to detail and an eye toward perfect construction, you can make your sweaters look fabulous. You can learn new techniques and valuable skills. You can repair and rejuvenate. And you can take the old and make it new again.

Finishing School is never out of session. ■

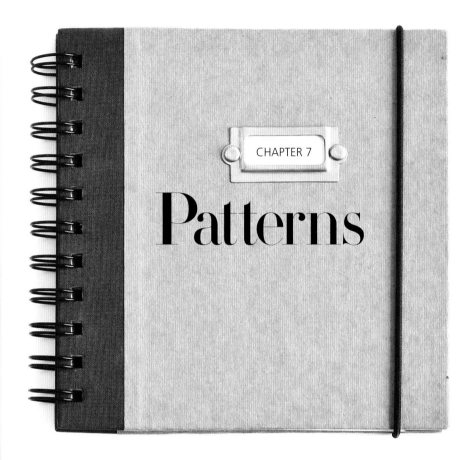

CHAPTER 7

Patterns

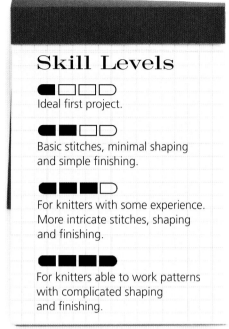

Skill Levels

■□□□
Ideal first project.

■■□□
Basic stitches, minimal shaping and simple finishing.

■■■□
For knitters with some experience. More intricate stitches, shaping and finishing.

■■■■
For knitters able to work patterns with complicated shaping and finishing.

Take time to save time. Always check your gauge!

Abbreviations

approx	approximately
beg	begin(ning)
CC	contrasting color
ch	chain
cm	centimeter(s)
cn	cable needle
cont	continu(e)(ing)
dec	decreas(e)(ing)
dpn(s)	double-pointed needle(s)
foll	follow(s)(ing)
g	gram(s)
inc	increas(e)(ing)
k	knit
k2tog	knit 2 stitches together
kwise	knitwise
LH	left-hand
lp(s)	loop(s)
m	meter(s)
M1	make 1 (knit stitch)
M1 p-st	make 1 purl stitch
MC	main color
mm	millimeter(s)
oz	ounce(s)
p	purl
p2tog	purl 2 stitches together
pat(s)	pattern(s)
pm	place marker
p2sso	pass 2 slip stitches over
psso	pass slip stitch over
pwise	purlwise
rem	remain(s)(ing)
rep	repeat
rev St st	reverse stockinette stitch
RH	right-hand
rnd(s)	round(s)
RS	right side(s)
S2KP	slip 2 stitches together, knit 1, pass 2 slip stitches over knit 1
SKP	slip 1, knit 1, pass slip stitch over
SK2P	slip 1, knit 2 together, pass slip stitch over the knit 2 together
sl	slip
sl st	slip stitch
ssk	slip, slip, knit
sssk	slip, slip, slip, knit
st(s)	stitch(es)
St st	stockinette stitch
tbl	through back loop(s)
tog	together
WS	wrong side(s)
wyib	with yarn in back
wyif	with yarn in front
yd	yard(s)
yo	yarn over needle
*	repeat directions following * as many times as indicated
[ ]	repeat directions inside brackets as many times as indicated

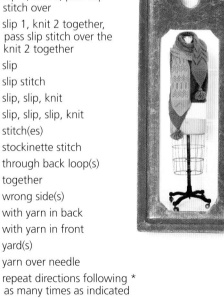

Lace Scarves

page 26   *page 28*

SIZE
Instructions are written for one size.

MEASUREMENTS
• CHUNKY SCARF Approx 11"/28cm wide x 70"/178cm long (before finishing)
• FINE-GAUGE SCARF Approx 9"/23cm wide x 50"/127cm long (before finishing)

MATERIALS
CHUNKY SCARF
• Blue Sky *Bulky* (alpaca/wool), 3½oz 100g, 45yd/41m: #1213 (Jasmine)—6 skeins
• One pair each size 13 (9mm) and 15 (10mm) knitting needles *or size needed to obtain gauge*

FINE-GAUGE SCARF
• Blue Sky *Royal* (alpaca), 3½oz/100g, 288yd/263m: #708 (Seaglass)—2 hanks
• One pair size 4 (3.5mm) knitting needles *or size needed to obtain gauge*

GAUGE
CHUNKY SCARF
9 sts and 11 rows over 4"/10cm in Lace pat using size 15 (10mm) needles and Blue Sky *Bulky*
FINE-GAUGE SCARF
23 sts and 30 rows over 4"/10cm in Lace pat using size 4 (3.5mm) needles and Blue Sky *Royal*
Take time to save time—check your gauge.

GARTER SITICH
(over any number of sts)
Knit every row.

STOCKINETTE STITCH (ST ST)
(over any number of sts)
Knit RS rows, purl WS rows.

REVERSE STOCKINETTE STITCH (REV ST ST)
(over any number of sts)
Purl RS rows, knit WS rows.

LACE PATTERN
(multiple of 10 sts plus 3)
Row 1 (RS) K1, *yo, ssk, k8; rep from *, end yo, ssk, k7, k2tog, yo, k1.
Rows 2, 4, 6, 8, 10, 12, 14, 16, 18, 20 and 22 Purl.
Row 3 K1, *k1, yo, ssk, k5, k2tog, yo; rep from *, end k2.
Row 5 K1, *k2, yo, ssk, k3, k2tog, yo, k1; rep from *, end k2.
Row 7 K1, *(yo, ssk, k1) 2 times, k2tog, yo, k2; rep from *, end (yo, ssk, k1) 2 times, k2tog, yo, k1, k2tog, yo, k1.
Row 9 K1, *k1, yo, ssk, k1, yo, SK2P, yo, k1, k2tog, yo; rep from *, end k2.
Row 11 Rep row 5.
Row 13 Rep row 7.
Row 15 Rep row 9.
Row 17 Rep row 5.
Row 19 K1, *k3, yo, ssk, k1, k2tog, yo, k2; rep from *, end k2.
Row 21 K1, *k4, yo, SK2P, yo, k3; rep from *, end k2.
Row 23 K1, *p1, ssk, k2, yo, k1, yo, k2, k2tog; rep from *, end p1, k1.
Rows 24, 26, 28, 30, 32 and 34 (WS) P1, k1, *p9, k1; rep from *, end p1.
Rows 25, 27, 29, 31, 33 and 35 (RS) Rep row 23.
Row 36 Same as row 24.
Rows 37–58 Rep rows 1–22.
Rows 59 and 61 Knit.
Rows 60 and 62 Purl.
Rep rows 1–62 for Lace pat.

CHUNKY SCARF
With Blue Sky *Bulky* and size 15 (10mm) needles, cast on 25 sts. Beg with a WS (purl) row and work 5 rows in St st.
Next row (RS) K1, work row 1 of Lace pat over 23 sts, end k1.
Keeping first and last st in St st, work in Lace pat until 3 reps are completed. Bind off.

FINISHING
Lay scarf flat and, working in manageable sections, steam with iron and a damp press cloth. Allow each section to dry slightly before removing from pressing surface.

TRIANGULAR END TRIMS
With RS facing and size 13 (9mm) needles, pick up 24 sts along short end of scarf.

Knit 3 rows.
Next (dec) row (RS) K1, ssk, k to last 3 sts, k2tog, k1. Knit WS row. Rep the last 2 rows until 4 sts rem.
Next row (RS) K1, k2tog, k1. Knit WS row.
Next row (RS) SK2P. Cut 8" and pull through last st. Rep for second end.

FINE-GAUGE SCARF
With Blue Sky *Royal* and size 4 (3.5mm) needles, cast on 53 sts.
Est pats (WS) K5, beg with a WS (purl) row and work center 43 sts in St st, end k5.
Keeping first and last 5 sts each side in Garter st, work 4 rows more.
Next row (RS) K5, work row 1 of Lace pat over center 43 sts, end k5.
Keeping first and last 5 sts in Garter st, work in Lace pat until 6 reps are complete. Bind off.

FINISHING
Note Pick up directly into each of the 5 Garter sts at each end, and in the center St st section, pick up into the front loop only of each bound-off st along edge. When picking up along the cast-on edge, do the same, picking up into the front loop only in center St st section.
With RS facing, pick up 53 sts along bound-off end of scarf. Knit 2 rows.
Row 1 (WS) K26, p1, k26.
Row 2 (RS) K24, k2tog, yo, k1, yo, ssk, k24.
Row 3 K24, p5, k24.
Row 4 K23, k2tog, yo, k3, yo, ssk, k23.
Row 5 K23, p7, k23.
Row 6 K22, (k2tog, yo) twice, k1, (yo, ssk) twice, k22.
Row 7 K22, p9, k22.
Row 8 K21, (k2tog, yo) twice, k3, (yo, ssk) twice, k21.
Row 9 K21, p4, k1, p1, k1, p4, k21.
Row 10 K20, (k2tog, yo) twice, k5, (yo, ssk) twice, k20.
Row 11 K20, p4, k2, p1, k2, p4, k20.
Row 12 K19, (k2tog, yo) twice, k3, yo, k1, yo, k3, (yo, ssk) twice, k19—55 sts.
Row 13 K19, p4, k3, p3, k3, p4, k19.

BEG TO SHAPE TRIANGULAR POINT
Row 14 K2, ssk, yo, ssk, k5, yo, ssk, k5, (k2tog, yo) twice, k5, yo, k1, yo, k5, (yo, ssk) twice, k5, k2tog, yo, k5, k2tog, yo, k2tog, k2.
Row 15 K2, p3, k5, p2, k5, p4, k4, p5, k4, p4, k5, p2, k5, p3, k2.
Row 16 K2, ssk, yo, ssk, k5, yo, ssk, k3, (k2tog, yo) twice, k7, yo, k1, yo, k7, (yo, ssk) twice, k3, k2tog, yo, k5, k2tog, yo, k2tog, k2.

133

Row 17 K2, p3, k5, p2, k3, p4, k5, p7, k5, p4, k3, p2, k5, p3, k2.

Row 18 K2, ssk, yo, ssk, k5, yo, ssk, k1, (k2tog, yo) twice, k9, yo, k1, yo, k9, (yo, ssk) twice, k1, k2tog, yo, k5, k2tog, yo, k2tog, k2.

Row 19 K2, p3, k5, p2, k1, p4, k6, p9, k6, p4, k1, p2, k5, p3, k2.

Row 20 K2, ssk, yo, ssk, k5, yo, SK2P, yo, k2tog, yo, k7, ssk, k5, k2tog, k7, yo, ssk, yo, k3tog, yo, k5, k2tog, yo, k2tog, k2.

Row 21 K2, p3, k5, p5, k7, p7, k7, p5, k5, p3, k2.

Row 22 K2, ssk, yo, ssk, k16, ssk, k3, k2tog, k16, k2tog, yo, k2tog, k2.

Row 23 K2, p3, k16, p5, k16, p3, k2.

Row 24 K2, ssk, yo, ssk, k15, ssk, k1, k2tog, k15, k2tog, yo, k2tog, k2.

Row 25 K2, p3, k15, p3, k15, p3, k2.

Row 26 K2, ssk, yo, ssk, k14, SK2P, k14, k2tog, yo, k2tog, k2—39 sts; end of central pattern.

COMPLETE POINT DECREASING
Next row (WS) K2, p3, k to last 5 sts, p3, k2.

Next row (RS) K2, ssk, yo, ssk, k to last 6 sts, k2tog, yo, k2tog, k2.
Rep the last 2 rows until 11 sts rem, end WS.
Next row (RS) K2, ssk, yo, SK2P, yo, k2tog, k2.
WS K2, p5, k2.
RS K2, ssk, k1, k2tog, k2.
WS K7.
RS K2, SK2P, k2.
Bind off rem 5 sts.
Rep for cast-on edge.

BLOCKING
Steam the main section of scarf in sections, allowing steam to permeate fabric, opening up the fabric gently with your fingers and flattening with your palm; do not allow iron to touch fabric. For the triangular tip sections, steam and open only lace areas with fingers; do not flatten or stretch Garter st section. Pinch embossed leaves to emphasize shape; do not flatten. ■

page 33   *page 31*

Tunics

SIZES
To fit sizes Small (Medium, Large, X-Large, XX-Large). Shown in size Medium.

MEASUREMENTS
• BUST AT UNDERARM 32 (36, 40, 44, 48)"/81 (91.5, 101.5, 111.5, 122)cm
• COTTON/BAMBOO TUNIC LENGTH 22"/56cm
• LINEN TUNIC LENGTH 27½"/70cm

MATERIALS
COTTON/BAMBOO TUNIC
• Classic Elite *Cotton Bam Boo* (cotton/bamboo), 1¾oz/50g, 130yd/118m: #3648 (Heron Blue)—6 (6, 7, 8, 8) balls
LINEN TUNIC
• Louet *Euroflax Sport Weight* (linen), 3½oz/100g, 270yd/246m: #05 (Goldilocks)—3 (4, 4, 4, 4) hanks
• One pair size 4 (3.5mm) knitting needles *or size needed to obtain gauge*
• Size 4 (3.5mm) circular knitting needle, 36"/91.5cm long, *or size needed to obtain gauge*
• Size 3 (3.25cm) circular knitting needle, 36"/91.5cm long (for linen tunic)
• Stitch holders (for cotton/bamboo tunic; optional)
• Stitch markers

GAUGE
COTTON/BAMBOO TUNIC
24 sts and 32 rows over 4"/10cm in Lace Rib and Textured Lace pats using size 4 (3.5mm) needles and Classic Elite *Cotton Bam Boo*
LINEN TUNIC
24 sts and 28 rows over 4"/10cm in Lace Rib and Textured Lace pats using size 4 (3.5mm) needles and Louet *Euroflax Sport Weight*
Take time to save time—check your gauge.

A triangular edging is a nice way to add detail to a rectangular scarf. Just pick up stitches along the end, work a wrong-side row, then decrease one stitch at each end of every right-side row. It can be as simple as a plain garter-stitch point on the heavy purple scarf, or more ornate like this one.

STOCKINETTE STITCH (ST ST)
(over any number of sts)
Knit RS rows, purl WS rows.

LACE RIB PATTERN
(multiple of 12 sts plus 1)
Row 1 (RS) *P1, k2tog, yo, k1, yo, ssk, p2, k3, p1; rep from * to last st, p1.
Rows 2 *K2, p3, k2, p5; rep from * to last st, k1.
Row 3 *P1, k1, yo, k3tog, yo, k1, p2, k3, p1; rep from * to last st, p1.
Row 4 Same as row 2.
Row 5 (RS) Same as row 1.
Row 6 Same as row 2.
Row 7 *P2, k3, p2, k2tog, yo, k1, yo, ssk; rep from * to last st, p1.
Row 8 K1, *p5, k2, p3, k2; rep from * to end.
Row 9 *P2, k3, p2, k1, yo, k3tog, yo, k1; rep from * to last st, p1.
Row 10 Same as row 8.
Row 11 (RS) Same as row 7.
Row 12 Same as row 8.
Rep rows 1–12 for Lace Rib pat.

TEXTURED LACE PATTERN
(multiple of 12 sts plus 1)
Rows 1 and 3 (RS) *K1, yo, ssk, p7, k2tog, yo; rep from *, end k1.
Rows 2 and 4 P1, *p2, k7, p3; rep from *.
Rows 5 and 7 *K2, yo, ssk, p5, k2tog, yo, k1; rep from *, end k1.
Rows 6 and 8 P1, *p3, k5, p4; rep from *.
Rows 9 and 11 *K3, yo, ssk, p3, k2tog, yo, k2; rep from *, end k1.
Rows 10 and 12 P1, *p4, k3, p5; rep from *.
Row 13 *K4, yo, ssk, p1, k2tog, yo, k3; rep from *, end k1.
Row 14 P1, *p5, k1, p6; rep from *.
Rows 15 and 17 *P4, k2tog, yo, k1, yo, ssk, p3; rep from *, end p1.
Rows 16 and 18 K1, *k3, p5, k4; rep from *.
Rows 19 and 21 *P3, k2tog, yo, k3, yo, ssk, p2; rep from *, end p1.
Rows 20 and 22 K1, *k2, p7, k3; rep from *.
Rows 23 and 25 *P2, k2tog, yo, k5, yo, ssk, p1; rep from *, end p1.
Rows 24 and 26 K1, *k1, p9, k2; rep from *.
Row 27 *P1, k2tog, yo, k7, yo, ssk; rep from *, end p1.
Row 28 K1, *p11, k1; rep from *.
Rep rows 1–28 for Textured Lace pat.

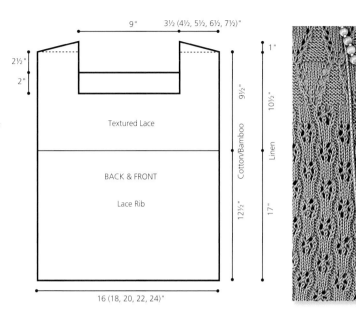

BACK
With size 4 (3.5mm) needles, cast on 101 (113, 125, 137, 149) sts.
Est pat (RS) K2 (St st seam sts), work row 1 of Lace Rib pat over center 97 (109, 121, 133, 145) sts, end k2 (St st seam sts).
Work even as est until 102 rows of pat are completed (12-row rep 8 times plus rows 1–6)—approx 12½"/31.5cm (cotton/bamboo tunic); approx 17"/43cm (linen tunic).

YOKE/CHANGE PAT (RS)
Row 1 K2 (St st seam sts), work row 1 of Textured Lace pat over center 97 (109, 121, 133, 145) sts, end k2 (St st seam sts).
Work even as est until 56 rows of pat are completed (28-row rep 2 times)—approx 7"/18cm (cotton/bamboo tunic); approx 8"/20.5cm (linen tunic).

NECKLINE SHAPING
Mark center 55 sts.
Next row (RS) K2 (St st seam sts), work in Textured Lace pat over 19 (25, 31, 37, 43) sts, k2 (now St st seam sts), join a second ball of yarn, bind off center 55 sts, k2 (now St st edge sts), work in Textured Lace pat over 19 (25, 31, 37, 43) sts to last 2 sts, end k2 (St st seam sts)—23 (29, 35, 41, 47) sts rem each side.
Working both sides at the same time with separate balls of yarn, work even in pats as est until 76 rows of pat are completed— approx 9½"/24cm (cotton/bamboo tunic); approx 10½"/26.5cm (linen tunic).

SHOULDER SHAPING (RS)— COTTON/BAMBOO TUNIC
Bind off 23 (29, 35, 41, 47) sts each side, or place on holders for 3-needle bind-off.

SHOULDER SHAPING (RS)—LINEN TUNIC
Bind off 8 (10, 12, 14, 16) sts from each shoulder edge twice, then 7 (9, 11, 13, 15) sts once.

FRONT
Work same as for back until 42 rows of textured lace yoke are completed—approx 5"/13cm (cotton/bamboo tunic); approx 6"/15cm (linen tunic).

NECKLINE SHAPING
Work same as for back.
Work even until front is same as back to shoulder.
SHOULDER SHAPING (RS)
Work same as for back.

FINISHING
Sew front to back at shoulder seams (linen tunic), OR work 3-needle bind-off (cotton/bamboo tunic).

ARMHOLE TRIM
Place markers on front and back 6½ (7, 7½, 8, 8½)" down from shoulders. With size 4 needles, pick up 84 (88, 92, 96, 100) sts between markers. Knit 3 rows. Bind off.
Sew side seams, joining armhole trim edges where they meet.

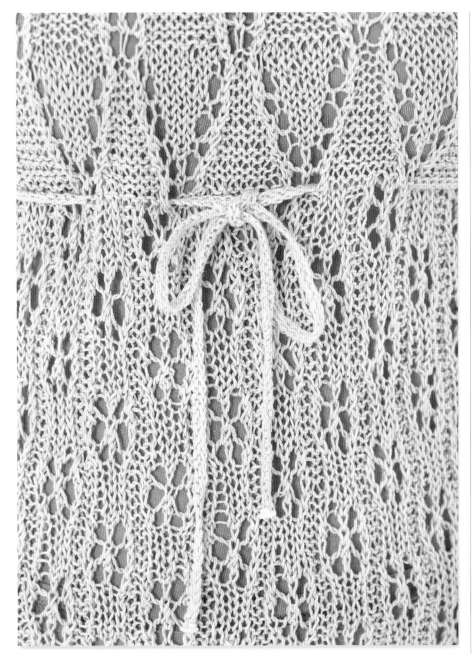

I felt the linen tunic would benefit from a little detail, so I made a very fine L-cord (see page 97) to thread through the line of eyelets where the two stitch patterns meet.

NECKLINE TRIM

Note Use size 4 (3.5mm) circular needle for cotton/bamboo tunic or size 3 (3.25mm) circular needle for linen tunic.

With circular needle and RS facing, starting at right shoulder seam, pick up 11 sts to back corner, pick up 1 st in corner and mark it, pick up 48 sts evenly along back neck edge to corner, pick up 1 st in corner and mark it, pick up 11 sts to shoulder and 24 sts more to front corner, pick up 1 st in

corner and mark it, pick up 48 sts evenly along front neck edge to corner, pick up 1 st in corner and mark it, pick up 24 sts to shoulder—170 sts.

Place marker for beg of rnd and join. (Purl 1 rnd, knit 2 rnds) twice, p1 rnd AND AT THE SAME TIME, work dec at each corner marked st every other rnd as follows: Work to 1 st before corner, sl 2 sts tog kwise, k1, p2sso. Bind off. ■

page 47   page 45

Cables & Eyelets Pullovers

FITTED-SLEEVE PULLOVER

SIZES
To fit Small (Medium, Large, X-Large, XX-Large). Shown in size Medium.

MEASUREMENTS
BUST AT UNDERARM 33 (36, 39, 42, 45½)"/84 (91.5, 99, 106.5, 115.5)cm
LENGTH 24½ (25, 25½, 26, 26½)"/62 (63.5, 64.5, 66, 67)cm
SLEEVE WIDTH AT UPPER ARM 12 (12, 13½, 15, 16½)"/30.5 (30.5, 34, 38, 42)cm

MATERIALS
• Classic Elite *Lush* (angora/wool), 1¾oz/50g, 124yd/113m: #4408 (Easter Egg)—10 (11, 13, 14, 15) skeins
• One pair size 8 (5mm) knitting needles or *size needed to obtain gauge*
• Size 7 (4.5mm) circular knitting needle, 24"/60cm long
• Cable needle (cn)
• Stitch markers

GAUGE
26 sts and 26 rows over 4"/10cm in Cable Rib, using size 8 (5mm) needles
20 sts and 25 rows over 4"/10cm in Eyelet Block pat, using size 8 (5mm) needles
Take time to save time—check your gauge.

EYELET BLOCK PATTERN
(multiple of 10 sts plus 8)
Row 1 (RS) P1, *yo, ssk, k4, p4; rep from *, end p1 instead of p4.
Row 2 and all WS rows K1, p6, *k4, p6; rep from *, end k1.
Row 3 P1, *k1, yo, ssk, k3, p4; rep from *, end p1 instead of p4.
Row 5 P1, *k2, yo, ssk, k2, p4; rep from *, end p1 instead of p4.
Row 7 P1, *k3, yo, ssk, k1, p4;

rep from *, end p1 instead of p4.
Row 9 P1, *k4, yo, ssk, p4; rep from *, end p1 instead of p4.
Row 10 Same as row 2.
Rep rows 1–10 for Eyelet Block pat.

CABLE RIB
(multiple of 10 sts plus 8)
Back Cross (BC) Sl next 2 sts to cn and hold in back, k2, then k2 from cn.
Row 1 (RS) P1, *p1, k4, p2, k2, p1; rep from *, end p1, k4, p2.
Row 2 and all WS rows Knit the k sts and purl the p sts as they present themselves.
Row 3 Same as row 1.
Row 5 P1, *p1, BC, p2, k2, p1; rep from *, end p1, BC, p2.
Row 7 Same as row 1.
Row 9 P1, *p2, k2, p2, k4; rep from *, end p2, k2, p3.
Row 11 Same as row 9.
Row 13 P1, *p2, k2, p2, BC; rep from *, end p2, k2, p3.
Row 15 Same as row 9.
Row 16 Knit the k sts and purl the p sts as they present themselves.
Rep rows 1–16 for Cable Rib pat.

STOCKINETTE STITCH (ST ST)
(over any number of sts)
Knit on RS, purl on WS.

BACK
With size 8 (5mm) needles, cast on 112 (122, 132, 142, 152) sts.
Est pat (RS) K2 (St st seam sts), work row 1 of Eyelet Block pat over center 108 (118, 128, 138, 148) sts, end k2 (St st seam sts). Work even in Eyelet Block pat until piece measures approx 12"/30.5cm, end with a WS row 10 of pat.
Change pat (RS) K2 (St st seam sts), work row 1 of Cable Rib over center 108 (118, 128, 138, 148) sts, end k2 (St st seam sts). Work even as est until piece measures 17½"/44.5cm, end with a WS row.

ARMHOLE SHAPING (RS)
Bind off 5 (6, 6, 8, 8) sts at beg of next 2 rows. Keeping seam sts, work even for 4 rows.
Next (dec) row (RS) K1, ssk, work in pats to last 3 sts, k2tog, k1.
WS rows P2, work to last 2 sts, end p2.
Rep dec row every RS row 6 (8, 11, 12, 15) more times—88 (92, 96, 100, 104) sts.
Work even until armhole measures 4 (4½, 5, 5½, 6)"/10 (11.5, 12.5, 14, 15)cm, end with a WS row.

BACK NECK SHAPING
Mark center 28 sts.
Next row (RS) Work to marked sts, join a second ball of yarn and bind off center 28 sts, work to end. Working both sides at the same time, bind off at each neck edge 2 sts 5 times—20 (22, 24, 26, 28) sts rem each side.
Work even until armhole measures 7 (7½, 8, 8½, 9)"/17.5 (19, 20.5, 21.5, 23)cm, end with a WS row.

SHOULDER SHAPING (RS)
Bind off from each shoulder 6 (8, 8, 8, 10) sts once, then 7 (7, 8, 9, 9) sts twice.

FRONT
Work same as for back until armhole measures 1½ (2, 2½, 3, 3½)"/4 (5, 6.5, 7.5, 9)cm, end with a WS row.

FRONT NECK SHAPING
Mark center 28 sts.
Next row (RS) Cont armhole shaping as for back and work to marked sts, join a second ball of yarn and bind off 28 sts, work to end. Working both sides at the same time, bind off at each neck edge 2 sts 5 times—20 (22, 24, 26, 28) sts rem each side. When piece measures same as back to shoulders, work shoulder shaping as for back.

SLEEVES
With size 8 (5mm) needles, cast on 82 (82, 92, 102, 112) sts.
Est pats (RS) K2 (St st seam sts), work row 1 of Eyelet Block pat over center 78 (78, 88, 98, 108) sts, k2 (St st seam sts). Work even until piece measures approx. 7"/17.5cm, end with a WS row 10 of pattern.
Change pat (RS) K2 (St st seam sts), work row 1 of Cable Rib over center 78 (78, 88, 98, 108) sts, end k2 (St st seam sts). Work even until piece measures 12½"/31.5cm, end with a WS row.

CAP SHAPING (RS)
Bind off 5 (6, 6, 8, 8) sts at beg of next 2 rows. Bind off 2 sts at beg of next 4 (2, 4, 4, 6) rows.
Next (dec) row (RS) K1, ssk, work to last 3 sts, k2tog, k1.
WS rows P2, work to last 2 sts, p2. Rep the last 2 rows 12 (16, 15, 17, 17) more times. Bind off 3 sts at the beg of the next 4 (2, 4, 4, 6) rows—26 (26, 28, 30, 30) sts. Bind off.

FINISHING
Sew front to back at shoulders. Sew in sleeves. Sew side and sleeve seams.

NECK FINISHING
With circular needle and RS facing, pick up 182 sts evenly around neckline. Est rib: *K1, p1; rep from * around. Work 1 rnd more. Bind off in rib. ■

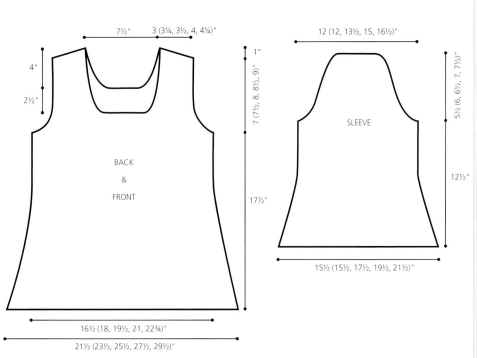

GATHERED-SLEEVE PULLOVER

SIZES
To fit Small (Medium, Large, X-Large, XX-Large). Shown in size Medium.

FINISHED MEASUREMENTS
BUST AT UNDERARM 33 (36, 39, 42, 45½)"/84 (91.5, 99, 106.5, 115.5)cm
LENGTH 20½ (21, 21½, 22, 22½)"/52 (53.5, 54.5, 56, 57)cm
SLEEVE WIDTH AT UPPER ARM 18 (18, 18, 20, 20)"/45.5 (45.5, 45.5, 51, 51)cm

MATERIALS
• Classic Elite *Lush* (angora/wool), 1¾oz/50g, 124yd/113m: #4420 (Aqua Foam)—8 (9, 10, 11, 12) skeins
• One pair size 8 (5mm) knitting needles *or size needed to obtain gauge*
• Size 7 (4.5mm) circular knitting needle, 16"/40cm length
• Cable needle (cn)
• Stitch markers

GAUGE
26 sts and 26 rows over 4"/10cm in Cable Rib, using size 8 (5mm) needles
20 sts and 25 rows over 4"/10cm in Eyelet Block pat, using size 8 (5mm) needles
Take time to save time—check your gauge.

EYELET BLOCK PATTERN
See instructions for Fitted-Sleeve Pullover (page 136).

CABLE RIB
See instructions for Fitted-Sleeve Pullover.

STOCKINETTE STITCH (ST ST)
See instructions for Fitted-Sleeve Pullover.

BACK
With size 8 (5mm) needles, cast on 112 (122, 132, 142, 152) sts.
Est pat (RS) K2 (St st seam sts), work row 1 of Eyelet Block pat over center 108 (118, 128, 138, 148) sts, end k2 (St st seam sts). Work even until 10 rows of Eyelet Block pat are complete.
Change pat (RS) K2 (St st seam sts), work row 1 of Cable Rib over center 108 (118, 128, 138, 148) sts, end k2 (St st seam sts). Work even until back measures 13½"/34cm, end with a WS row.

ARMHOLE SHAPING (RS)
Bind off 5 (6, 6, 8, 8) sts at beg of next 2 rows. Keeping seam sts, work even for 4 rows.
Next (dec) row (RS) K1, ssk, work in pats to last 3 sts, k2tog, k1.
WS rows P2, work to last 2 sts, end p2.
Rep dec row every RS row 6 (8, 11, 12, 15) more times—88 (92, 96, 100, 104) sts.
Work even until armhole measures 4 (4½, 5, 5½, 6)"/10 (11.5, 12.5, 14, 15)cm, end with a WS row.

BACK NECK SHAPING
Mark center 28 sts.
Next row (RS) Work to marked sts, join a second ball of yarn and bind off center 28 sts, work to end. Working both sides at once, bind off at each neck edge 2 sts 5 times—20 (22, 24, 26, 28) sts rem each side. Work even until armhole measures 7 (7½, 8, 8½, 9)"/17.5 (19, 20.5, 21.5, 23)cm, end with a WS row.

SHOULDER SHAPING (RS)
Bind off from each shoulder 6 (8, 8, 8, 10) sts once, then 7 (7, 8, 9, 9) sts twice.

FRONT
Work same as for back until armhole measures 1½ (2, 2½, 3, 3½)"/4 (5, 6.5, 7.5, 9) cm, end with a WS row.

FRONT NECK SHAPING
Mark center 28 sts.
Next row (RS) Cont armhole shaping as for back and work to marked sts, join a second ball of yarn and bind off center 28 sts, work to end.
Working both sides at the same time, bind off at each neck edge 2 sts 5 times—20 (22, 24, 26, 28) sts rem each side. When piece measures same as back to shoulders, work shoulder shaping as for back.

SLEEVES
With size 8 (5mm) needles, cast on 92 (92, 92, 102, 102) sts.
Est pats (RS) K2 (St st seam sts), work row 1 of Eyelet Block pat over center 88 (88, 88, 98, 98) sts, k2 (St st seam sts). Work even until piece measures 6½"/16.5 cm, end with a WS row.

CAP SHAPING (RS)
Bind off 5 (6, 6, 8, 8) sts at beg of next 2 rows. Keeping seam sts, work even for 4 more rows.
Next (dec) row (RS) K1, ssk, work to last 3 sts, k2tog, k1.
WS rows P2, work to last 2 sts, p2. Keeping seam sts, work 2 rows even.
Rep the last 4 rows 2 (4, 6, 5, 7) more times, then rep dec row every RS row 9 (6, 4, 8, 6) times, working WS rows as est—58 sts. Bind off 3 sts at the beg of the next 2 rows AND AT THE SAME TIME, p2tog twice in each p4 rib across RS row—40 sts. Bind off 3 sts at the beg of the next 2 rows AND AT THE SAME TIME, p2tog once in each p2 rib across RS row—30 sts. Bind off.

FINISHING
Sew front to back at shoulders. Sew in sleeves. Sew side and sleeve seams.

NECK FINISHING
With circular needle and RS facing, pick up 168 sts evenly around neckline.
Est pat Working in the rnd, work rows 1–10 of Eyelet Block pat. **Note** Work in the rnd by changing rnd 2 and every other rnd to knit the k sts and purl the p sts as they appear. Bind off in pat. ■

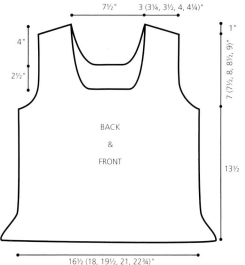

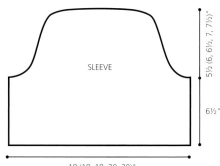

Cabled Patchwork Scarf ◼◼◼◻

page 49

MEASUREMENTS
Approx 9"/23cm wide x approx 54"/137cm long

MATERIALS
• Berroco *Peruvia* (wool), 3½oz/100g, 174yd/160m: #7122 (Avocado)—3 hanks
• One pair size 10 (6mm) knitting needles *or size to obtain gauge*
• Size 10 (6mm) circular needle, 24"/60cm long
• Cable needle (cn)
• Scrap yarn for markers
• Tapestry needle

GAUGE
20 sts and 16 rows over 4"/10cm in Cable Unit using size 10 (6mm) needles
Take time to save time—check your gauge.

CABLE PANEL (over 12 sts)
Row 1 (WS) K4, p4, k4.
Row 2 P4, k4, p4.
Row 3 K4, p1, sl 2 wyif, p1, k4.
Row 4 P2, sl next 3 sts to cn and hold in back, k1, (p1, k1, p1) from cn, sl next st to cn and hold in front, k1, p1, k1, k1 from cn, p2.
Rows 5, 7 and 9 K2, (p1, k1) 3 times, p2, k2.
Rows 6, 8 and 10 P2, (k1, p1) 3 times, k2, p2.
Row 11 K2, sl 1 wyif, (k1, p1) 3 times, sl 1 wyif, k2.
Row 12 P2, sl next st to cn and hold in front, p2, k1, k1 from cn, sl next 3 sts to cn and hold in back, k1, (k1, p2) from cn, p2.
Rows 13 and 15 Same as row 1.

Rows 14 and 16 Same as row 2.
Rep rows 1–16 for Cable Panel.

STOCKINETTE STITCH (ST ST)
(over any number of sts)
Knit RS rows, purl WS rows.

NOTE Each Cable Unit of the scarf is made of two Blocks. The first Block is worked, then the sts for the second Block are picked up along one side edge and worked as for the first Block.
   The scarf is made of 2 Cable Units, sewn together, with a single Block sewn at the end to make the scarf symmetrical.

CABLE UNIT
BLOCK #1
With size 10 (6mm) needles, cast on 46 sts.
Next row (WS) P3 (St st edge sts), [work Cable Panel over 12 sts, p2 sts and keep in St st] twice, work Cable Panel over 12 sts, end p3 (St st edge sts). Work even for 3 reps of Cable Panel, then work rows 1–13 of Cable Panel, bind off on RS row 14 of pat.

BLOCK #2
With RS of Block #1 facing and size 10 (6mm) needles, pick up 46 sts evenly along side edge. Work as for Block #1. One Cable Unit is complete. Work 1 more Cable Unit. Work 1 more single Block.

FINISHING
Steam each unit so that the fabric is damp, then with your fingers, open up the fabric to ease out the patterns. *Do not flatten.* With RS facing, using markers as in photo on page 51, sew units together so that the row side of one unit meets the bound-off edge of the other unit. Sew the row side of the last single block to the other bound-off end of the joined units.

SIDE TRIM
With RS facing, beg at the corner of one long side, *pick up 35 sts evenly along stitch side of the first block, then 42 sts along row side of next block; rep from *, end by picking up 35 sts evenly along stitch side of last block—189 sts. Knit every row for 1"/2.5cm. Bind off. Rep trim on the other long side.

END TRIM
With RS facing, beg at corner of trim on one short end, pick up 48 sts evenly along edge. Knit every row for 1"/2.5cm. Bind off. Rep trim on other short side. ◼

Preppy Vest ◼◼◻◻

page 53

SIZES
To fit Child's sizes 4 (6, 8, 10).
Shown in size 6.

FINISHED MEASUREMENTS
CHEST 25 (28, 31, 34)"/63.5 (71, 78.5, 86.5)cm
LENGTH 13 (13½, 16, 17½)"/33 (34, 40.5, 44.5)cm

MATERIALS
• Debbie Bliss *Cashmerino DK* (merino wool/microfiber/cashmere), 1¾oz/50g, 121yd/110m:
A #28 (Teal)—2 (2, 3, 3) balls
B #33 (Teal Green)—2 (2, 3, 3) balls
C #30 (Mustard)—1 (1, 2, 2) balls
• One pair size 6 (4mm) knitting needles *or size needed to obtain gauge*
• Two size 5 (3.75mm) circular knitting needles, each 16"/40.5cm long
• One wooden button, ½"/1.25cm
• Stitch holders

GAUGE
20 sts and 42 rows over 4"/10cm in Garter stitch using size 6 (4mm) needles
Take time to save time—check your gauge.

GARTER STITCH
(any number of sts)
Knit every row.

STRIPED PATTERN
(worked in Garter st)
*6 rows A, 2 rows C, 2 rows A, 6 rows B, 2

rows C, 2 rows B; rep from * for Striped pat.

BACK
With size 6 (4mm) needles and A,
cast on 64 (72, 78, 86) sts.
Working in Garter st and Striped pat,
work until piece measures 12 (13½, 15,
16½)"/30.5 (34, 38, 42)cm, end with a WS
row.

BACK NECK SHAPING
Mark center 22 (24, 26, 28) sts.
Next row (RS) Work to center marked sts,
join a second ball of yarn and bind off
center sts, work to end—21 (24, 26, 29) sts
rem each side.
Working both sides at the same time with
separate balls of yarn, work WS row.
Next (dec) row (RS) K to last 4 sts in first
section, k2tog, k2, for second section,
k2, ssk, k to end—20 (23, 25, 28) sts.
Rep dec row every RS row 4 more times—
16 (19, 21, 24) sts. Work WS row—neckline
depth measures 1"/2.5cm, piece measures
13 (14½, 16, 17½)"/33 (36.5, 40.5,
44.5)cm.
Sl shoulder sts to stitch holders.

FRONT
Work same as for back until piece measures
11 (12½, 14, 15½)"/28 (32, 35.5, 39)cm,
end with a WS row.

FRONT NECK SHAPING (RS)
Work same neck shaping as for back. Work
even until neckline depth measures 2"/5cm,
end with a WS row. Piece measures 13
(14½, 16, 17½)"/33 (36.5, 40.5, 44.5)cm. Sl
shoulder sts to yarn holders.

FINISHING
Slip sts for left shoulders to size 6 (4mm)
needles and with WS facing and color B,
join by 3-needle bind-off (see page 42).

NECKLINE TRIM
With RS facing, size 5 (3.75mm) needle and
A, pick up 42 (45, 47, 49) sts along back
neck, and 52 (56, 57, 58) sts along front
neck—94 (101, 104, 107) sts. K 3 rows.
Change to B and k 1 row. Bind off on WS.
Join right shoulder with 3-needle bind-off
method. Sew neckline trim where it meets.

LEFT ARMHOLE TRIM
Tie yarn markers 5½ (6, 7, 8)"/14 (15, 18,
20.5cm) down from shoulder on front and
back. With RS facing, size 5 (3.75mm)

needle and A, pick up 1 st for every Garter
ridge between markers. K 3 rows. Change
to B and k 1 row. Bind off on WS.

RIGHT ARMHOLE TRIM
With RS facing, size 5 (3.75mm) needle and
C, pick up 1 st for every Garter ridge
between markers. K 3 rows. Change to A
and k 1 row. Bind off on WS.

JOIN SIDES
Refer to photo on page 54. With RS of
front facing, size 5 (3.75mm) circular needle
and B, starting at lower edge of left side,
pick up 1 st for every Garter ridge along
edge and armhole trim. Cut yarn with a
4"/10cm length and set aside.
Rep on back side with second circular
needle, beg at armhole trim, pick up to
lower edge. Cut yarn with a 4"/10cm
length.
With WS tog, holding needles tog with RS
facing, using size 6 needles and B, bind off
the sides using the 3-needle bind-off to
join. Rep for right seam using color A.

FALSE POCKET FLAP
Measure 2"/5cm from armhole and down
4" from shoulder, mark row and st.
With RS facing slip smaller needle into
bump of st and with A, pick up a st in each
bump until you have 13 sts. Change to size
6 (4mm) needle. Work in Garter st for
1"/2.5cm, end WS. Dec 1 st each end of
every RS row until 3 sts rem.
Next RS row SK2P. Pull yarn through and
cut strand.
With RS of flap facing, size 6 (4mm) needle
and C, beg at pick-up row and pick up 9 sts
to point, then 2 sts in point, then 9 sts to
pick-up row. Knit WS row, purl RS row,
increasing 1 st at point.
Bind off in knit. Weave in ends.
Sew button on pocket flap. ∎

Crochet-Edge Pullover

page 55

SIZES
To fit Child's sizes 4 (6, 8, 10).
Shown in size 6.

MEASUREMENTS
CHEST 25 (28, 31, 34)"/63.5
(71, 78.5, 86.5)cm
LENGTH 13 (13½, 16, 17½)"/33
(34, 40.5, 44.5)cm
WRIST TO WRIST WIDTH
Approx 28½ (30, 32½, 35)"/72.5
(76, 82.5, 89)cm

MATERIALS
• Debbie Bliss *Cashmerino DK*
(merino wool/microfiber/cashmere),
50g/1¾oz, 121yd/110m:
A #23 (Apricot)—3 (3, 4, 5) balls
B #17 (Light Lilac)—3 (3, 4, 5) balls
C #14 (Burnt Orange)—2 (2, 3, 3) balls
• One pair each size 5 (3.75)
and 6 (4mm) knitting needles *or size
needed to obtain gauge.*
• Size H/8 (5mm) crochet hook
• Tapestry needle

GAUGE
20 sts and 42 rows over 4"/10cm in Garter
stitch using size 6 (4mm) needles
Take time to save time—check your gauge.

GARTER STITCH
(any number of sts)
Knit every row.

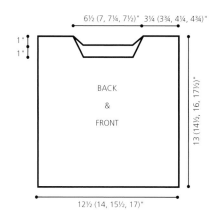

6½ (7, 7¼, 7½)"   3¼ (3¾, 4¼, 4¾)"

BACK
&
FRONT

1"
1"

13 (14½, 16, 17½)"

12½ (14, 15½, 17)"

STRIPED PATTERN

(worked in Garter st)

*6 rows A, 2 rows C, 2 rows A, 6 rows B, 2 rows C, 2 B; rep from * for Striped pat.

BACK

With size 6 (4mm) needles and A, cast on 64 (72, 78, 86) sts.

Working in Garter st and Striped pat, work until piece measures 8 (8½, 9, 9½)"/20.5 (21.5, 23, 24)cm, end with a WS row.

CAST ON FOR SLEEVES

Using cable cast-on method, cast on 40 (40, 43, 45) sts at the beg of the next 2 rows—144 (152, 164, 176) sts.

Work even until piece measures 12 (13½, 15, 16½)"/30.5 (34, 38, 42)cm, end with a WS row.

BACK NECK SHAPING

Mark center 22 (24, 26, 28) sts.

Next row (RS) Work to center marked sts, join a second ball of yarn and bind off center 22 (24, 26, 28) sts, work to end—61 (64, 69, 74) sts rem each side.

Working both sides at the same time with separate balls of yarn, work WS row.

Next (dec) row (RS) K to last 4 sts in first section, k2tog, k2, for second section, k2, ssk, k to end—60 (63, 68, 73) sts.

Rep dec row every RS row 4 more times—56 (59, 64, 69) sts. Work WS row. Bind off. Piece measures 13 (14½, 16, 17½)"/33 (36.5, 40.5, 44.5)cm.

FRONT

Work same as for back until piece measures 11 (12, 14, 15½)"/28 (30.5, 35.5, 39.5)cm, end with a WS row.

FRONT NECK SHAPING

Work same neck shaping as for back. Work even until neckline depth measures 2"/5cm, end with a WS row—56 (59, 64, 69) sts. Bind off. Piece measures 13 (14½, 16, 17½)"/33 (36.5, 40.5, 44.5)cm.

FINISHING

Note All crochet for seams is done with RS facing, so that crochet sts look the same on all edges.

With WS of front and back pieces tog and with RS of fronts facing, with crochet hook and C, single crochet (sc) front and back tog at shoulders. With C, sc along lower sleeves, sc front and back tog at side seams, then sc around neck edge.

POCKET

With size 6 (4mm) needles and A, cast on 23 sts. Work flower chart for 28 rows. Bind off. With C and crochet hook, sc along cast-on edge. With B and tapestry needle, chain a circle at center of flower, as indicated on chart. With RS of pocket facing, size 5 (3.75mm) needles and C, pick up 1 st for every bound-off st along top of pocket. Knit 2 rows. Change to B, knit 2 rows. Bind off. Pin pocket on front and sew in place. ■

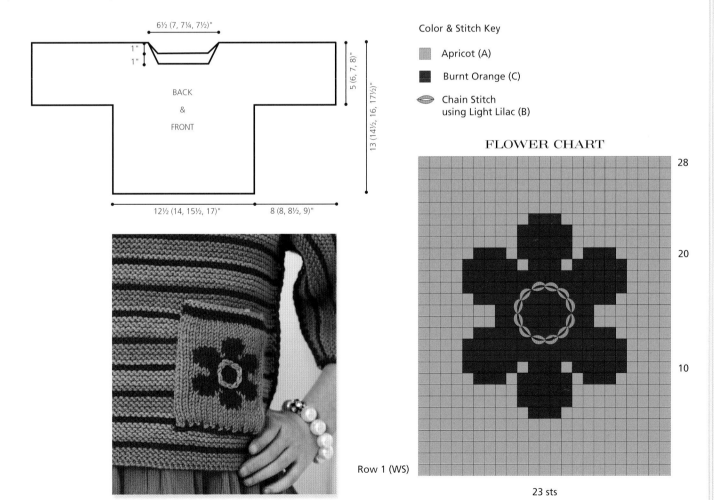

Color & Stitch Key

Apricot (A)

Burnt Orange (C)

Chain Stitch using Light Lilac (B)

FLOWER CHART

Row 1 (WS)

23 sts

Striped Turtleneck

page 52

SIZES
To fit Child's sizes 4 (6, 8, 10).
Shown in size 6.

FINISHED MEASUREMENTS
CHEST 25 (28, 31, 34)"/63.5
(71, 78.5, 86.5)cm
LENGTH 13 (13½, 16, 17½)"/33
(34, 40.5, 44.5)cm
WRIST TO WRIST WIDTH Approx 36½
(38½, 40½, 43)"/93 (98, 103, 109)cm

MATERIALS
• Debbie Bliss *Cashmerino DK* (merino
wool/microfiber/cashmere), 50g/1¾oz,
121yd/110m:
A #11 (Green)—5 (5, 7, 8) balls
B #33 (Teal Green)—2 (2, 2, 2) balls
C #30 (Mustard)—1 (1, 1, 1) ball
D #14 (Burnt Orange)—2 (3, 3, 3) balls
• One pair size 6 (4mm) knitting needles *or
size needed to obtain gauge*
• Size 6 (4mm) circular knitting needle,
16"/40.5cm long
• Tapestry needle

GAUGE
20 sts and 42 rows over 4"/10cm in Garter
stitch using size 6 (4mm) needles
Take time to save time—check your gauge.

GARTER STITCH
(over any number of sts)
Knit every row.

STRIPED BAND
(worked in Garter st)
*6 rows A, 2 rows B, 2 rows A,
6 rows C, 2 rows B, 2 rows C, 6 rows D,
2 rows B, 2 rows D; rep from * once, then
work 6 rows A, 2 rows B.

BACK
With size 6 (4mm) needles and A, cast on
64 (72, 78, 86) sts. Work Striped Band. Cut
all yarns except A and cont in Garter st until
piece measures 8 (8½, 9, 9½)"/20.5 (21.5,
23, 24)cm, end with a WS row.

CAST ON FOR SLEEVES
Using the cable cast-on method, cast on 60
(60, 63, 65) sts at the beg of the next 2
rows—184 (192, 204, 216) sts. Work even
until piece measures 12 (13½, 15,
16½)"/30.5 (34, 38, 42)cm,
end with a WS row.

BACK NECK SHAPING
Change to D. Mark center 22
(24, 26, 28) sts.
Next row (RS) Work to center marked sts,
join a second ball of yarn and bind off
center 22 (24, 26, 28) sts, work to end—81
(84, 89, 94) sts rem each side.
Working both sides at the same time with
separate balls of yarn, work WS row.
Next (dec) row (RS) K to last 4 sts in first
section, k2tog, k2, for second section, k2,
ssk, k to end. Rep dec row every RS row 4
more times—76 (79, 84, 89) sts each side.

Work WS row.
Neckline depth measures 1"/2.5cm, piece
measures 13 (14½, 16, 17½)"/33 (36.5,
40.5, 44.5)cm.
Do not cut D, with B knit 2 rows to form a
contrasting ridge, to indicate shoulder line.

FRONT
With D, cont to work both sides at the
same time, work in Garter st for 10 rows,
end with a WS row.

FRONT NECK SHAPING
Inc row (RS) Change to A, work to last 2
sts in first section, M1, k2, for second
section, k2, M1, k to end. Rep inc row
every RS row 4 more times—81 (84, 89, 94)
sts each side.

JOIN PIECES TO COMPLETE
FRONT NECK
Work to end of first section, cast on 22 (24,
26, 28) sts, then k to end—184 (192, 204,
216) sts. Work even until there are the
same number of rows on Front as for back
to blue ridge at shoulder, end with a WS
row.

END SLEEVES (RS)
Bind off 60 (60, 63, 65) sts, work center 64
(72, 78, 86) sts, bind off rem 60 (60, 63,
65) sts. Cut yarn. Turn and join yarn at beg
of WS row.
Work in Garter st until there are the same
number of rows on Front as for back above

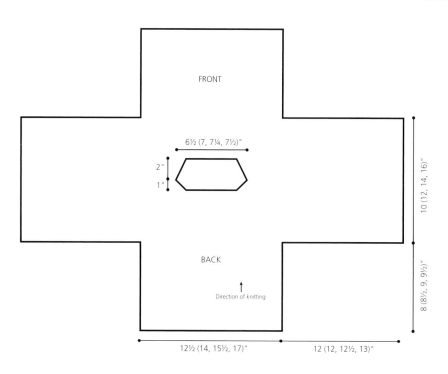

FRONT

6½ (7, 7¼, 7½)"

2"

1"

BACK

↑
Direction of knitting

10 (12, 14, 16)"

8 (8½, 9, 9½)"

12½ (14, 15½, 17)"   12 (12, 12½, 13)"

Striped Border, to the blue ridge at shoulder.
Work Striped Border in reverse, end with a WS row. Bind off.

FINISHING
SLEEVE TRIM
With RS facing, size 6 (4mm) needle and B, pick up 1 st for each Garter ridge along sleeve edge. (K1 row, p1 row) 3 times. Bind off in knit leaving a long end. Allow to roll to WS. Using long end and tapestry needle, sew trim down invisibly to WS of sleeve. Rep for second sleeve.
Fold sweater at shoulder line. Sew side seams and under-sleeve seams, joining sleeve trim where they meet; refer to photo on page 52 for seaming Garter st edges.

TURTLENECK COLLAR
With RS facing, circular needle and D, pick up 120 (126, 132, 132) sts evenly around neckline edge.
Est rib *K3, p3; rep from * around.
Rep this rnd until collar measures 5"/12.5cm. Change to C and work 1"/2.5cm more. Bind off. ■

Striped Cardigan Vest

page 73

SIZES
To fit Small (Medium, Large, X-Large, XX-Large). Shown in size Medium.

MEASUREMENTS
BUST AT UNDERARM 32 (36, 40, 44, 50)"/81 (91.5, 101.5, 112, 127)cm

LENGTH BEFORE FINISHING 24½ (25, 25½, 26, 26½)"/62 (63.5, 64.5, 66, 67.5)cm

MATERIALS
• Debbie Bliss *Donegal Luxury Tweed* (wool/angora), 1¾oz/50g, 97yd/88m:
A #04 (Scarlet)—4 (4, 4, 4, 5) balls
B #06 (Eggplant)—3 (3, 4, 4, 4) balls
C #17 (Raspberry)—3 (3, 4, 4, 4) balls
D #16 (Maroon)—3 (3, 4, 4, 4) balls
• One pair each size 6 (4mm) and 7 (4.5mm) knitting needles *or size needed to obtain gauge.*
• Size 6 (4mm) circular knitting needle, 36"/91.5cm long
• Four 1¼"/3cm buttons
• Cable needle (cn)
• Stitch markers

GAUGE
20 sts and 26 rows to 4"/10cm in Textured pat, using size 7 (4.5mm) needles.
Cable Panel over 12 sts measures approx 1½"/4cm wide
Take time to save time—check your gauge.

STOCKINETTE STITCH (ST ST)
(over any number of sts)
Knit RS rows, purl WS rows.

COLOR SEQUENCE
*12 rows A, 12 rows B, 12 rows C, 12 rows D; rep from * for Color Sequence.

TEXTURED PATTERN
(multiple of 3 sts)
Rows 1 and 3 (RS) Knit.
Rows 2 and 4 Purl.
Rows 5 and 7 K1, *p1, k2; rep from *, end p1, k1.
Rows 6 and 8 P1, *k1, p2; rep from *, end k1, p1.
Rows 9 and 11 *P2, k1; rep from *.
Rows 10 and 12 *P1, k2; rep from *.
Rep rows 1–12 for Textured pat.

CABLE PANEL (over 12 sts)
Rows 1 and 3 (RS) P2, k8, p2.
Row 2 and all WS rows K2, p8, k2.
Row 5 P2, sl 4 sts to cn and hold in back, k4, k4 from cn, p2.
Rows 7, 9 and 11 Same as row 1.
Row 12 K2, p8, k2.
Rep rows 1–12 for Cable Panel.

BACK
Note The lower back is made in two pieces, which are then joined together, with sts cast on between them, at given length. The back is completed in one piece.

RIGHT LOWER BACK
With size 7 (4.5mm) needles and A, cast on 54 (60, 66, 72, 78) sts.
Est pats (RS) K2 (St st side seam sts), place marker (pm), work row 1 of Cable Panel over 12 sts, pm, work row 1 of Textured pat over 18 (21, 24, 27, 30) sts, pm, work row 1 of Cable Panel over 12 sts, pm, work row 1 of Textured pat over 9 (12, 15, 18, 21) sts, pm, end k1 (St st mid back edge st).
Work even in pats as est and Color Sequence AND AT THE SAME TIME, when 12 rows are complete, end with a WS row.
Side shaping (dec) row (RS) Work 14 sts, sl marker, ssk, work to end. Rep dec row every 12th row for a total of 6 decs at side edge AND AT THE SAME TIME, when 60 rows are complete and piece measures approx 9"/23cm, end with a WS row.
Do not cut yarn. Set piece aside.

LEFT LOWER BACK
With size 7 (4.5mm) needles and A, cast on 54 (60, 66, 72, 78) sts.
Est pats (RS) K1 (St st mid back edge st), PM, work row 1 of Textured pat over 9 (12, 15, 18, 21) sts, pm, work row 1 of Cable Panel over 12 sts, pm, work row 1 of Textured pat over 18 (21, 24, 27, 30) sts, pm, work row 1 of Cable Panel over 12 sts, pm, end k2 (St st side seam sts).
Work even in pats as est and Color Sequence AND AT THE SAME TIME, when 12 rows are complete, end with a WS row.
Side shaping (dec) row (RS) K1 (edge), work 9 (12, 15, 18, 21) sts in Textured pat, work 12 sts of Cable Panel, work to last 2 sts of 2nd Textured pat section, k2tog, sl marker, work 14 sts to end.
Rep dec row every 12th row for a total of 6 decs at side edge AND AT THE SAME TIME, when 60 rows are complete and piece measures approx 9"/23cm, end with a WS row. Join back pieces.
Next row (RS) Cont side decs if necessary, work across all sts of right lower back as est, cast on 7 sts, with same yarn, work across left lower back as est to end.
Next row (WS) Cont in pats as est, working center 27 (33, 39, 45, 51) sts in Textured pat. Work in pats as est until piece measures 14"/35.5cm, end with a WS row—103 (115, 127, 139, 151) sts.

ARMHOLE SHAPING (RS)
Bind off 10 (12, 12, 12, 12) sts at the beg of the next 2 rows, then 2 sts at the beg of the

next 2 (2, 2, 4, 4) rows.
Next (dec) row (RS) K1, ssk, work in pats as est to last 3 sts, end k2tog, k1.
Next row (WS) P2, work in pats as est to last 2 sts, end p2.
Rep the last 2 rows 5 (6, 9, 10, 13) times—67 (73, 79, 85, 91) sts. Work even until armhole measures 8½ (9, 9½, 10, 10 ½)"/21.5 (23, 24, 25.5, 26.5)cm, end with a WS row.

BACK NECK SHAPING
Mark center 15 (17, 19, 21, 23) sts.
Next row (RS) Work as est to marked sts, join a second ball of yarn and bind off center 15 (17, 19, 21, 23) sts, work to end. Working both sides at the same time with separate balls of yarn, bind off from each neck edge 5 sts 2 times, end with a WS row—16 (18, 20, 22, 24) sts rem each side.

SHOULDER SHAPING (RS)
Bind off from each shoulder edge 5 (6, 7, 7, 8) sts 2 times, then 6 (6, 6, 8, 8) sts once.

LEFT FRONT
With size 7 (4.5mm) needle and A, cast on 54 (60, 66, 72, 78) sts.
Next row (RS) K2 (St st side seam sts), pm, work row 1 of Cable Panel over 12 sts, pm, work row 1 of Textured pat over 18 (21, 24, 27, 30) sts, pm, work row 1 of Cable Panel over 12 sts, pm, work row 1 of Textured pat over 9 (12, 15, 18, 21) sts, pm, end k1 (St st front edge st).

Work even in pats as est and Color Sequence AND AT THE SAME TIME, when 12 rows are complete, end with a WS row.
Side shaping (dec) row (RS) Work 14 sts, sl marker, ssk, work to end.
Rep dec row every 12th row for a total of 6 decs at side edge—48 (54, 60, 66, 72) sts. Work in pats until piece measures 14"/35.5cm, end with a WS row.

ARMHOLE SHAPING (RS)
Bind off 10 (12, 12, 12, 12) sts at the beg of the next RS row (tie a marker at the beg of this row), then bind off 2 sts at the beg of the next 1 (1, 1, 2, 2) RS row.
Next (dec) row (RS) K1, ssk, work in pats as est to end.
Next row (WS) Work in pats as est to last 2 sts, end p2. Rep the last 2 rows 5 (6, 9, 10, 13) more times—30 (33, 36, 39, 42) sts. Work even until front measures 5½ (6, 6½, 7, 7½)"/14 (15, 16.5, 18, 19)cm above armhole shaping, end with a RS row.

FRONT NECK SHAPING (WS)
Bind off 3 sts at the beg of the next WS row, 2 sts at the beg of the next 5 (6, 6, 7, 7) WS rows, then 1 (0, 1, 0, 1) sts at the beg of the next WS row—16 (18, 20, 22, 24) sts rem.
Work even until armhole measures same as Back to shoulder, end with a WS row.

SHOULDER SHAPING (RS)
Bind off at shoulder edge 5 (6, 7, 7, 8) sts twice, then 6 (6, 6, 8, 8) sts once.

RIGHT FRONT
Work same as for Left Front, reversing placement of patterns and all shaping.

FINISHING
Sew fronts to back at shoulders.

ARMHOLE TRIM
With RS facing, size 6 (4mm) needles and D, pick up 109 (113, 117, 121, 125) sts evenly along entire armhole edge. Work in Garter st in the following color sequence: 1 row D, 2 rows A, 2 rows B, 1 row C. Bind off in knit on WS. Rep for second armhole edge.
Sew side seams including trim.

NECKLINE TRIM
With RS facing, size 6 (4mm) needles and A, beg at right front edge and pick up 30 sts to shoulder seam, 35 (37, 39, 41, 43) sts along back neck, then 30 sts to left front edge—95 (97, 99, 101, 103) sts. Work in Garter st in the following color sequence: 1 row A, 2 rows B, 2 rows C, 1 row D. Bind off in knit on WS.

LEFT FRONT BUTTONBAND
With RS facing, size 6 (4mm) circular needle and D, beg at neckline edge and pick up 100 (102, 104, 106, 108) sts to lower edge, pm, pick up 2 sts in corner, pm, pick up 90 (94, 98, 104, 108) sts along lower edge to back placket corner, pm, pick up 2 sts in corner, pm, pick up 48 sts along back placket edge—242 (248, 254, 262, 268) sts.
Keeping the marked corner sts in St st, work in Garter st AND AT THE SAME TIME, inc 1 st before and after corner sts every RS row, keeping incs in Garter st.
Work in the following color sequence: 3 rows D, 4 rows C, 4 rows B, 3 rows A. Bind off in knit on WS.

RIGHT FRONT BUTTONHOLE BAND
Work as for left front band for 4 rows.
Next buttonhole row (WS) K5, *work 6 st buttonhole (see page 85 for one-row buttonhole), k21; rep from * 3 times, work to end. Complete as for left front band. With RS facing, sew side of one band edge to upper placket opening. Sew second band edge to underside of placket opening along ridge formed by seam. Sew buttons to left front band opposite buttonholes. ∎

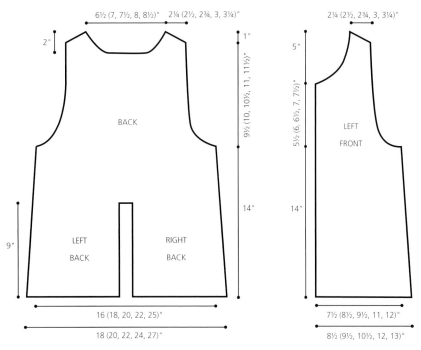

Cowl-Neck Pullover

page 75

SIZES
To fit sizes Small (Medium, Large, X-Large, XX-Large). Shown in size Medium.

MEASUREMENTS
BUST AT UNDERARM
40 (43, 46, 49, 52)"/101.5 (109, 117, 124.5, 132)cm
LENGTH FROM BACK NECK TO TOP OF CABLED YOKE 27 (27½, 28, 28½, 29)"/68.5 (70, 71, 72.5, 73.5)cm
SLEEVE WIDTH AT UPPER ARM
14 (14, 15½, 15½, 17)"/35.5 (35.5, 39.5, 39.5, 43)cm

MATERIALS
• Nashua Handknits *Ecologie Wool* (wool), 1¾oz/50g, 87yd/79m: #NFW.0086 (Logwood)—18 (19, 21, 23, 25) balls
• One pair size 10 (6mm) knitting needles *or size needed to obtain gauge*
• Cable needle (cn)
• Two size 10 (6mm) circular needles, 24"/60cm long
• One 2"/5cm button (optional)
• Small amount of lightweight yarn, in a similar color, for pocket lining, and needles to give a gauge of 6 sts over 1"/2.5cm
• Scrap yarn for markers

GAUGE
17 sts and 25 rows to 4"/10cm in Checked Rib using size 10 (6mm) needles Cable Panel over 25 sts is approx 5"/12.5cm wide

---

Take time to save time—check your gauge.

TWIN RIB
(multiple of 6 sts)
Row 1 (WS) *K3, p3; rep from *.
Row 2 *K1, p1; rep from *.
Rep rows 1–2 for Twin Rib.

CHECKED RIB
(multiple of 4 sts plus 2)
Rows 1 and 3 (WS) K2, *p2, k2; rep from *.
Rows 2 and 4 P2, *k2, p2; rep from *.
Rows 5 and 6 Knit.
Rows 7 and 9 P2, *k2, p2; rep from *.
Rows 8 and 10 K2, *p2, k2; rep from *
Rows 11 and 12 Knit.
Rep rows 1–12 for Checked Rib.

STOCKINETTE STITCH (ST ST)
(over any number of sts)
Knit RS rows, purl WS rows.

REVERSE STOCKINETTE STITCH (REV ST ST)
(over any number of sts)
Purl RS rows, knit WS rows.

CABLE PANEL
(over 25 sts)
Front Purl Cross (FPC) Sl 2 k sts to cn and hold in front, p1, k2 from cn.
Back Purl Cross (BPC) Sl 1 p st to cn and hold in back, k2, p1 from cn.
Front Knit Cross (FKC) Sl 2 k sts to cn and hold in front, k1, k2 from cn.
Front Double Knit Cross (FDKC) Sl 2 k sts to cn and hold in front, k2, k2 from cn.
Back Double Knit Cross (BDKC) Sl 2 k sts to cn and hold in back, k2, k2 from cn.
Row 1 (WS) P2, k6, p4, (k1, p1) 3 times, p4, k3.
Row 2 P2, BPC, FPC, (k1, p1) twice, BPC, FKC, p4, BPC.
Row 3 and all WS rows Knit all the knit sts and purl all the purl sts.
Row 4 P1, BPC, p2, FPC, k1, p1, BPC, k1, p1, FKC, p2, BPC, p1.
Row 6 BPC, p4, FPC, BPC, (k1, p1) twice, FKC, BPC, p2.
Row 8 K2, p6, BDKC, (k1, p1) 3 times, BDKC, p3.
Row 10 FPC, p4, BPC, FKC, (k1, p1) twice, BPC, FPC, p2.
Row 12 P1, FPC, p2, BPC, k1, p1, FKC, k1, p1, BPC, p2, FPC, p1.
Row 14 P2, FPC, BPC, (k1, p1) twice, FKC, BPC, p4, FPC.

Row 16 P3, FDKC, (k1, p1) 3 times, FDKC, p6, k2.
Rep rows 1–16 for Cable Panel.

CUFFS (MAKE TWO)
With size 10 (6mm) needles, cast on 27 sts.
Est pat (RS) P1 (Rev St st edge st), work Cable Panel over center 25 sts, p1 (Rev St st edge st). Work even until cuff measures 14 (14, 15½, 15½, 17)"/35.5 (35.5, 39.5, 39.5, 43)cm, unstretched, end with a WS row. Bind off.

YOKE CABLE
With size 10 (6mm) needles, cast on 27 sts.
Est pat (RS) P1 (Rev St st edge st), work Cable Panel over center 25 sts, p1 (Rev St st edge st). Work even until yoke measures 46 (48, 49, 51, 53)"/117 (122, 124.5, 129.5, 134.5)cm, unstretched, end with a WS row. Bind off.

BACK
With size 10 (6mm) needles, cast on 88 (94, 100, 108, 114) sts.
Est rib (WS) P2 (St st seam sts), work Row 1 of Twin Rib over 84 (90, 96, 104, 110) sts, end p2 (St st seam sts). Work in pat as est until rib measures 5"/12.5cm, end with a WS row.
Knit RS row.
Change pat (WS) P2 (St st seam sts), work Row 1 of Checked Rib over 84 (90, 96, 104, 110) sts, end p2 (St st seam sts).
Work even in pat for 4 more rows, ending with a WS row.

POCKET FACING (RS)
Using backward loops, cast on 5 sts at beg of row, k5, k first edge st, then sl 2nd edge st wyib, work to last 2 sts, sl1 wyib, k1, cast on 5 sts at end of row—98 (104, 110, 118, 124) sts.
Next row (WS) P7, work to last 7 sts, end p7.
Next row (RS) K6, sl1 wyib, work to last 7 sts, sl1 wyib, end k6.
Rep the last 2 rows until pocket depth is 6"/15cm, end with a WS row.
Bind off 5 sts at the beg of the next 2 rows—88 (94, 100, 108, 114) sts.
Resume 2 St st seam sts, work in pat until Back measures 19"/48cm, end with a WS row.

RAGLAN SHAPING (RS)
Bind off 4 sts at the beg of the next 2 rows, then 0 (0, 0, 2, 2) sts at beg of next 2 rows.

Next (dec) row (RS) K2, ssk, work to last 4 sts, k2tog, k2.
WS rows P3, work in pat as est to last 3 sts, end p3.
Rep the last 2 rows 5 (6, 8, 8, 9) more times—68 (72, 74, 78, 82) sts.

BACK NECK SHAPING
Mark center 24 (28, 30, 34, 38) sts.
Next row (RS) K2, ssk, work to marked sts, join a second ball of yarn and bind off center 24 (28, 30, 34, 38) sts, work to last 4 sts, k2tog, k2.
Working both sides with separate balls of yarn, bind off 6 sts at each neck edge 3 times AND AT THE SAME TIME, dec 1 st at each armhole edge as est 2 times more, end off rem st each side.

FRONT
Work same as for back to armhole, end with a WS row.

RAGLAN SHAPING (RS)
Bind off 4 sts at the beg of the next 2 rows, then 0 (0, 0, 2, 2) sts at beg of next 2 rows.
Next (dec) row (RS) K2, ssk, work to last 4 sts, k2tog, k2.
WS rows P3, work in pat as est to last 3 sts, end p3.
Rep the last 2 rows 3 (4, 6, 6, 7) more times—72 (76, 78, 82, 86) sts.

FRONT NECK SHAPING
Mark center 22 (26, 28, 32, 36) sts.
Next row (RS) K2, ssk, work to marked sts, join a second ball of yarn and bind off

center 22 (26, 28, 32, 36) sts, work to last 4 sts, k2tog, k2.
Working both sides with separate balls of yarn, bind off 7 sts at each neck edge 3 times AND AT THE SAME TIME, dec 1 st at each armhole edge as est 2 times more, end off rem st each side.

RIGHT SLEEVE
With RS of cuff facing, pick up 62 (62, 70, 70, 74) sts evenly spaced along long edge of cuff, one st in from edge.
Est pat (WS) P2 (St st seam sts), work row 1 of Checked Rib over 58 (58, 66, 66, 70) sts, end p2 (St st seam sts). Work even until sleeve measures 15½"/39.5cm, end with a WS row.

RAGLAN CAP SHAPING (RS)
Bind off 4 sts at the beg of the next 2 rows, then 0 (0, 0, 2, 2) sts at beg of next 2 rows.
Next (dec) row (RS) K2, ssk, work to last 4 sts, end k2tog, k2.
WS rows P3, work in pat as est to last 3 sts, end p3.
Rep the last 2 rows 6 (7, 9, 9, 10) more times—40 (38, 42, 38, 40) sts.

TOP OF CAP SHAPING (RS)
Bind off 13 (12, 14, 12, 13) sts, work to last 4 sts, end k2tog, k2.
WS row P3, work in pat as est to end.
Next (dec) row (RS) Bind off 13 (12, 14, 12, 13) sts, work to last 4 sts, end k2tog, k2.
WS row P3, work in pat as est to end.
Bind off rem 12 sts.

LEFT SLEEVE
Work same as for right sleeve, reversing all top of cap shaping by beginning one row later, on a WS row.

FINISHING
LOWER SLEEVE TRIM
With RS facing, pick up 64 (64, 70, 70, 76) sts evenly along lower sleeve.
Est rib (WS) P2 (St st seam sts), work row 1 of Twin Rib over 60 (60, 66, 66, 72) sts, end p2 (St st seam sts). Cont in pats as est until rib measures 2"/5cm. Bind off in pat. Rep for second sleeve.
Sew front and back to sleeves along raglan lines. Sew side seams above and below pocket facings. Sew cast-on and bound-off edges of pocket extensions tog where they meet, front to back.

ATTACH YOKE CABLE
Sew short ends of yoke cable together. Lay the folded yoke cable flat and align with the upper edge of flat sweater (with front of sweater facing) with yoke cable seam aligned with back right raglan seam. Tie yarn markers at intervals matching the yoke cable with the upper edge of sweater: Refer to photo on page 78. With RS facing, sew yoke cable firmly to body, matching markers.

COWL
Lay sweater flat with front facing. Tie yarn markers where the yoke cable folds at shoulder lines.
With RS of back facing and circular needle, pick up 102 (102, 108, 108, 114) sts evenly

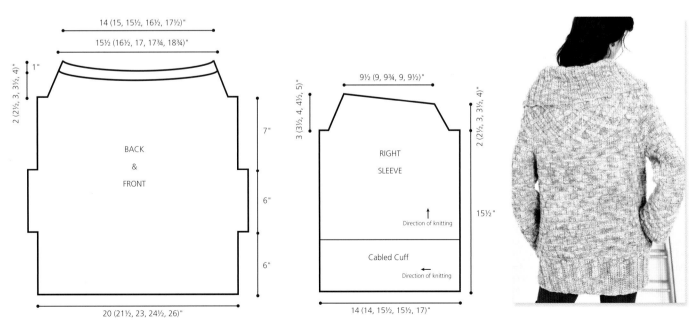

along back neck between markers. Mark center 30 (30, 36, 36, 42) sts. Turn and work WS row of Twin Rib across all sts.

WORK SHORT ROWS
Turn and work 36 sts as est in Twin Rib, then work across center 30 (30, 36, 36, 42) sts, then bring yarn forward, sl 1, bring yarn to back, sl st back to LH needle and turn. *Work to 6 sts after marked center sts, wrap st as before and turn; rep from * working 6 more sts each side of center marked sts every row AND AT THE SAME TIME, when you come to a wrapped st, work wrap tog with st that it surrounds, cont as est until all sts have been worked, ending with a WS row.
With RS facing and a second circular needle, beg at side marker, pick up 96 (96, 102, 102, 108) sts evenly along front neck to second marker, then cont in pat across back sts to marker, dropping first circular needle, work 24 sts in pat from beg of second circular needle. Turn and using cable cast on, cast on 10 sts. Turn.
Next row (WS of collar) K4 (keep these sts in Garter st: knit every row), work 24 sts in pat, sl marker, work 102 (102, 108, 108, 114) back sts in pat, sl marker, work 72 (72, 78, 78, 84) sts in pat as est. Turn.
Next row (RS of collar) Using backward loops, cast on 4 sts. K4 (keep these sts in Garter st), then working back and forth on all 212 (212, 224, 224, 236) sts, cont in pats as est until collar measures approx 10"/25cm. Bind off in pat.
Allow edges of cowl to overlap at base and sew cast-on sections in place at base of cowl above yoke cable. Sew button in place through all layers where desired, or use a piece of jewelry to close.

POCKET LININGS
Turn sweater inside out. With knit side of front pocket extension facing, using smaller needles and lighter-weight yarn, pick up 38 sts evenly along the long edge of pocket extension. Beg with a purl row and work in St st until piece measures approx 5"/13cm, end with a purl row. Purl next row to form a fold line, then purl next row and resume St st for 5"/13cm more. Bind off. Sew bound-off edge to other side of front pocket extension, allowing pocket lining to fold in half along purl row. Sew side seams of pocket lining. Rep for second pocket.
Optional If desired, tack upper edges of pocket linings loosely to WS of front. ■

Fitted Colorblock Jacket

page 92

SIZES
To fit Small (Medium, Large, X-Large, XX-Large). Shown in size Medium.

MEASUREMENTS
BUST AT UNDERARM 32 (36, 40, 44, 48)"/81 (91.5, 101.5, 112, 122)cm
LENGTH 21½ (22, 22½, 23, 23½)"/54.5 (56, 57, 58.5, 59.5)cm
SLEEVE WIDTH AT UPPER ARM 11 (12, 13, 14, 15)"/28 (30.5, 33, 35.5, 38)cm

MATERIALS
• Stacy Charles/Filatura Di Crosa *Zara* (merino superwash wool), 1¾oz/50g, 137yd/125m:
A #1481 (Denim)—4 (4, 4, 5, 5) balls
• Stacy Charles/Filatura Di Crosa *Zara Chiné* (merino superwash wool), 1¾oz/50g, 137yd/125m
B #1901 (Ebony Chiné)—5 (5, 6, 6, 7) balls
C #27 (Silver Chiné)—4 (5, 5, 6, 6) balls
• One pair each size 5 (3.75mm) and 6 (4mm) knitting needles *or size needed to obtain gauge*
• Stitch markers
• One separating zipper, 21½ (22, 22½, 23, 23½)" long
• Two closed-end zippers, 7"/18cm long
• One closed-end zipper, 4"/10cm long (**Note** Custom-length zippers are available from zipperstop.com.)
• Sewing needle and black cotton thread (avoid cotton/polyester thread as it tends to knot easily)
• Straight pins
• Small amount of fabric lining for pocket—approx 10" x 6" (25.5cm x 15cm) [optional]

GAUGE
24 sts and 26 rows over 4"/10cm in Block and Ridged pats using size 6 (4mm) needles
Take time to save time—check your gauge.

BLOCK PATTERN
(multiple of 6 sts plus 2)
Row 1 (RS) K2, *p4, k2; rep from *.
Row 2 P2, *k4, p2; rep from *.
Rows 3, 5 and 7 P2, *k4, p2; rep from *.
Rows 4, 6 and 8 K2, *p4, k2; rep from *.
Rep rows 1–8 for Block pat.

STOCKINETTE STITCH (ST ST)
(over any number of sts)
Knit RS rows, purl WS rows.

K2, P2 RIB
(multiple of 4 sts plus 2)
Row 1 (WS) P2, *k2, p2; rep from *.
Row 2 (RS) K2, *p2, k2; rep from *.
Rep rows 1–2 for K2, P2 Rib.

RIDGED PATTERN
(over an odd number of sts)
Row 1 (RS) Knit.
Row 2 Purl.
Row 3 K1, *p1, k1; rep from *.
Row 4 P1, *k1, p1; rep from *.
Row 5 Knit.
Row 6 Purl.
Row 7 P1, *k1, p1; rep from *.
Row 8 K1, *p1, k1; rep from *.
Rep rows 1–8 for Ridged pat.

BACK
With size 6 (4mm) needles and A, cast on 102 (114, 126, 138, 150) sts.
Est pat (RS) K2 (St st seam sts), place marker (pm), work Row 1 of Block pat over center 98 (110, 122, 134, 146) sts, pm, end k2 (St st seam sts).
Work even until piece measures approx 5"/12.5cm, end with row 2 of pat. Change to color B.
Next (inc) row (RS) Knit, inc 20 (20, 24, 28, 32) sts evenly spaced—122 (134, 150, 166, 182) sts.
Change pat (WS) Work row 1 of K2, P2 Rib over all 122 (134, 150, 166, 182) sts. Work even in K2, P2 Rib until piece measures 13"/33cm, end with a RS row. Change to color C.

The different stitch patterns used in this design are clearly visible in this back view.

Next (dec) row (WS) Purl, dec 21 (21, 25, 29, 33) sts evenly spaced—101 (113, 125, 137, 149) sts.
Change pat (RS) K2 (St st seam sts), pm, work row 1 of Ridged pat over 97 (109, 121, 133, 145) sts, end k2 (St st seam sts). Work even as est until piece measures 14½"/37cm, end with a WS row.

ARMHOLE SHAPING (RS)
Bind off 5 (6, 6, 7, 7) sts at the beg of the

next 2 rows.
Next (dec) row (RS) K1, ssk, work to last 3 sts, end k2tog, k1.
WS row P2, work in pat as est to last 2 sts, end p2.
Rep the last 2 rows 5 (7, 10, 12, 15) more times—79 (85, 91, 97, 103) sts.
Keeping 2 seam sts each side, work in pat as est until armhole measures 7 (7½, 8, 8½, 9)"/17.5 (19, 20.5, 21.5, 23)cm, end with a WS row.

SHOULDER AND BACK NECK SHAPING
Mark center 23 (23, 25, 25, 29) sts.
Next row (RS) Bind off 6 (7, 8, 9, 9) sts, work to marked sts, join a second ball of yarn and bind off center 23 (23, 25, 25, 29) sts, work to end.
Working both sides at the same time with separate balls of yarn, bind off 6 (7, 8, 9, 9) sts from the next 5 (5, 3, 3, 5) shoulder edges, then 0 (0, 7, 8, 0) sts from the next 2 shoulder edges AND AT THE SAME TIME, bind off from each neck edge 5 sts 2 times.

LEFT FRONT
With size 6 (4mm) needles and A, cast on 53 (59, 65, 71, 77) sts.
Est pat (RS) K2 (St st side seam sts), pm, work row 1 of Block pat over center 50 (56, 62, 68, 74) sts, pm, end k1 (St st front edge st). Work even until piece measures approx 5"/12.5cm, end with row 2 of pat.
Change to color B.
Next (inc) row (RS) Knit, inc 9 (11, 13, 11, 13) sts evenly spaced—62 (70, 78, 82, 90) sts.
Change pat (WS) Work row 1 of K2, P2

Rib over all 62 (70, 78, 82, 90) sts.
Work even in K2, P2 Rib until piece measures 13"/33cm, end with a RS row.
Change to color C.
Next (dec) row (WS) Purl, dec 10 (12, 14, 12, 14) sts evenly spaced—52 (58, 64, 70, 76) sts.
Change pat (RS) K2 (St st side seam sts), pm, work row 1 of Ridged pat over 49 (55, 61, 67, 73) sts, end k1 (St st front edge st). Work even as est until piece measures 14½"/37cm, end with a WS row.

ARMHOLE SHAPING (RS)
Bind off 5 (6, 6, 7, 7) sts at the beg of the next RS row.
Work WS row as est.
Next (dec) row (RS) K1, ssk, work as est to end.
WS row P1, work as est to last 2 sts, end p2.
Rep the last 2 rows 5 (7, 10, 12, 15) more times—41 (44, 47, 50, 53) sts.
Keeping edge sts on each end, work in pat as est until armhole measures 3½"/9cm, end with a WS row 4 or 8 of pat.

POCKET OPENING
Next row (RS) Cont armhole shaping if necessary and work 7 (7, 9, 11, 13) sts, bind off 24 sts, work as est to end.
Next row (WS) Purl to bound-off sts, cast on 24 sts, purl to end.
Cont in pat as est until armhole measures 5 (5½, 6, 6½, 7)"/12.5 (14, 15, 16.5, 18)cm, end with a RS row.

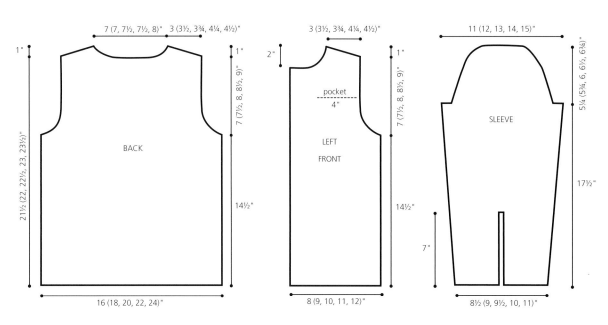

NECKLINE SHAPING (WS)
Bind off 5 (5, 6, 6, 8) sts at the beg of the next WS row, then 3 sts at the beg of the next 6 WS rows—18 (21, 23, 26, 27) sts. Keeping 2 edge sts on each end, work in pat until armhole measures 7 (7½, 8, 8½, 9)"/17.5 (19, 20.5, 21.5, 23)cm, end with a WS row.

SHOULDER SHAPING (RS)
Bind off 6 (7, 8, 9, 9) sts at the beg of the next 3 (3, 2, 2, 3) RS rows, then 0 (0, 7, 8, 0) sts at the beg of the next RS row.

RIGHT FRONT
Work same as for left front, reversing all shaping and omitting pocket opening.

SLEEVES
With size 6 (4mm) needles and B, cast on 25 (27, 29, 31, 33) sts, then with a second ball of B cast on 25 (27, 29, 31, 33) sts—50 (54, 58, 62, 66) sts total.
Est pat (RS) K2 (St st seam sts), work row 1 of Ridged pat over 21 (23, 25, 27, 29) sts, k2 (St st seam sts); then with second strand (to form second separate section), k2 (St st seam sts), work row 1 of Ridged pat over 21 (23, 25, 27, 29) sts, end k2 (St st seam sts). Working both sides separately, work in pat until 7 more rows are complete, ending with a WS row.
Next (inc) row (RS) K2, M1, work as est to last 2 sts in second section, M1, end k2— 26 (28, 30, 32, 34) sts in each section. Working incs into Ridged pat, rep inc row every 8th row for a total of 4 incs each side—29 (31, 33, 35, 37) sts in each section AND AT THE SAME TIME, cont until sleeve measures 7"/18cm, end with a WS row. Change to color C.

CLOSE OPENING
Next (inc) row (RS) Knit across both sections with same ball of yarn AND AT THE SAME TIME, inc 12 sts evenly spaced—70 (74, 78, 82, 86) sts. Cut extra strand at center.
Change pat (WS) Work row 1 of K2, P2 Rib over all 70 (74, 78, 82, 86) sts. Work even in Rib until sleeve measures 13"/33cm, end with a RS row. Change to color A.
Purl next WS row, dec 10 (8, 6, 4, 2) sts evenly spaced—60 (66, 72, 78, 84) sts.
Change pat (RS) K2 (St st seam sts), pm, work row 1 of Block pat over center 56 (62, 68, 74, 80) sts, pm, end k2 (St st seam sts).

Work in pat until 5 more rows are complete, ending with a WS row.
Next (inc) row (RS) K2 (seam sts), M1, work as est to last 2 sts, M1, end k2 (seam sts).
Working incs into Block pat, rep inc row every 6th row for a total of 4 incs each side—68 (74, 80, 86, 92) sts. Work even until sleeve measures 17½"/44.5cm, end with a WS row.

CAP SHAPING (RS)
Bind off 5 (6, 6, 7, 7) sts at the beg of the next 2 rows.
Next row (RS) K1, ssk, work in pat to last 3 sts, end k2tog, k1.
WS rows P2, work in pat to the last st, end p2.
Rep the last 2 rows 14 (16, 16, 16, 16) more times.
Bind off 2 sts at the beg of the next 2 (2, 2, 4, 4) rows, then 0 (0, 3, 3, 3) sts at the beg of the next 0 (0, 2, 2, 4) rows.
Bind off rem 24 sts.

FINISHING
LOWER SLEEVE ZIPPER OPENING
With RS facing, size 6 (4mm) needles and A, pick up 40 sts evenly along one edge of opening at lower sleeve. Trim: Bind off in knit carefully so edge does not flare or draw in, trim must be flat and even. Rep on other side of opening. Join trims at top and weave in all ends away from trim. Lay closed 7" zipper under the trim and pin in place so the tabs of the zipper extend beyond lower edge of sleeve and teeth are even with lower edge. Pin so the trim is away from the teeth and zipper may open and close easily. With RS facing and threaded sewing needle, beg at lower edge of one side, sew in the "dent" between the trim and the main fabric of the sleeve, using "stab" stitches, by inserting needle straight up from the WS, then straight down from the RS. Lock sewing sts by back stitching every few sts. When one side is complete, sew other side in the same direction, from lower edge. Sew tabs of zipper to the side on the diagonal, at lower edge. Rep for second sleeve.
Sew sleeve seams.

LEFT FRONT POCKET OPENING
With RS facing, size 6 (4mm) needle and A, pick up 1 st for every bound-off st along lower edge of opening. Work trim as for lower sleeve. Rep along upper opening of

pocket, picking up 1 st for every cast on st. Work trim. Weave in ends away from trim. Pin closed short zipper in place and sew as for lower sleeve zipper.

BODY
Sew front to back at shoulders. Sew side seams.

COLLAR
With RS facing, size 6 (4mm) needles and B, pick up 136 (136, 140, 140, 144) sts evenly along entire neckline edge.
Est rib (WS) P3, k2, *p2, k2; rep from * to last 3 sts, p3. Work even in rib until collar measures 3½"/9cm. Change to A and work in rib for 1"/2.5cm more. Bind off. Tie marker at the center of collar along the front edges.

RIGHT FRONT EDGE TRIM
With RS facing, size 6 (4mm) needles and A, beg at lower edge, pick up 33 sts along lower section to ribbed waist, pick up 44 sts along waist section, pick up 44 (47, 50, 53, 56) sts to collar, then pick up 16 sts along collar to marker. Bind off in knit on WS row, taking care that edge does not flare or draw in. Rep on left front edge reversing directon of picked-up sts. Weave in all ends away from trim. Pin closed zipper in place along the trim edges, placing the tabs of the zipper to extend beyond upper edge of trim at collar and lower zipper is even with lower edge. Pin so that the trim is away from the teeth and zipper may open and close easily. With RS facing and threaded sewing needle, beg at lower edge of one side. Sew in the "dent" between the trim and the main fabric of front, as for lower sleeve. Sew second side in the same direction, from lower edge.
Fold collar to the inside and with tapestry needle and yarn, loosely sew inner untrimmed edges of collar along side of zipper, sewing lightly into the ribbing.
Sew the bound off edges evenly along the ridge formed by the picked-up sts, along base of collar.
Sew sleeve caps into armholes.
Weave in all ends.
Optional Make pocket lining for upper pocket and sew in place. ∎

Plaid Accents Cardigan ■■■■

page 105

SIZES
To fit sizes Small (Medium, Large, X-Large, XX-Large). Shown in size Small.

MEASUREMENTS
FINISHED BUST AT UNDERARM, BUTTONED 36 (39, 42, 45, 48)"/ 91.5 (99, 106.5, 114.5, 122)cm
LENGTH 23 (23½, 24, 24½, 25)"/ 58.5 (59.5, 61, 62, 63.5)cm
SLEEVE WIDTH AT UPPER ARM 12½ (13½, 14½, 15½, 16½)"/ 32 (34, 37, 39, 42)cm

MATERIALS
• Rowan *Lima* (baby alpaca/merino wool/nylon), 1¾oz/50g, 109 yd/100m:
MC #888 (Lima)—12 (13, 14, 16, 17) balls
1 ball each in the following colors:
A #885 (Machu Picchu) B #886 (Puno)
C #884 (Cusco)   D #882 (Chile)
E #889 (Peru)   F #887 (Nazca)
• One pair each size 7 (4.5mm) and 8 (5mm) knitting needles *or size to obtain given gauge*
• Cable needle (cn)
• Size H (3.75mm) crochet hook
• Seven ¾"/2cm buttons
• Tapestry needle

GAUGE
22 sts and 32 rows over 4"/10cm in Textured pat using size 8 (5mm) needles
Take time to save time—check your gauge.

NOTE
After I finished knitting the pieces for this cardigan, I decided I liked the "wrong" side of the fabric better than the "right" side (see page 111 for a photo that shows the right side of the fabric). I assembled the sweater with the wrong side showing. The schematic and pattern reflect my original plan. You can decide for yourself which side of the fabric you like best. This will determine how the cardigan buttons.

STOCKINETTE STITCH (ST ST)
(over any number of sts)
Knit RS rows, purl WS rows.

TEXTURED PATTERN
(multiple of 3 sts plus 2)
Rows 1, 3, 5, 7, 9, 11 and 13 (RS) Purl.
Rows 2, 4, 6, 8, 10, 12 and 14 *K2, p1; rep from *, end k2.
Rows 15, 19 and 23 (RS) Knit.
Rows 16, 18, 20, 22, 24 and 26 *K2, p1; rep from *, end k2.
Rows 17, 21 and 25 *P2, k1; rep from *, end p2.
Row 27 Knit.
Row 28 *K2, p1; rep from *, end k2.
Rep rows 1–28 for Textured pat.

CABLE PATTERN
(panel of 20 sts)
T3B (twist 3 back) Sl next st to cn and hold in back, k2, p1 from cn.
T3F (twist 3 front) Sl next 2 sts to cn and hold in front, p1, k2 from cn.
Row 1 (RS) K2, p5, T3B, T3F, p5, k2.
Row 2 P2, k5, p2, k2, p2, k5, p2.
Row 3 K2, p4, T3B, p2, T3F, p4, k2.
Row 4 P2, k4, p2, k4, p2, k4, p2.
Row 5 K2, p3, T3B, p4, T3F, p3, k2.
Row 6 P2, k3, p2, k6, p2, k3, p2.
Row 7 K2, p2, T3B, p6, T3F, p2, k2.
Row 8 P2, k2, p2, k8, p2, k2, p2.
Rep rows 1–8 for Cable pat.

PLAID PATTERN
(multiple of 13 sts)
Row 1 (RS) [K4, p1] 2 times, k2, p1; rep from *.
Row 2 (WS) Knit the knit sts and purl the purl sts as they appear.
Work rows 1–2 in the following color sequence: *2 rows E, 6 rows A, 1 row D, 3 rows B, 2 rows C, 1 row E, 2 rows F, 2 rows B, 1 row D and 6 rows MC; rep from *.
Chain vertical lines With RS facing and crochet hook, working from right to left, work a row of chain sts into each of the vertical purl channels in the following color sequence: *D, A, F, MC, B, C and E; rep from *.

BACK
With size 8 (5mm) needles and MC, cast on 102 (111, 120, 129, 138) sts.
Est pats (RS) K2 (St st seam sts), work row 1 of Textured pat over 98 (107, 116, 125, 134) sts, end k2 (St st seam sts). Work even in pats until back measures 3"/7.5cm, end with a WS row.
Waist shaping (dec) row (RS) K1, ssk, work in pat as est to last 3 sts, k2tog, k1.
WS rows P2, work in pat to last 2 sts, p2. Rep dec row every 8th row for a total of 4 decs each side—94 (103, 112, 121, 130) sts.
Work even until back measures 9"/23cm, end with a WS row.
Waist shaping (inc) row (RS) K2 (seam sts), M1, work in pat as est to last 2 sts, M1, k2 (seam sts). Working incs into pat, rep inc row every 8th row for a total of 4 incs each side—102 (111, 120, 129, 138) sts. Work even until back measures 15½"/39.5cm, end with a WS row.

ARMHOLE SHAPING (RS)
Bind off 6 sts at the beg of the next 2 rows.
Next (dec) row (RS) K1, ssk, work in pat as est to last 3 sts, k2tog, k1.
WS rows P2, work to last 2 sts, end p2. Rep the last 2 rows 5 (7, 9, 11, 12) more times—78 (83, 88, 93, 100) sts.
Cont 2 seam sts each side and work even in pat until armhole measures 7½ (8, 8½, 9, 9½)"/19 (20.5, 21.5, 23, 24)cm, end with a WS row.

SHOULDER AND BACK NECK SHAPING (RS)
Mark center 24 (25, 26, 27, 28) sts.
Next row (RS) Bind off 5 (7, 7, 7, 8) sts, work to center marked sts, join a second ball of yarn and bind off center 24 (25, 26, 27, 28) sts, complete row. Working both sides at the same time with separate balls of yarn, bind off 5 (7, 7, 7, 8) sts at the beg of the next row, then 6 (6, 7, 8, 9) sts at the beg of the next 4 rows AND AT THE SAME TIME, bind off from each neck edge 5 sts twice.

LEFT FRONT
With size 8 (5mm) needles and MC, cast on 47 (53, 56, 59, 65) sts.

Est pats (RS) K2 (St st seam sts at side seam), work row 1 of Textured pat over 44 (50, 53, 56, 62) sts, end k1 (St st edge st at front edge).

Work even in pats until left front measures 3"/7.5cm, end with a WS row.

Waist shaping (dec) row (RS) K1, ssk, work in pat as est to end.

WS rows P1, work in pat to last 2 sts, end p2.

Rep dec row every 8th row after for a total of 4 decs at side—43 (49, 52, 55, 61) sts

Work even until left front measures 9"/23cm, end with a WS row.

Waist shaping (inc) row (RS) K2, M1, work in pat as est to end.

Working incs into pat, rep inc row every 8th row for a total of 4 incs at side—47 (53, 56, 59, 65) sts.

Work even until left front measures 15½"/39.5cm, end with a WS row.

ARMHOLE SHAPING (RS)

Bind off 6 sts at the beg of the next RS row.

Next (dec) row (RS) K1, ssk, work in pat as est to end.

WS rows P1, work to last 2 sts, end p2.
Rep the last 2 rows 5 (7, 9, 11, 12) more times—35 (39, 40, 41, 46) sts.
Keeping edge sts in St st as est, work even until Armhole measures 5½ (6, 6½, 7, 7½)"/ 14 (15, 16.5, 18, 19)cm, end with a RS row.

NECKLINE SHAPING (WS)

Bind off 4 (6, 5, 4, 6) sts at the beg of the row, then bind off 2 sts at the beg of the next 7 WS rows—17 (19, 21, 23, 26) sts.
Work even until left front measures same as back to shoulder, end with a WS row.

Shape shoulder (RS) Bind off 5 (7, 7, 7, 8) sts at the beg of row, then 6 (6, 7, 8, 9) sts at the beg of next 2 RS rows.

RIGHT FRONT

With size 8 (5mm) needles and MC, cast on 74 (83, 92, 98, 107) sts.

Est pats (RS) K1 (St st edge st at front edge), work row 1 of Textured pat over 71 (80, 89, 95, 104) sts, end k2 (St st seam sts at side seam).

Work even in pats until right front measures 3"/7.5cm, end with a WS row.

Waist shaping (dec) row (RS) K1, work in pat as est to last 3 sts, k2tog, k1.

WS rows P2, work in pat to last st, end p1.
Rep dec row every 8th row after for a total of 4 decs at side—70 (79, 88, 94, 103) sts.

Work even until right front measures 9"/23cm, end with a WS row.

Waist shaping (inc) row (RS) K1, work as est to last 2 sts, M1, end k2 (seam sts).

Working incs into pat, rep inc row every 8th row for a total of 4 incs at side—74 (83, 92, 98, 107) sts.

Work even until right front measures 15½"/39.5cm, end with a RS row.

ARMHOLE SHAPING (WS)

Bind off 6 sts at the beg of the next row.

Next row (RS) Work in pat as est to last 3 sts, end k2tog, k1.

WS rows P2, work to last st, end p1.
Rep the last 2 rows 5 (7, 9, 11, 12) more times—62 (69, 76, 80, 88) sts.
Keeping edge sts in St st as est, work even until armhole measures 5½ (6, 6½, 7, 7½)"/ 14 (15,16.5,18,19)cm, end with a WS row.

NECKLINE SHAPING (RS)

Bind off 31 (36, 41, 43, 48) sts at the beg of row, then bind off 2 sts at the beg of the next 7 RS rows—17 (19, 21, 23, 26) sts.
Work even until right front measures same as back to shoulder, end with a RS row.

SHOULDER SHAPING (WS)

Bind off 5 (7, 7, 7, 8) sts at the beg of the next row, then 6 (6, 7, 8, 9) sts at the beg of the next 2 WS rows.

SLEEVES (MAKE 2)

Note The sleeve is deliberately narrow. The cabled strip that follows will be sewn along the sleeve's side edges to widen it to full width.

With size 8 (5mm) needles and MC, cast on 39 (45, 45, 48, 48) sts.

Est pats (RS) K2 (St st seam sts), work row 1 of Textured pat over 35 (41, 41, 44, 44) sts, end k2 (St st seam sts). Work even in pats until sleeve measures 2"/5cm, end with a WS row.

Next (inc) row (RS) K2, M1, work in pat as est to last 2 sts, M1, k2.

Working incs into pat, rep inc row every 10th (10th, 8th, 6th, 6th) row 10 (10, 10, 6, 14) more times, then every 0 (0, 10th, 8th, 8th) row 0 (0, 2, 8, 2) times—61 (67, 71, 78, 82) sts.

Work even until sleeve measures 17"/43cm, end with a WS row.

CAP SHAPING (RS)

K1, ssk, work in pat as est to last 3 sts, k2tog, k1.

Rep dec row every RS row 18 (21, 23, 25, 27) more times—23 (23, 23, 26, 26) sts. Bind off on next RS row.

CABLED STRIP TO WIDEN SLEEVE (MAKE 2)

With size 8 (5mm) needles and MC, cast on 20 sts. Work in Cable pat until piece measures 17"/43cm, end with a WS row. Bind off.

Sew 1 cabled strip along one side edge of each sleeve, between lower edge and cap shaping.

FINISHING

See note at beginning of pattern about choosing right or wrong side of pattern stitch.

Sew fronts to back at shoulder seams. Sew side seams.

NECKLINE TRIM

With RS facing, size 7 (4.5mm) needles and D, beg at right front, pick up 24 (24, 26, 28, 30) sts to shoulder, 46 (46, 48, 50, 52) sts along back neck, then 47 (47, 49, 51, 53) sts to end—117 (117, 123, 129, 135) sts. Knit WS row, purl RS row, bind off in k on WS.

COLLAR

With size 8 (5mm) needles and E, cast on 91 (91, 91, 104, 104) sts. Purl 1 row.
Beg Plaid pat and work for 1"/2.5cm, end with a WS row.

Next (dec) row (RS) K1, ssk, work in pat to last 3 sts, k2tog, k1. Keeping first and last 2 sts in St st, rep dec row every 4th row 3 more times—83 (83, 83, 96, 96) sts. Cont as est until 34 rows of Plaid pat are complete, end with a WS row.

Change to MC and Garter st, omitting purl channels.

NECKLINE EDGE SHAPING (WS)

Bind off 4 sts at the beg of row, work to end.

Next row (RS) Bind off 3 sts at the beg of row, work to end. Rep the last 2 rows 6 more times. Bind off rem 34 (34, 34, 47, 47) sts. Work chained vertical lines.

SEW COLLAR IN PLACE

With WS of body facing and RS of collar, pin collar along ridge formed by picked up sts at base of neckline edge and approx ½"/1cm away from untrimmed front edges. Sew collar in place. Refer to photo on page 99 for detail of sewing collar.

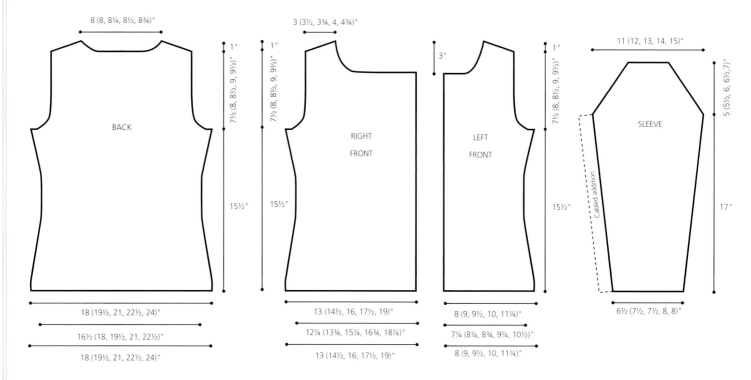

BACK

8 (8, 8¼, 8½, 8¾)"

1"

7½ (8, 8½, 9, 9½)"

15½"

18 (19½, 21, 22½, 24)"

16½ (18, 19½, 21, 22½)"

18 (19½, 21, 22½, 24)"

RIGHT
FRONT

3 (3½, 3¾, 4, 4¾)"

1"

7½ (8, 8½, 9, 9½)"

15½"

13 (14½, 16, 17½, 19)"

12¼ (13¾, 15¼, 16¾, 18¼)"

13 (14½, 16, 17½, 19)"

LEFT
FRONT

3"

1"

7½ (8, 8½, 9, 9½)"

15½"

8 (9, 9½, 10, 11¼)"

7¼ (8¼, 8¾, 9¼, 10½)"

8 (9, 9½, 10, 11¼)"

SLEEVE

11 (12, 13, 14, 15)"

5 (5½, 6, 6½, 7)"

17"

Cabled addition

6½ (7½, 7½, 8, 8)"

CUFFS

With size 8 (5mm) needles, WS facing and E, pick up 52 (56, 56, 60, 60) sts along bottom of sleeve. Purl 1 row (this is now the WS as cuff will be folded up). Beg Plaid pat (not all sizes are a mult of 13; end all RS rows at the same st) and work for 5"/12.5cm, end with a WS row. Bind off. Work chained vertical lines. Rep for second sleeve.

Sew sleeve seams, sewing cuff seams in opposite direction. Sew sleeve caps into armholes.

RIGHT FRONT BAND

The band is knitted for the same number of rows as the front: Knit the band a few inches, then sew it on and repeat to end. With size 7 (4.5mm) needles and C, cast on 7 sts.

Row 1 (RS) K2, p1, k1, p1, k2.

WS row P2, k1, p1, k1, p2.

Rep these 2 rows for pat, working the ribbing firmly, tugging at the first st of every row. Work in the following color sequence. Work C for 4½"/11.5cm, B for 3½"/9cm, F for 6"/15cm, E for ¾"/2cm, A for 2"/5cm, then work D for rem. Bind off and sew in place. Place markers for 6 buttons, the lower one at 2"/5cm from bottom edge and the top one at ½"/1cm down from top edge, then 4 more evenly spaced between.

LEFT FRONT BUTTONHOLE BAND

With size 7 (4.5mm) needles and A, cast on 7 sts. Work as for right front band in the following colors AND AT THE SAME TIME, work buttonholes opposite button markers as follows: When you reach a marker for buttonhole, end with a WS row and work the buttonhole rows.

Buttonhole row 1 (RS) K1, ssk, yo, p2tog, k2.

Buttonhole row 2 (WS) P2, k1, (p1, k1) into yo of previous row, p2.

COLOR SEQUENCE FOR LEFT BAND

Work A for 5"/12.5cm, C for 3"/7.5cm, E for 1"/2.5cm, D for 2"/5cm, B for 3"/7.5cm, D for 2"/5cm, E for ½"/1cm, then work A for rem. Bind off and sew in place.

REINFORCING CHAIN FOR BUTTONS ON RIGHT FRONT

Lay the sweater flat, or try it on, and overlap the fronts to make the collar meet. Lift the right front slightly and mark the vertical ridge in the pattern that is closest to the line of buttonholes. Mark the top of the ridge where it is even with the uppermost buttonhole. With the RS facing, MC and crochet hook, starting at lower edge, chain a line into the marked vertical ridge, keeping the chain the same as the knitting so it does not pull. Chain until you reach the marker. Pull the yarn through, cut and weave to back. Sew buttons opposite buttonholes, sewing into the reinforcing chain.

POCKET

Measure 3"/7.5cm from lower edge and 2"/5cm from side seam. Using a crochet hook or point of needle, with A pick up 23 sts over a 4"/10cm width (see photo on page 103). Using size 8 (5mm) needles, purl WS row, inc 1 st—24 sts.

Est pat (RS) K5, p1, k4, p1, k2, p1, k4, p1, k5.

WS rows Knit the knit sts and purl the purl sts as they appear. Rep these 2 rows for Plaid pat and work color sequence as foll: 4 rows A, 1 row D, 3 rows B, 2 rows C, 1 row E, 2 rows F, 2 rows B, 1 row D, 6 rows MC, 2 rows E; rep from * until pocket measures approx. 6"/15cm. Bind off. Work chained vertical lines. Sew sides of pocket to front. Weave in ends.

BUTTON LOOP

With size 7 (4.5mm) needles and D, cast on 13 sts. Bind off. Sew ends together and then to center of pocket. Sew on button. Refer to photo on page 106. ∎

Asian-Inspired Vest

page 119

SIZES
To fit sizes Small (Medium, Large). Shown in size Small.

MEASUREMENTS (AFTER FELTING)
BUST AT UNDERARM, BUTTONED
Approx 40 (44, 48)"/101.5 (112, 122)cm
LENGTH Approx 22½ (23, 25)"/57 (58.5, 63.5)cm

MATERIALS
• Nashua Handknits *Julia* (wool/alpaca/mohair), 1¾oz/50g, 93yd/85m:
• MC #3983 (Delphinium)—13 (15, 17) skeins
• CC #1890 (Peony)—1 skein
• Size 9 (5.5mm) and 10 (6mm) circular knitting needles, 24"/61cm or 36"/91.5cm long
• Stitch holders
• Size 1 (2.25mm) or 2 (2.75mm) circular knitting needle, 36" (91.5cm) long
• Three 2"/5cm long toggle buttons
• Three approx ¾"/2cm anchor buttons

MATERIALS NEEDED FOR FELTING
• 12"/30.5 long piece of slippery cotton yarn that will not felt or bleed color
• Mild liquid soap, such as baby shampoo, or delicate wool cleanser
• Baking soda to add if your local water is hard
• Automatic washing machine with warm-water setting

GAUGE
16 sts and 32 rows over 4"/10cm in Garter st using size 10 (6mm) circular needle (before felting)
Approx 18 sts and 30 rows over 4"/10cm in Garter st using size 10 (6mm) circular needle (after felting)
Take time to save time—check your gauge.

FELTING/SWATCH INSTRUCTIONS
In order to get an accurate gauge so that your vest will shrink to the proper size, you need to work a very large swatch. This swatch should go through the felting process so that you can see that your gauge is approximately the same as the gauge given in this pattern.
   Work your swatch in Garter st over 40 sts and 80 rows, to the given gauge of 4 sts per inch.

WORK TRIM ON THE SWATCH
Beg with RS lower edge facing and circular needle (same size as for swatch), * pick up 1 st for every st along the edge, then slide a thin needle into a "bump" in each ridge (see photo on page 60) along the side edge, and k1 into each bump; rep from * along bound off edge and other side. Turn and knit WS row, then bind off on RS row. Join corner.

FELTING
Put your swatch in the washer with some mild detergent (I used a small amount of baby shampoo), and a lint-free bath towel. If your water is hard, add ½ cup of baking soda. Set water temperature for warm (not hot), and run the swatch through a normal cycle. Remove swatch and dry flat on a dry towel. Check your felted gauge.

GARTER STITCH
(over any number of sts)
Knit every row.
Note 1 "ridge" equals 2 rows.

NOTES
1) The vest is worked in one piece, back and forth on size 10 (6mm) circular needle, to the underarm. Then the back and fronts are worked separately.
2) The armhole extensions are picked up and knitted from the armhole edge before the shoulders are seamed.
3) The shoulder seams are sewn, then the edgings are picked up with size 9 (5.5mm) circular needle and worked before the vest is washed and felted.

ONE-ROW BUTTONHOLE/POCKET OPENING
Work to where you want the buttonhole/pocket to be. Slip next stitch, move yarn to the back of work, slip second stitch, pass first slipped stitch over the second, slip next stitch, pass second stitch over the third, and repeat until desired width of buttonhole is reached. Turn work and, by using the cable cast-on method (see page 161), cast on the number of stitches bound off plus one. Turn work again. Slip the next stitch to the right-hand needle and pass the extra cast-on stitch over the slipped stitch.

BODY
With size 10 (6mm) circular needles and MC, cast on 218 (244, 272) sts.
Work in Garter st until there are 30 rows, or 15 ridges, end with a WS row.
Buttonhole row (RS) K6, work a 7 st one-row buttonhole (see above) loosely, k to end. Rep buttonhole row at this edge after 60 rows (30 ridges) from beg, and again after 90 rows (45 ridges) from beg AND AT THE SAME TIME, work until 46 rows (23 ridges) are complete, end with a WS row.

POCKET OPENING (RS)
K64 (72, 82) sts for right front, place marker (pm), k90 (100, 108) sts for back, pm, k5 sts, work a 22-st one-row pocket opening (see above), then k rem sts for left front—64 (72, 82) sts after second marker—218 (244, 272) sts.
Sl markers and cont buttonholes as described, knit until 68 rows (34 ridges) are complete, end with a WS row.

DIVIDE FOR ARMHOLES
Next row (RS) Knit 64 (72, 82) sts to marker, turn, knit back over the right front 64 (72, 82) sts. Slip 90 (100, 108) sts to holder for back and 64 (72, 82) sts to holder for left front.

RIGHT FRONT
Cont to knit over 64 (72, 82) sts, working buttonhole rows as est, until 98 rows (49 ridges) are complete, end with a WS row.

V-NECK SHAPING
Dec row (RS) K2, ssk, k to end.
Knit WS row.
Rep the last 2 rows 35 (38, 45) more times—28 (33, 36) sts.
Piece should be 170 (176, 190) rows, or 85 (88, 95) ridges, from beg. Knit RS row.

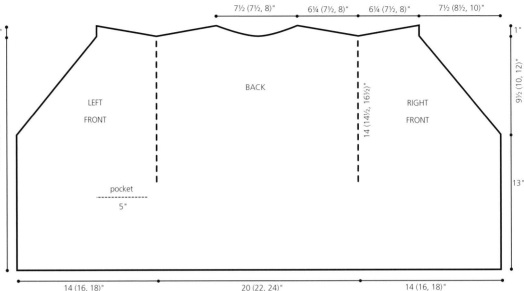

7½ (7½, 8)"   6¼ (7½, 8)"   6¼ (7½, 8)"   7½ (8½, 10)"

1"

BACK

LEFT FRONT

14 (14½, 16½)"

RIGHT FRONT

1"

9½ (10, 12)"

22½ (23, 25)"

13"

pocket

5"

14 (16, 18)"   20 (22, 24)"   14 (16, 18)"

SHOULDER SHAPING (WS)
Bind off 7 (9, 9) sts at the beg of the next 4 (1, 4) WS rows, then 0 (8, 0) sts at beg of next 3 WS rows.

BACK
Attach yarn to back sts at beg of RS row. With RS facing, knit 90 (100, 108) sts, turn, knit WS row. Leave sts for left front on holder. Work even until back has same number of rows as right front to shoulder, minus 1 row, so end with a WS row. Piece should be 170 (176, 190) rows, or 85 (88, 95) ridges, from beg.

BACK NECK AND SHOULDER SHAPING
Mark center 16 (16, 18) sts.
Next row (RS) Bind off 7 (9, 9) sts, k to marked sts and join second ball of yarn and bind off center 16 (16, 18) sts, k to end. Working both sides at the same time with separate balls of yarn, bind off 7 (9, 9) sts at the beg of the next 7 (1, 7) shoulder edges, then 0 (8, 0) sts at the next 6 shoulder edge AND AT THE SAME TIME, bind off from each neck edge 3 sts 3 times. Attach yarn at beg of RS row for beg of left front.

LEFT FRONT
With RS facing, k64 (72, 82) sts.
Knit until left front has same number of rows as right front to beg of V-neck shaping, end with WS row.

V-NECK SHAPING
Dec row (RS) K to last 4 sts, end k2tog, k2.
Knit WS row.
Rep the last 2 rows 35 (38, 45) more times—28 (33, 36) sts.

Piece should be same number of rows as back to shoulder, ending with a WS row.

SHOULDER SHAPING
Bind off 7 (9, 9) sts at the beg of the next 4 (1, 4) RS rows, then 0 (8, 0) st at beg of the next 3 RS rows.

ARMHOLE EXTENSION
With RS of back left armhole facing, size 10 (6mm) needle and MC, beg at shoulder, pick up 1 st for every ridge along back armhole to underarm—51 (54, 61) sts, then pick up 2 sts in underarm, then pick up 1 st for every ridge along left front armhole to shoulder 51 (54, 61) sts—104 (110, 124) sts. Knit every row for 16 rows, ending with a WS row. Bind off. Rep for second armhole.

FINISHING
Work all trim as follows BEFORE felting.

ARMHOLE TRIM
Note Trim is worked before sewing shoulder seams.
With size 9 (5.5 mm) needle, RS facing and CC, pick up 1 st for every bound-off st along extension edge. Knit WS and bind off on RS. Sew fronts to back at shoulders, including top of extensions and trim where it meets.

LOWER EDGE TRIM
With size 9 (5.5 mm) needle, RS facing and CC, pick up 1 st for every cast-on st along lower edge. Work trim as before.

FRONT EDGE TRIM
With size 9 (5.5 mm) needle, RS facing, CC and beg at right front edge, first slip a very

fine needle (size 1 or 2) into edge loops from beg of neck shaping to lower edge, then with CC knit each loop, then slip the fine needle into edge loops from shoulder to beg of neck shaping, with CC knit each loop, pick up 34 (34, 36) sts along back neck, then rep picking up to lower edge on other side. Work trim as before, increasing 1 st at the corners of the front neck shaping on bind-off row. Join trims at lower corners where they meet.

POCKET TRIM
With size 9 (5.5 mm) needle, RS facing and CC, pick up 24 sts evenly along every cast-on st at lower opening. Work trim as before. Sew pocket opening closed for the felting process with a slippery cotton yarn, tying each end securely.

FELTING
Weave in all ends before felting. With washer set to normal cycle, follow felting instructions for swatch. Remove vest and dry flat on a towel. You can insert a towel between layers to absorb excess water. Allow to dry thoroughly.

POCKET LINING
With size 9 (5.5 mm) needle and CC, cast on 25 sts. Keeping first and last 2 sts in Garter st, work in St st for 4"/10cm. Bind off. Remove cotton yarn from pocket. Sew top of lining to upper WS edge. Pin lining in place and sew around edge with thin needle, penetrating felted fabric only partway through. Mark button placement. Sew buttons in place, sewing through fabric, attaching "anchor button" on WS. ■

Fair Isle Cardigan

page 123

SIZES
To fit sizes Small (Medium, Large, X-Large). Shown in size Medium.

MEASUREMENTS
BUST AT UNDERARM (including 1½"/4cm front band) 36½ (40, 44½, 48½)"/93 (101.5, 113, 123)cm
LENGTH FROM BACK NECK 21½ (22, 22½, 23)"/54.5 (56, 57, 58.5)cm
SLEEVE WIDTH AT UPPER ARM 13 (14, 15, 16)"/33 (35.5, 38, 40.5)cm

MATERIALS
• Berroco *Ultra Alpaca* (alpaca/wool), 3½oz/100g, 215yd/195m)
BACKGROUND COLORS
A #6249 (Fennel)—3 (3, 3, 4) hanks
B #6224 (Steel Blue)—3 (3, 3, 4) hanks
PATTERN COLORS
C #6219 (Iris)—3 (3, 3, 4) hanks
D #6235 (Fuchsia)—3 (3, 3, 4) hanks
E #62172 (Cobalt Mix)—3 (3, 3, 3) hanks
F #6261 (Ultramarine)—3 (3, 3, 3) hanks
G #6258 (Cyclamen)—3 (3, 3, 3) hanks
H #6285 (Oceanic Mix)—4 (4, 4, 4) hanks
• Size 8 (5mm), 9 (5.5mm) and 10 (6mm) circular knitting needles, 24"/61cm or 36"/91.5cm long, *or size needed to obtain gauge*
• One set each size 8 (5mm), 9 (5.5mm) and 10 (6mm) double-pointed needles (dpns)
• Sewing thread
• Sewing machine or sewing needle

• Two 1½"/4cm wooden buttons
• Two ½"/1.25cm anchor buttons
• One wooden buckle (with center bar, but without prong), approx 2"/5cm wide
• Six small buttons for ends of ties
• Tapestry needle
• Sharp scissors

GAUGE
20 sts and 21 rnds to 4"/10cm in charted Fair Isle pat using size 10 (6mm) needles
Take time to save time—check your gauge.

NOTES
1) Sleeves and body are worked in the round on larger needles. Beg sleeves with dpns and change to circular needle when possible.
2) Steeks are worked at front edge, and for armholes, as well as for sleeve cap.
3) Steeks are reinforced by hand or sewing machine stitching before being cut.
4) Sleeve caps are then sewn in place, collar and trimmed edges are worked last.
5) Size 9 (5.5mm) needle is used for trim.

FAIR ISLE COLORWORK CHART
(worked in St st)
Read all chart rnds from right to left, beg and end where stated for chosen size. Rep rnds 1–52 for pat. Carry yarns not in use loosely across back of fabric, twisting when necessary to avoid long floats.

STOCKINETTE STITCH (ST ST; IN THE RND)
(over any number of sts)
Knit every rnd.

STOCKINETTE STITCH (ST ST; BACK AND FORTH)
(over any number of sts)
Knit RS rows, purl WS rows.

SEAM PATTERN
(over 3 sts)
Rnd 1 K1 pattern color, k1 background color, k1 pattern color.
Rep this rnd for Seam pat.

STEEK PATTERN
(over 5 sts)
Rnd 1 K1 background color, (k1 pattern color, k1 background color) 2 times.
Rnd 2 K1 pattern color, (k1 background color, k1 pattern color) 2 times.
Rep rnds 1 and 2 over 5 sts to form Steek pat.

SEED STITCH (IN THE ROUND)
(over an even number of sts)
Rnd 1 *K1, p1; rep from *.
Rnd 2 *P1, k1; rep from *.
Rep rnds 1–2 for seed st.

SEED STITCH (BACK AND FORTH)
(over an odd number of sts)
Rnd 1 K1, *p1, k1; rep from *.
Rep row 1 for seed st.

BODY
With size 10 (6mm) needles and A, cast on 180 (198, 220, 240) sts. Place marker (pm) for beg of rnd and join.
Est pats Sl beg marker, work 3 sts in Seam pat, pm, beg Fair Isle chart with rnd 1 and st #20 (24, 13, 16) and work to last 8 sts of rnd, ending at st #6 (2, 13, 10), pm, work 3 sts in Seam pat, pm, work Steek pat over last 5 sts .
Next rnd (place side seam markers) Sl beg marker, work 42 (47, 52, 57) sts (Seam pat and Fair Isle pat) for right front, pm (for side seam), work 91 (99, 111, 121) sts for back, pm for second side seam, work 42 (47, 52, 57) sts for left front, (Fair Isle pat and Seam pat), sl last marker, work Steek pat over last 5 sts. Work in pats as est until piece measures 12"/30.5cm.

V-NECK SHAPING
Remove the 2 markers between Seam pats and Fair Isle pats. Next (dec) rnd Sl beg marker, work 2 sts in Seam pat, ssk [the last Seam pat st with the first st of Fair Isle pat (in pattern color)], work in pat as est to 1 st before second Seam pat sts, then k2tog [the last Fair Isle pat st tog with first Seam pat st (in pattern color)], work 2 rem Seam pat sts, sl last marker, work Steek pat over last 5 sts. Keeping Seam pat sections intact over 3 sts each, work 2 rnds even and rep dec rnd on next rnd and every 3 rnds after for a total of 14 (15, 15, 16) decs at each neckline edge [total of 28 (30, 30, 32) decs] AND AT THE SAME TIME, cont until piece measures 14½"/37cm.

SHAPE ARMHOLES AND DIVIDE FRONTS FROM BACK
Next rnd (bind off at armholes) Cont neckline decs as est, work to 4 sts before side seam marker, then bind off 8 sts, work until there are 83 (91, 103, 113) sts after bind offs, then bind off 8 sts (4 sts before and 4 sts after second side marker), work as est to end—back 83 (91, 103, 113) sts.

FAIR ISLE CHART

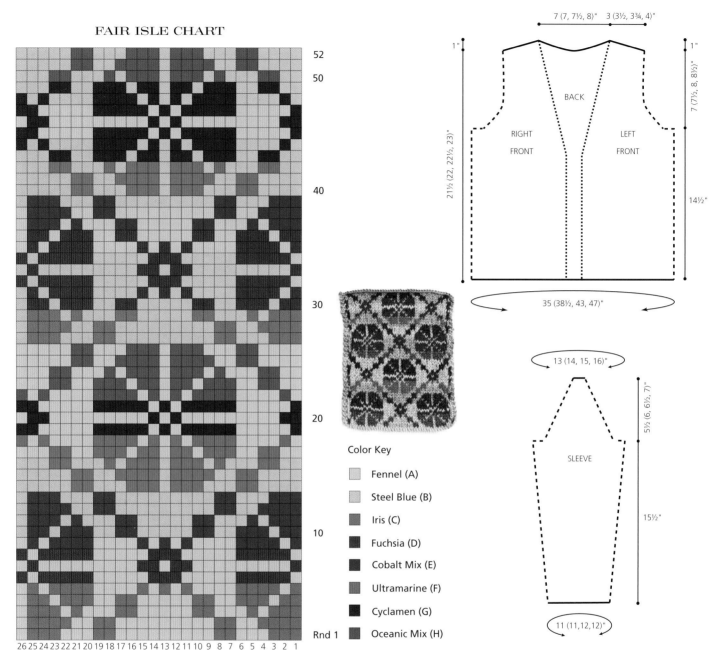

52
50
40
30
20
10
Rnd 1

26 25 24 23 22 21 20 19 18 17 16 15 14 13 12 11 10 9 8 7 6 5 4 3 2 1

26-st and 52-rnd rep

Color Key

▨ Fennel (A)

▨ Steel Blue (B)

▨ Iris (C)

■ Fuchsia (D)

■ Cobalt Mix (E)

▨ Ultramarine (F)

■ Cyclamen (G)

▨ Oceanic Mix (H)

7 (7, 7½, 8)"   3 (3½, 3¾, 4)"

1"   1"

BACK

7 (7½, 8, 8½)"

RIGHT   LEFT
FRONT   FRONT

21½ (22, 22½, 23)"

14½"

35 (38½, 43, 47)"

13 (14, 15, 16)"

5½ (6, 6½, 7)"

SLEEVE

15½"

11 (11,12,12)"

Next rnd (create steek) Cont in pats as est, work to first bound-off section, pm, cast on 5 sts with backward loops in alternating colors, pm, work to second bound-off section, pm, cast on 5 sts with backward loops in alternating colors, pm, work as est to end.
Keeping in pats, cont decs at neckline edge and work Steek pat in newly cast-on 5 sts for each armhole edge.
Next (armhole dec) rnd Work to 2 sts before first armhole Steek, k2tog, sl marker, work Steek pat over 5 sts, sl marker, ssk,

work to 2 sts before second armhole steek, k2tog, sl marker, work Steek over 5 sts, sl marker, ssk, work as est to end.
Work 1 rnd even.
Rep last 2 rnds 8 (9, 13, 15) more times for a total of 9 (10, 14, 16) decs on both sides of armhole steeks.
Cont as est until armhole measures 7 (7½, 8, 8½)"/17.5 (19, 20.5, 21.5)cm. Fronts have 15 (18, 19, 21) sts for each shoulder and 65 (71, 75, 81) sts for back (not counting steek sts).

SHOULDER AND BACK NECK SHAPING
Next (bind-off steeks) rnd Work to first armhole steek, bind off 5 sts, work in pat to second armhole steek and bind off 5 sts, work to last center front steek and bind off 5 sts, *do not cut yarns.*

RIGHT FRONT SHOULDER SHAPING
Next row (RS) Keeping in pat, work 15 (18, 19, 21) sts, turn.
Bind off 5 (6, 6, 7) sts at the beg of the next 3 (3, 2, 3) WS rows, then 0 (0, 7, 0) sts at beg of next WS row.

BACK NECK SHAPING

Attach yarns at beg of RS row. Mark center back 15 (15, 17, 19) sts.

Next row (RS) Keeping in pat, bind off 5 (6, 6, 7) sts, work to center marked sts, bind off 15 (15, 17, 19) sts, join a second set of yarns, work to end of back.

Working both sides at the same time with separate balls of yarn, bind off 5 (6, 6, 7) sts at the beg of the next 5 (5, 3, 5) shoulder edges, then 0 (0, 7, 0) sts at the beg of next 2 shoulder edges AND AT THE SAME TIME, bind off 5 sts from each neck edge twice.

LEFT FRONT SHOULDER SHAPING

Attach yarns at beg of RS row.

Keeping in pat, bind off 5 (6, 6, 7) sts at the beg of the next 3 (3, 2, 3) RS rows, then 0 (0, 7, 0) sts at beg of next RS row.

SLEEVES

With size 10 (6mm) dpns and A, cast on 56 (56, 60, 60) sts. Divide sts over dpns, pm and join.

Est pats Beg Fair Isle chart with rnd 1 and st #26 (26, 24, 24) and work to last 3 sts, ending at st #26 (26, 2, 2), place 2nd marker, work 3 sts in Seam pat. Work in pats as est for 15 rnds.

Next (inc) rnd Sl beg of rnd marker, M1 in pat, work to 2nd marker, M1 in pat, work 3 sts in Seam pat.

Working incs into Fair Isle pat, work 13 (9, 8, 6) more rnds, then rep inc rnd on next rnd, and every 14th (10th, 9th, 7th) rnds after for a total of 5 (7, 8, 10) inc rnds—66 (70, 76, 80) sts. Work even until sleeve measures approx 15½"/40cm.

SLEEVE CAP SHAPING

Work rnd to 4 sts before 3 seam sts, bind off these 4 sts, then bind off 3 seam sts, remove marker, and bind off 4 sts, then work to end—55 (59, 65, 69) sts.

Next (cast-on for steek) rnd Replace beg marker, cast on 5 sts at end of rnd, (alternate pattern color and background color) for steek, pm, then work in Fair Isle pat as est to end of rnd—60 (64, 70, 74) sts.

Next (beg steek pat) rnd Sl marker, work Steek pat over 5 sts, sl marker, work in Fair Isle pat to end.

Cap shaping (dec) rnd Sl marker, work Steek pat over 5 sts, sl marker, ssk, work to 2 sts before next marker, k2tog. Rep dec rnd. Work 1 rnd even.

Rep the last 3 rnds 7 (8, 9, 10) more times,

changing to dpns when necessary—28 (28, 30, 30) sts rem.

Next rnd Bind off 5 Steek sts, work to end of rnd, turn.

WS Bind off 2 sts, work to end of row, turn.

RS Bind off 2 sts, work to end, turn. Bind off rem 19 (19, 21, 21) sts.

FINISHING

Steam pieces lightly and flatten with the palms of your hands to even out the surface of the knitting.

STEEKS

For the body piece, with RS facing, a tapestry needle and contrasting yarn, sew a line of large sts down the middle of the center st of the steek as a marker. With a small machine st, sew down the center of the marked st. Sew down the center of the st to each side of marked st. You may also sew these lines by hand with sewing needle and thread, taking small stitches and back stitching often. Rep on sleeve cap and armhole steeks. When all lines of sewing are complete, with a sharp scissor and RS facing, cut down the center st of each steek.

LOWER SLEEVE CUFF

With RS facing, size 8 (5mm) dpns and E, pick up 64 (64, 68, 68) sts evenly around. Divide sts over 4 dpns. Work in seed st for the entire cuff, in the following color sequence: 4 rnds E, 3 rnds D, change to size 9 (5.5mm) dpns and work 3 rnds H, 1 rnd F, 2 rnds G, then work in C until cuff measures approx 2¼"/5.5cm. Bind off in pat with size 10 (6mm) needle. Steam edge lightly.

FRONT RUFFLED TRIM

Tie a marker on each side of beg of V-neck shaping. With RS facing, size 8 (5mm) circular needle and E, beg at lower right front edge, pick up 1 st next to the steek sts every row to shoulder seam, pick up 41 (41, 43, 45) sts along back neck, then pick up 1 st for every row from shoulder to lower left front (odd number of sts).

WS row Working back and forth in seed st and color sequence as for sleeve cuffs, and when you reach the marker at beg of V-neck, keeping to pat, inc 6 sts evenly between marker and shoulder, work in Seed st over back sts, then, keeping to pat, inc 6 sts evenly between shoulder and left

front V-neck, then work to end in Seed st. Cont in Seed st and color sequence as for sleeve cuff, changing needle sizes when indicated.

CORDS (MAKE 2)

With size 8 (5mm) needle and E, cast on 50 sts. Change to G and purl 1 row. Bind off with F.

Sew 1 button on each side of front, just below bust, sewing through an anchor button on WS too. Sew end of cord underneath button on RS. Sew 3 small buttons to ends of each cord. Tie at front.

BELT STRAPS (MAKE 2)

With size 8 (5mm) needle and E, cast on 31 sts. Knit 2 rows each in the following colors: E, D, H, A, G, C, B and E. Bind off. The wrong side of the Garter st (broken stripes, not solid stripes) is the RS.

Weave in ends to WS of belt. Slip straps through belt buckle and center. Pin ends of belts at waist on back at desired spot. Sew ends of straps to back. With WS facing, yarn and tapestry needle, sew front steeks to inside, keeping edges even. Steam edge and trim lightly. ■

Embellished Cardigan ◼◼◼▶

page 126

SIZES
To fit sizes Small (Medium, Large, X-Large, XX-Large). Shown in size Medium.

MEASUREMENTS
BUST AT UNDERARM
34 (37, 40, 45, 48)"/86.5 (94, 101.5, 114, 122)cm
LENGTH BEFORE FINISHING
20½ (21, 21½, 22, 22½)"/52 (53.5, 54.5, 56, 57)cm
SLEEVE WIDTH AT UPPER ARM
12 (13, 14, 15, 16)"/30.5 (33, 35.5, 38, 40.5)cm

MATERIALS
• Classic Elite *Fresco* (wool/baby alpaca/angora), 1¾oz/50g, 164yd/149m: MC #5336 (Oatmeal)—8 (9, 10, 11, 12) hanks
• CC #5301 (Parchment)—1 hank
• One pair each size 5 (3.75mm) and 7 (4.5mm) knitting needles *or size to obtain gauge*
• Size 5 (3.75mm) circular knitting needle, 24"/60cm
• One extra size 7 (4.5mm) knitting needle

FINISHING MATERIALS
SWAROVSKI ELEMENTS CRYSTALS:
• Sixty-three 8mm crystals: Item 6301 (Golden Shadow)
• Eighty-three 6mm crystals: Item 6301 (Golden Shadow)

1¾ (1¾, 2, 2, 2 1/4) yards of 100-percent silk organza fabric (54"/137cm wide) in Sandy Beige (available at silkfabric.etsy.com)
• Small piece of silk lining fabric, approx 8" x 12"/20 x 30.5cm
• Sharp scissors
• Tapestry needle
• Sewing needle
• Cotton thread in color to match the organza
• Straight dressmaker's pins

GAUGE
22 sts and 38 rows to 4"/10cm in Honeycomb pat using size 7 (4.5mm) needles
Take time to save time—check your gauge.

STOCKINETTE STITCH (ST ST)
(over any number of sts)
Knit RS rows, purl WS rows.

HONEYCOMB PATTERN
(multiple of 4 sts plus 1)
Rows 1, 3 and 5 (WS) Purl.
Rows 2 and 4 K1, *sl 3 wyif (holding yarn loosely), k1; rep from *.
Row 6 K2, *insert the RH needle under the long strands of 2 previous rows and knit the next st (taking the long strands over as you k the st), k3; rep from *, end k2 instead of k3.
Rows 7, 9, and 11 Purl.
Rows 8 and 10 K3, *sl 3 wyif, k1; rep from *, end k2.
Row 12 K4, *insert the RH needle under the long strands of 2 previous rows and knit the next st, k3; rep from *, end k1.
Rep rows 1–12 for Honeycomb pat.

BACK
With size 7 (4.5mm) needles and MC, cast on 95 (103, 111, 127, 135) sts.
Est pat (WS) P1 (St st edge st), work row 1 of Honeycomb pat over 93 (101, 109, 125, 133) sts, end p1 (St st edge st). Work even until piece measures 13½"/34cm, end with a WS row.

ARMHOLE SHAPING (RS)
Bind off 5 (5, 6, 6, 6) sts at the beg of the next 2 rows. Work even for 4 rows.
Next (dec) row (RS) Ssk, work in pat to last 2 sts, end k2tog.
WS rows P1, work in pat to the last st, end p1.
Rep the last 4 rows 5 (6, 7, 7, 7) more times, then rep last 2 rows 0 (0, 0, 5, 6)

times—73 (79, 83, 89, 95) sts. Work even until armhole measures 7 (7½, 8, 8½, 9)"/18 (19, 20, 21.5, 23)cm.

SHOULDER AND BACK NECK SHAPING
Mark center 23 (23, 25, 29, 29) sts.
Next row (RS) Bind off 3 (4, 5, 5, 5) sts, work to marked sts, join a second ball of yarn and bind off center 23 (23, 25, 29, 29) sts, work to end.
Working both sides with separate balls of yarn, bind off 3 (4, 5, 5, 5) sts from the next 5 (9, 1, 3, 9) shoulder edges, then 4 (0, 4, 4, 0) sts from the next 4 (0, 8, 6, 0) shoulder edges AND AT THE SAME TIME, bind off 2 sts from each neck edge 4 times.

LEFT FRONT
With size 7 (4.5mm) needles and MC, cast on 47 (51, 55, 63, 67) sts.
Est pat (WS) P1 (St st edge st), work row 1 of Honeycomb pat over 45 (49, 53, 61, 65) sts, end p1 (St st edge st). Work even until piece measures 10"/25.5cm, end with a WS row.

V-NECKLINE SHAPING
Next (dec) row (RS) Work to the last 2 sts, k2tog.
WS rows P1, work as est to the last st, end p1.
Work even in pat for 2 more rows, end with a WS row.
Rep dec row on the next row, then after 5 more rows, then alternately every 4th and 6th row after for a total of 19 (19, 20, 22, 22) decs at neckline edge AND AT THE SAME TIME, when piece measures 13½"/34cm, end with a WS row.

ARMHOLE SHAPING (RS)
Cont front neck decs as est and bind off 5 (5, 6, 6, 6) sts at the beg of the next RS row. Work as est for 5 rows.
Next row (RS) Ssk, work as est to end.
WS rows P1, work as est to the last st, end p1.
Rep the last 4 rows 5 (6, 7, 7, 7) more times, then rep last 2 rows 0 (0, 0, 5, 6) times. When armhole measures same as back to shoulder, end with a WS row—17 (20, 21, 22, 25) sts.

SHOULDER SHAPING (RS)
Keeping in pat, bind off 3 (4, 5, 5, 5) sts at the beg of the next 3 (5, 1, 2, 5) RS rows, then 4 (0, 4, 4, 0) sts at the beg of the next 2 (0, 4, 3, 0) RS rows.

RIGHT FRONT

Work same as for left front until piece measures approx 5"/12.5, end with pat row 1 or 7.

RIGHT FRONT POCKET FACING

With an extra size 7 (4.5mm) needle and MC, cast on 35 sts. Keeping first and last st in St st for edging, work in Honeycomb pat over center 33 sts until piece measures approx 1½"/4cm, end with pat row 1 or 7. Set aside.

POCKET OPENING (WS)

Work 8 (10, 12, 16, 18) sts, bind off 31 sts, work rem 8 (10, 12, 16, 18) sts to end.
Next (facing) row (RS) Work 7 (9, 11, 15, 17) sts, with RS of pocket facing toward you, work the next st tog, in pat, with the first st of pocket facing, then work in pat to the last st of pocket facing and work this st tog, in pat, with the next st, work in pat to end.
Work rem right front same as for left front, reversing all shaping.

SLEEVES

With size 7 (4.5mm) needles and MC, cast on 53 (53, 57, 61, 65) sts.
Est pat (WS) P2 (St st seam sts), work row 1 of Honeycomb pat over 49 (49, 53, 57, 61) sts, end p2 (St st seam sts).
Work until 25 rows (2 reps plus WS row 1) are complete.
Next (inc) row (RS) K2, M1, work row 2 of pat to last 2 sts, M1, end k2.
Working incs into pat when possible, rep inc row every 20th (12th, 12th, 10th, 10th)

row, until 7 (10, 11, 12, 13) incs have been worked each side—67 (73, 79, 85, 91) sts. Work even until sleeve measures 16½"/42cm, end with a WS row.

SLEEVE CAP (RS)

Bind off 5 (5, 6, 6, 6) sts at the beg of the next 2 rows. Work even for 4 rows.
Next row (RS) Ssk, work in pat to last 2 sts, end k2tog.
WS rows P1, work in pat to the last st, end p1.
Work as est for 2 rows.
Rep the last 4 rows 3 (3, 3, 2, 1) more times.
Next row (RS) Ssk, work in pat to last 2 sts, end k2tog.
WS rows P1, work in pat to the last st, end p1.
Rep the last 2 rows 13 (16, 18, 22, 26) more times.
Bind off 21 sts on next RS row.

FINISHING

Steam all sweater pieces lightly, holding the iron approx 1"/2.5 above each piece. *Do not press or apply any pressure.* Do not steam edges; they will be evened out when seaming.

LOWER SLEEVE TRIM

With RS facing, size 5 (3.75mm) needles and MC, pick up 48 (48, 52, 54, 58) sts along lower edge of sleeve.
Trim pat Knit 2 rows MC, knit 2 rows CC, knit 4 rows MC. Bind off.
Rep for second sleeve.

RIGHT FRONT POCKET TRIM

With RS facing, size 5 (3.75mm) needle and MC, pick up 27 sts along lower edge of pocket opening. Work trim pat. Sew sides of trim to front. Sew fronts to back at shoulders. Sew side seams.

LOWER EDGE TRIM

With RS facing, circular needle and MC, pick up 44 (48, 52, 58, 62) sts across lower left front, 86 (94, 102, 118, 126) sts along lower back, the 44 (48, 52, 58, 62) sts along lower right front—174 (190, 206, 234, 250) sts. Work trim pat.

FRONT EDGES AND NECKLINE TRIM

With RS facing, circular needle and MC, beg at right front lower trim, pick up 58 sts to beg of V-neck shaping, 67 (70, 73, 76, 79) sts to shoulder, 37 (37, 40, 43, 43) sts along back neck, 67 (70, 73, 76, 79) sts to beg of V-neck, then 58 sts to lower left front trim—287 (293, 302, 311, 317) sts. Work trim pat.

POCKET LINING

Cut piece of lining fabric on straight grain of fabric to measure 6" x 10"/15cm x 25.5cm. Press under ¼"/.5cm on each short end. The knitted pocket facing extends 1" below the pocket opening, so one side of the lining must be 1" shorter than the other. Fold fabric in half and sew side seams so that *front* side of lining extends 1"/2.5cm. Turn inside out. Sew short *back* edge of lining to pocket facing, then sew longer *front* edge to ridge formed by picked-up sts of trim. Sew 5 large crystals evenly below pocket trim.

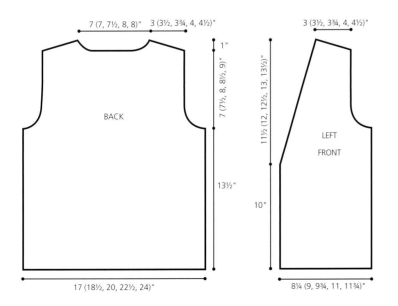

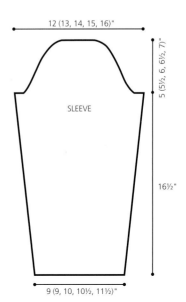

PREPARE ORGANZA TRIM

Press to eliminate wrinkles. Lay organza fabric flat, making sure fabric edges are at right angles. Refer to the illustrations on page 130 to prepare organza trim. Fold fabric along the bias. Pin approx 2"/5cm away from the fold and at various points on the layered fabric so that the layers do not shift. With very sharp scissors, cut along the folded bias line. Measure and lightly mark lines with a pencil 3"/7.5cm, apart, parallel to the fold line. Cut bias strips, 3"/7.5cm wide, along penciled lines. Sew ends of strips tog by hand with sewing needle and cotton thread, into longer lengths. Press seam allowances open. Make approx. 8 (8, 9, 9, 10) yards of strips. Cut long strip in half and layer the strips, sew tog to form 4 (4, 4½, 4½, 5) yards of double layered strips. Set aside.

MAKE FLOWERS

With sharp scissors, cut smaller ½-yard piece of organza into bias strips 1"/2.5cm wide. Each flower requires a 9"/23cm long strip. See illustrations on page 131 for how to make flowers. Sew 1 large crystal at center of each flower.

ATTACH RUFFLE TO LOWER SLEEVE

Gather a strip of bias trim slightly with its basting thread. With WS of sleeve facing, pin a length of loosely gathered ruffle along lower edge so that the shorter layer of ruffle is to the RS of sleeve. Ruffle should extend approx 2"/5cm below trim. Cut ends of ruffle ½"/1cm wide on each end. Sew ruffle in place, sewing into the "dent" between the trim and the main fabric of the sleeve.
Sew ends of ruffle together and sew sleeve seam. Rep for second sleeve.

ATTACH RUFFLE TO BODY

Beg at lower right side seam, pin slightly gathered ruffle along lower edges of back and to about 4"/10cm before left front corner. Gather ruffle a little more and pin in place so that it lies flat and there is no pulling as it turns around the corner. Cont to pin ruffle up left front; at V-neck allow a small amount of extra gathering, as well as along the back neck so that ruffle has some ease and does not pull. Cont to pin around entire remaining edges to beg, allowing extra at corners. Cut the ruffle allowing ½"/1cm seam allowance to seam the edges of the ruffle together where they meet. Sew ruffle in place, sewing into the "dent" between the trim and the main fabric of the body.

SEW SLEEVE CAPS INTO ARMHOLES

With sewing needle and cotton thread, sew flowers as in photos on page 129 and at left.
With sewing needle and cotton thread, sew 13 small crystals around the upper cap of each sleeve, approx ½"/1cm apart. Sew small crystals along all trimmed edges, sewing into the "dent" between trim and main fabric; do not cut thread between each attachment, but run the thread under the knitted fabric to the next spot where you want to attach the next crystal.

TIES (MAKE 2)

With size 5 (3.75mm) needles, cast on 40 sts. Bind off. Sew 1 large crystal to end. Sew one to each inside front edge approx 4"/10cm from bottom edge. ■

RESOURCES

Berroco, Inc.
1 Tupperware Drive
Suite 4
North Smithfield, RI
02896
berroco.com

Blue Sky Alpacas
P.O. Box 387
St. Francis, MN 55070
blueskyalpacas.com

Brown Sheep
Company
100662 County Rd. 16
Mitchell, NE 69357
brownsheep.com

Classic Elite Yarns
122 Western Avenue
Lowell, MA 01851
classiceliteyarns.com

Debbie Bliss
Distributed by KFI
debbieblissonline.com

Filatura Di Crosa
Distributed By
Tahki•Stacy Charles,
Inc.

KFI
P.O. Box 336
315 Bayview Avenue
Amityville, NY 11701
knittingfever.com

Louet North
America
808 Commerce Park
Drive
Ogdensburg, NY
13669
louet.com

Nashua Handknits
Distributed by
Westminster Fibers,
Inc.

Rowan Yarns
USA: Distributed by
Westminster Fibers,
Inc.
UK: Green Lane Mill
Holmfirth HD9 2DX
England
knitrowan.com

Silkfabric
silkfabric.etsy.com

Swarovski
crystallized.com

Tahki•Stacy Charles,
Inc.
70-30 80th Street,
Building 36
Ridgewood, NY 11385
tahkistacycharles.com

Westminster Fibers
165 Ledge Street
Nashua, NH 03060
westminsterfibers.com

ZipperStop
zipperstop.com

Cast-On How-tos

Throughout this book I have suggested several specific methods for casting on. The backward-loop cast-on is also used as an increase (for example, in mitered corners).

Long-Tail Cast-On

1. Make a slip knot on the right needle, leaving a long tail. Wind the tail end around your left thumb, front to back. Wrap the yarn from the ball over your left index finger and secure the ends in your palm.

2. Insert the needle upward in the loop on your thumb. Then with the needle, draw the yarn from the ball through the loop to form a stitch.

3. Take your thumb out of the loop and tighten the loop on the needle. Continue in this way until all the stitches are cast on.

Cable Cast-On

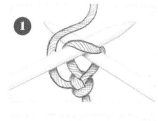

1. Make a slip knot on the left needle. *Insert the right needle knitwise into the stitch on the left needle. Wrap the yarn around the right needle as if to knit.

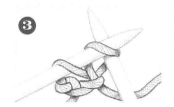

2. Draw the yarn through the first stitch to make a new stitch, but do *not* drop the stitch from the left needle.

3. Slip the new stitch to the left needle as shown. (Steps 1–3 are the knitting-on cast-on.)

4. *Insert the right needle between the two stitches on the left needle.

5. Wrap the yarn around the right needle as if to knit and pull the yarn through to make a new stitch.

6. Place the new stitch on the left needle as shown. Repeat from *, always inserting the right needle in between the last two stitches on the left needle.

Backward-Loop Cast-On

 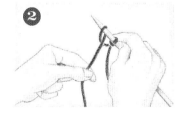 

1. Make a slip knot on the right needle, leaving a short tail. Wrap the yarn from the ball around your left thumb from front to back and secure it in your palm with your other fingers.

2. Insert the needle upward through the strand on your thumb.

3. Slip this loop from your thumb onto the needle, pulling the yarn from the ball to tighten it. Continue in this way until all the stitches are cast on.

PHOTOGRAPHY & ILLUSTRATION CREDITS

Model photography by Paul Amato for LVARepresents.com

Still-life photography by Marcus Tullis

Photographs from Vogue® Knitting: Paul Amato for LVARepresents.com: pp. 90, 96 and 100

Rose Callahan: pp. 37, 63, 83, 84, 98 and 101

How-to Illustrations by Deborah Newton

Schematics and charts by Barbara Khouri

Bella Mirror (pp. 77 and 119) courtesy of Ballard Designs ballarddesigns.com

Hair and Makeup by Alejandra using Bumble and Bumble for ArtistsbyTimothyPriano.com

Acknowledgments

I am grateful for the support of my friends in the yarn industry whose beautiful yarns are a pleasure to design with: Linda Pratt and Jessica LaCasse of Westminster Fibers, Susan Mills and Judy Croucher of Classic Elite Yarns, Norah Gaughan and Donna Yacino of Berroco Yarns, and Stacy Charles of Tahki Stacy Charles. A special thanks to everyone at Debbie Bliss, Blue Sky Alpacas, Brown Sheep Company, JCA Crafts and Louet for contributing their gorgeous materials to this book.

My deep gratitude to all my talented colleagues at Sixth&Spring Books. This amazing group of individuals has been so supportive of this book, and also of my design work over the years. I am especially appreciative of the support of the energetic and creative Trisha Malcolm, at the editorial helm of SoHo, out of whose talented mind popped the title for this book. An enormous thank-you to my terrific book editor Michelle Bredeson, whose clarity, creative organization and cheer were a great help during this challenging project. I am deeply grateful to my art director Diane Lamphron, whose delightful and detailed artistic vision makes everything she touches extra-special! I thank my longtime associate Carla Scott, whom I have known from the early days of *Vogue® Knitting,* and it is always a pleasure to work with Renée Lorion, who is an enormous help and always jumps in with the perfect yarn suggestion. Thanks to the gracious Wendy Williams for her kindness and support. And a long-overdue nod of appreciation to Joe Vior who has made my work look great on the pages of *Vogue Knitting* since it first appeared there in the 1980s.

I am grateful to stylist Sarah Liebowitz and photographers Paul Amato and Marcus Tullis for helping me to present the projects here in a beautiful, interesting and clear manner.

I love working with my longtime friend and gifted partner-in-technical-matters Barbara Khouri. She makes the challenging seem easy and lightens the load with her cheer and generous help.

Thanks to my friend Susan Moore for her decades of friendship and support. I am grateful to her for helping me proof this manuscript.

I could not, would not, do anything without the amazing group of knitting assistants who have worked so hard, with skill and perseverance, on the projects for this book. A special acknowledgment to Frances Scullin, Patricia Yankee and Lucinda Heller who have been there for me for many, many years, meeting challenge after knitting challenge with grace and mastery. I am also grateful to Laura Folden, Lynn Marlowe and Debbie O'Neill for their unflagging assistance on this book. It is these friends and others over the years too numerous to list here, all experts in their craft, who have brought my ideas to life. For their humor, concern and much appreciated expertise, I offer my greatest thanks.

Thanks to two shining mentors: Barbara G. Walker, whose immaculately clear volumes continue to influence me and other designers and knitters worldwide, and Christine Timmons, friend and editor of my book *Designing Knitwear,* who taught me so much.

No one could have a more supportive family than I do. Thanks to my brother, Jason Newton, my sister, Regina Orio, and my sister-in-law, Leslie Newton, who help, encourage and make space for my design work in the midst of our family's busy map business.

And to Paul—inspirational consort, cheer-giver, visionary and sharer of the rigors of the freelance life—all love and all thanks for your neverending help.